Material Meanings

Foundations of Archaeological Inquiry

James M. Skibo, series editor

Material Meanings
Critical Approaches to the Interpretation of Material Culture

Edited by Elizabeth S. Chilton

THE UNIVERSITY OF UTAH PRESS
SALT LAKE CITY

FOUNDATIONS OF ARCHAEOLOGICAL INQUIRY
James M. Skibo, editor

Manufactured in the United States of America
05   04   03   02   01   00   99   7   6   5   4   3   2   1

LIBRARY OF CONGRESS CATALOGING-IN-PUBLICATION DATA

Material meanings : critical approaches to the interpretation of
   material culture / edited by Elizabeth S. Chilton.
        p.   cm. — (Foundations of archaeological inquiry)
     Papers originally presented at the 1996 meeting of the Society for
   American Archaeology held in New Orleans, La.
     Includes bibliographical references (p.   ) and index.
     ISBN 0-87480-632-1 (alk. paper). — ISBN 0-87480-633-X (pbk. :
   alk. paper)
     1. Ethnoarchaeology.   2. Social archaeology.   3. Material culture.
   4. Ceramics—Analysis.   I. Chilton, Elizabeth S.   II. Series.
   CC79.E85M38   1999
   930.1—dc21   99-15804

Contents

Figures

Tables

Preface

The idea for this volume was originally conceived in 1995. At that time I planned to organize a two-day conference and subsequent edited volume entitled *New Approaches to the Interpretation of Material Culture*. The themes planned for that conference included (1) ethnoarchaeology and traditions of technology, (2) feminist theory and an archaeology of gender, (3) methodological approaches to the meaning of materials, and (4) efforts toward a theory of materiality. I am grateful to everyone who agreed to participate in the original conference, which included some of the authors in this volume (Dean Arnold, Philip Arnold, Cathy Costin, Hector Neff, Miriam Stark, and H. Martin Wobst), as well as Elizabeth Brumfiel, Michael Dietler, Joan Gero, Russell Handsman, Ian Hodder, Rosemary Joyce, Heather Lechtman, Bryan Pfaffenberger, Dwight Read, Michael Schiffer, James Skibo, and Anastasia Steffen. In the end the conference did not come to fruition.

Nevertheless, the momentum and enthusiasm generated by the preconference discussions prompted me to organize a symposium at the 1996 meeting of the Society for American Archaeology in New Orleans. That session bore the name of the current volume and included papers by Dean Arnold and Hector Neff, Philip Arnold, Cathy Costin, Dorothy Hosler, Miriam Stark, Bryan Pfaffenberger, James Skibo and Michael Schiffer, H. Martin Wobst, and myself, with Margaret Conkey as the discussant. The purpose of that session, as with this volume, was to bring together a group of diverse researchers to "explore the commonalities and divergences among current approaches to material culture and to assess future directions for the study of the material world." The high quality of the papers and the positive reception the session received prompted me to pull the papers together (with the addition and subtraction of a few others) to form this volume.

As with any set of conference papers, they needed to be expanded and integrated in order to create a cohesive edited volume. My thanks to the two anonymous reviewers, who helped all of the contributors stretch the boundaries of their contributions. I would also like to thank James Skibo, Foundations of Archaeological Inquiry series editor, for his interest in the session from the beginning, as well as Jeff Grathwohl, director of the University of Utah Press, for his patience throughout the review and revision process. A special thanks goes to Jessi Halligan, my research assistant at Harvard University, for chasing down bibliographic information and for providing clerical assistance throughout the editing of this volume. Finally, I wish to thank H. Martin Wobst for sparking my interest in the epistemology of classification and, thus, the meaning of materials.

Material Meanings and Meaningful Materials
An Introduction

Elizabeth S. Chilton

The challenge in material culture studies...is to give material objects life in the anthropological text, to conjure up an instant in a process.

—Christensen 1995:21

Having firm roots in antiquarianism, archaeology began as the study and collection of things. Like other scientific disciplines, in the early stages of the profession archaeologists collected data (objects) for their own sake (Trigger 1989:27). To this day objects take center stage in many areas of archaeological inquiry. In fact, "the study of artifacts in relation to past human behavior" serves as a general definition of archaeology (Lubar and Kingery 1993:ix).

Over the past few decades there has been an expansion and proliferation of the ways anthropological archaeologists analyze and interpret material culture. This development results from a decade of postprocessual approaches, more than two decades of processual and behavioral archaeology, nearly 30 years of feminist theory, and a renewed interest in materials science approaches. The purpose of this volume is to explore the commonalities and divergences among current archaeological approaches to material culture and to assess how far we have come in our attempts to understand the material world. What advances have archaeologists made in their interpretations of material culture, and what aspects of meaning still elude us? What do current approaches have in common, and in what ways do they differ?

The semantic distinction between "objects" and "materials" is important for the purpose of this volume: the terms *materials*

and *material culture* emphasize the constitutive process of artifact manufacture, use, and discard. As a result of theoretical changes in the broader field of anthropology in the 1970s and 1980s, culture itself has come to be viewed not as "something you have, but something that is continuously created" (Christensen 1995:9; see also Conkey 1989, 1992a). The impetus for this change originated outside of anthropology (e.g., Giddens 1979, 1982), but the notion of culture as constitutive has now permeated all of the social sciences. Archaeologists have applied this perspective to artifacts so that materials are viewed not only as "tools for survival" but as both embodying and shaping the identities of their makers and users (Csikszentmihalyi and Rochberg-Halton 1981:1; see also Appadurai 1986; Christensen 1995; Miller 1987; Shanks and Tilley 1987a). This view of the constitutive nature of materials is akin to the dialectic view of material culture as espoused by marxist archaeologists (see McGuire 1992).

Reflecting this new emphasis in archaeology, the essays that follow do not focus on artifacts themselves. Instead, the emphasis is on (1) the social and technical context in which materials are produced and (2) the interpretation of materials by researchers in the present. In this sense "materials" include raw materials, technology, tools, and techniques, as well as the finished products. Thus, most of the authors in this volume underscore "what is being created in the manufacturing process apart from physical objects" (Christensen 1995:10).

Although the authors' approaches all stem from the Americanist tradition of anthropological archaeology, the diversity of approaches represented here speaks generally to the relationship between people and the objects they create. The chapters represent a broad range of theoretical perspectives, methods, and data sets. Although a few of the chapters focus on methodological issues in the reconstruction of technical systems (P. Arnold, D. Arnold, Chilton), many of the chapters apply this understanding of technical systems to larger questions of social identity and ethnicity (Chilton, Stark, Costin, Dobres, Wobst). Some of the chapters draw on ethnoarchaeological data (P. Arnold, D. Arnold, and Stark), whereas others rely primarily on archaeological data (Chilton, Costin, Dobres). Despite these differences, the chapters share an awareness and appreciation of (1) the importance of historical context for interpreting artifact variability, (2) technical systems as a broader context for interpreting material culture, and (3) material culture as both product and precedent of human action. This emphasis on the importance of historical context does not exclude larger-scale models of cultural process, as demonstrated in the chapters by Philip Arnold and Dean Arnold (see also Arnold 1985; Arnold 1991).

Another commonality in this volume is that many of the chapters rely on ceramic data. In fact, this volume touches on all of the major trends in ceramic studies as outlined by Rice (1996a:182): function, style, composition, and production. This emphasis on ceramics was not a conscious choice on my part; much of the research being done on technical systems deals with ceramic production in an ethnoarchaeological context. Because ceramic production is an additive process, a pot embodies many of the choices made in the production sequence. These "technical choices [are]...elected in a rich context of tradition, value, alternatives, and compromises" (Rice 1996b:140). Thus, pots are a choice medium for the study of technical systems, subsistence, social interaction, the organization of production, social identity and hierarchy, and style.

In the rest of this chapter I lay out the major themes that run through this volume. As will become apparent, many of the chapters transcend and even defy these thematic boundaries, underscoring the overdetermined nature of materials.

ETHNOARCHAEOLOGY

Over the past two decades the emphasis by some archaeologists on *behavior* as the key to archaeological understanding has facilitated the connection between ethnography and archaeology in the form of ethnoarchaeology (Skibo and Schiffer 1996). One manifestation of ethnoarchaeology is ceramic ecology, which emphasizes the interaction between ceramics and their natural and sociocultural context (Arnold 1993:5). Several chapters in this volume utilize ethnoarchaeological data and reflect this tradition of ceramic ecology (D. Arnold et al., P. Arnold, and Stark).

Ethnoarchaeology, in all of its incarnations, has contributed much to the way that archaeologists view materials—particularly how they view the relationship between human behavior and the production and use of materials. In many ways ethnoarchaeology is the mother of all constitutive theories of material culture. Ethnoarchaeologists have repeatedly shown that artifacts reside in a complex web of meanings and can only be interpreted with respect to their unique historic and cultural context (e.g., Graves 1985; Hardin 1970, 1977, 1979; Hodder 1981, 1991a; Longacre 1981, 1991). Initially some archaeologists criticized ethnoarchaeology for purportedly failing to contribute to social theory and for contributing little more than cautionary tales (e.g., Conkey 1989; Miller 1983). However, recent ethnoarchaeological research has contributed greatly to understanding the relationship between material culture and human action (Longacre and Skibo 1994:11; see also Arnold 1991; Childs 1991; Stark 1998).

TECHNICAL SYSTEMS

The study of technical systems is a logical outgrowth of ethnoarchaeological research. Heather Lechtman (1977) originated the concept of "technological style," which focuses on the many elements that constitute technological behavior: learned techniques, attitudes toward the materials, organization of labor, ritual practices, and so forth. It is the entire "package" of these things that is viewed as stylistic in nature (Lechtman 1977:6). Technology, then, is seen not merely as a means of survival or adaptation but as a means of "creating and maintaining a symbolically meaningful environment" (Lechtman 1977:17).

How, then, do we get from "technology" to "technical systems"? There has been a modern semantic shift away from the term *technique* and toward the term *technology*: *technique* is often used to refer to the skills or choices of individuals, whereas *technology* connotes public, shared knowledge (Ingold 1990). Ingold (1990) considers this distinction to be "symptomatic of the disembedding of the [modern] forces of production from their social matrix." In this volume we do not differentiate between techniques and technology; both terms are taken to mean, simply, how things are made, in the broadest sense. Contrary to being a phenomenon outside culture, technology, as defined here, is "a phenomenon that marries the material, social and the symbolic in a complex web of associations" (Pfaffenberger 1988:249).

A focus on *how* things are made departs somewhat from traditional anthropology. In fact, the study of techniques is often regarded as an area of inquiry outside anthropology (Mahias 1993:157; Pfaffenberger 1988:237). In archaeology it was certainly the influence of "symbolic anthropology" and the focus on "style" (particularly decoration) that led archaeologists to reject or ignore the more "technical" aspects of material culture (Lemonnier 1989:157). The explicit study of techniques represents a union of ethnology and archaeology and has deep roots in the work of French archaeologist, Leroi-Gourhan (Stark 1998; see Leroi-Gourhan 1993). An important implication of the notion of technological style is that the focus is not on *things* but on the makers and users of objects as a window into social relations (Wright 1993:245; see also Chilton, and Stark, this volume).

Two chapters in this volume deal explicitly with technical systems, although the authors use vastly different data and methods. Miriam Stark's chapter, "Social Dimensions of Technical Choice in Kalinga Ceramic Traditions," uses ethnographic examples from the Philippines to illustrate commonalities between two seemingly divergent technologically oriented approaches: (1) the *techniques et culture* school, which explores links between cognition, technical choice, and material culture patterning; and (2) the analysis of formal variation as expressed in the goods of everyday life (often termed "isochrestic variation" or "technological style"). Stark applies the notion of technological style to a detailed analysis of Kalinga social boundaries and material culture patterning. She concludes by calling for an explicit material culture theory for archaeology, one that is based on innovative methods and "how technological behavior generates and reflects social boundaries" (Stark, this volume).

My own chapter proposes an alternative to the typological approach for analyzing prehistoric ceramics in New England. I demonstrate that New England ceramics are so diverse and are produced in such a wide variety of social and ecological contexts that a typological approach is simply not warranted or useful. Instead, I employ an "attribute analysis of technical choice" as a means to highlight the axes of choice for prehistoric New England potters. As a result of a focus on technical choices, ceramics are shown to provide a window into subsistence, settlement, political organization, social integration, and social boundaries. This study underscores the need for an awareness of the many agents of variation in material culture, which include knowledge, tradition, ability, production scale and context, intended use, and ideology.

MATERIALS SCIENCE APPROACHES

Materials science approaches, born of processual archaeology, have found a new home in analyses of technical systems and the burgeoning anthropological interest in technology. As Lechtman (1977:14) puts it: "The history of the manipulation of...materials is locked into their physical and chemical structure; the methods of material science can interpret that technical history." The analysis of materials using scientific techniques can inform not only on the "how-to's" of manufacture and the distribution of artifacts after manufacture but on the meanings of such contextual variables as sound and color (see Hosler 1995).

In the chapter by Dean Arnold et al., "Testing Interpretative Assumptions of Neutron Activation Analysis: Contemporary Pottery in Yucatán, 1964–1994," the authors demonstrate the potential contributions of materials science approaches to interpretations of material culture. Using neutron activation analysis (NAA) of contemporary, ethnographic pottery, they suggest that differences in trace element patterning over time and space represent a change in the resource areas used by Yucatecan potters. The authors demonstrate that NAA "works" in the sense that production communities utilizing different resource areas can be identified using NAA. The authors also demonstrate that paste preparation techniques and the addition of nonplastic temper materials are less significant in trace element patterning than are clay sources and tempers that contain clay minerals. One of the primary contributions of this chapter is that it demonstrates the potential for ethnoarchaeological and, thus, archaeological data to be linked to human behavior via a materials science approach.

THE ORGANIZATION OF PRODUCTION

With the advent of behavioral archaeology, ethnoarchaeology, and the study of technical systems, the organization of artifact production has received much more attention by anthropological archaeologists in the last 20 years. In many ways the organization of production is an artifact itself: it has the potential to both reflect and constitute social and political relations (including social networks and social identity), technological systems, economy, and ideology. An archaeological study of the organization of production can be approached via production as encoded in finished objects (Costin, this volume) or by interpreting the evidence for activity areas and spatial patterning in the archaeological record, which is often greatly assisted by the use of contemporary ethnographic data (P. Arnold, this volume). Although all of the chapters in this volume touch on the organization of production to some degree, Cathy Costin's and Philip Arnold's chapters deal with the topic explicitly.

Cathy Costin's chapter, "Formal and Technological Variability and the Social Relations of Production: *Crisoles* from San José de Moro, Peru," adopts methodological and theoretical approaches from studies of production and exchange and applies these to mortuary data to examine the relationship among artifact variability, labor organization, and social structure. Costin interprets the organization of production by examining technological and iconographic variation in Northern Moche ceramic *crisoles*. Through her examination of *crisoles* she interprets artifact variability with respect to differences in social hierarchy and social networks. It is clear in this case that the organization of production both reflects and constitutes elements of social and political organization.

In his chapter, "On Typologies, Selection, and Ethnoarchaeology in Ceramic Production Studies," Philip Arnold views production organization as "a dynamic phenomenon in which technology...reflects the producer's past experiences and future and short-term goals" (P. Arnold, this volume). By using ethnoarchaeological data from southern Veracruz, Mexico, he offers a critique of and alternative to (1) typological approaches to the "stages" of production and (2) the neo-Darwinian selectionist view of change in material culture. P. Arnold suggests that both of these approaches foster a "progressive, functional, and linear" view of change that does not contribute much to an archaeological understanding of ceramic production, organization, and change. As an alternative, he applies an ethnoarchaeological model of the relationship between production technology and the organization of production to an ancient Mexican archaeological context. By doing so he demonstrates the important contribution of ethnoarchaeology as a means of understanding the dynamic relationship between artifacts and their makers. P. Arnold makes it clear that the archaeological record cannot be completely accounted for by the variation present in contemporary contexts; instead, he emphasizes the importance of understanding the differences between the past and the present. Ethnoarchaeological research, thus, serves as a means to isolate the behavioral variables that archaeologists seek to explain.

THE EPISTEMOLOGY OF THINGS

"[T]he artifact is less a text to be read than a story to be told."

—Wright 1993:245

Two chapters in this volume deal explicitly with the epistemology of interpreting material culture. Dobres's chapter addresses the epistemology of engendered archaeology. Nowhere is the constitutive role of culture (and material culture) clearer than in issues of gender; gender itself both constitutes and is constituted by social relations and identities. Feminist archaeology has certainly lagged behind research on women and gender in sociocultural anthropology and the other social sciences by 20 years or more. Conkey and Spector (1984) argue that in the search for general laws and answers to "big questions," systems theory and the processual approaches prevalent in the 1960s and 1970s precluded attention to such historically contextual phenomena as gender relations. Wylie (1991) blames the rejection of internal "ethnographic variables" (which include gender) on a particular brand of processualism: the "new archeology" as promoted by Binford. The lag is also due to the fact that archaeologists had (and have) a difficult time "seeing" gender. Often the focus is on gender attribution—the mechanics of relating gender to things—as a means of engendering the past (see Conkey and Gero 1991:11). Archaeologists have come to realize that gender needs to be viewed as much more than simply finding men and women in the archaeological record. Even though much of the literature remains "womanist," that is, concerned with the lives of women in the past (Joyce and Claassen 1997:1), gender is viewed increasingly as a primary structuring principle integral to the construction of personal and public identity, political economy, and social inequality. Therefore, an engendered past is not simply about assigning gender to the remains of the past—it is about the social dynamics of everyday life (Conkey and Gero 1991:15). (For some recent reviews of gender and archaeology see Claassen 1992, 1994; Gero and Conkey 1991; Joyce and Claassen 1997; Siefert 1991; Walde and Willows 1991; Wright 1996; Wylie 1991, 1992).

In the chapter "Of Paradigms and Ways of Seeing: Artifact Variability as if People Mattered," Marcia-Anne Dobres examines how European Upper Paleolithic material culture has been interpreted by normative archaeologists on the one hand and processualist archaeologists on the other. The goal of Dobres's chapter is to demonstrate how a focus on interpersonal social agency and, more specifically, gender dynamics can profoundly transform the methods for examining material culture and, therefore, its possible interpretations. Dobres refers to the effect of changing one's epistemology as "seeing differently." Thus, as Dobres argues, an engendered approach is not something that is tacked on to extant interpretations, nor is gender viewed as something to be treated separately from other aspects of society. Instead, Dobres's research focuses on social agency as manifest in material culture production and use "with the goal of understanding the dialectic of gendered practices and technical strategies" (Dobres 1995:25; see also Dobres and Hoffman 1998).

H. Martin Wobst's chapter, "Style in

Archaeology or Archaeologists in Style," focuses on what artifacts "say" or "do" within their social and historical context and, more important, how humans "interfere" with each other materially. This chapter sets the stage for a critical interpretation of material culture by outlining the history of style since his oft-cited 1977 article (Wobst 1977). Wobst reviews the past 20 years of archaeological analysis of archaeological materials, placing particular emphasis on the articulation between theory and practice in the analysis of style.

Wobst's 1977 article reflects to some degree the processualist view of the time, which perceived style as functional. Although the processual archaeologists of the 1960s and 1970s induced a profound change in the way cultures are viewed and studied, their attempt to distance themselves from the artifact-centered, cultural historians of the previous era created some negative effects on our understanding of the material world. In particular, material culture was largely viewed as a means to reveal society (i.e., through stylistic patterns); the relationship *between* humans and the material world was largely ignored (Conkey 1989:17). Thus, the search for cross-cultural patterns and "laws" inhibited to some degree inquiry into material culture on its own terms (Hodder 1982a).

A major exception to this general neglect of material culture was the proliferation of archaeological theory related to style (see Conkey and Hastorf 1990). Focusing on the active role of style in artifact variability, Wobst (1977) and others explored the role of information exchange and social messaging (e.g., Braun and Plog 1982; Conkey 1978; DeBoer and Moore 1982; Hodder 1977, 1979; Lathrap 1983; Wiessner 1983). Wobst (1977) is one of the most cited articles on style in archaeology, and his promotion of an "information exchange" theory of style has had a profound effect on Euro-American archaeology. Wobst refers to his 1977 article as a resolution of the "contradiction between

vacuous archaeological theory and rich ethnographic data" (Wobst, this volume). With the informational value of style as promoted by Wobst and others, the concept of style was "promoted from being a vague and residual source of variability…to a broad and predominant factor" (Conkey 1982: 116). Perhaps the most profound contribution of the information-exchange theory of style was that artifacts came to be seen as both products and precedents of human action (Wobst 1978:307; see also Miller 1985: 205).

In this volume Wobst clarifies and elaborates on certain points in his 1977 article; in doing so he places new emphasis on the all-persuasiveness of style, style as "interference," and style as a dynamic process. This broader view of style includes not only the most visible types and aspects of artifacts but also raw material extraction and movement, tool production, and artifact disuse.

CONCLUSIONS

As Margaret Conkey underscores so well in the concluding chapter of this volume, there is no unifying theory of materiality presented here. What unifies the chapters is not the questions asked, nor the methods of study, but an appreciation of material culture as infinitely complex, as context dependent, and as both product and precedent of human action. By bringing together anthropological archaeologists with diverse approaches and methods and by focusing on a critical common theme—the interpretation of material culture—this volume provides a forum for evaluating and strengthening current approaches to material culture. Rather than presenting a singular perspective on material culture—such as ethnoarchaeological, feminist, historical, stylistic, symbolic, technical, or typological—the papers in this volume examine material culture through all of these lenses to come to a fuller understanding of the meaning of materials and to generate ideas for future directions in the quest for material meanings.

2

Of Paradigms and Ways of Seeing
Artifact Variability as if People Mattered

MARCIA-ANNE DOBRES

As the new archaeology came into its own in the 1970s and 1980s, a debate raged between Anglo-American archaeologists studying the European Paleolithic and European (specifically French) archaeologists studying their own turf. This difference of opinion can be characterized in many ways, but the most familiar turns on whether (prehistoric) cultures were structured by normative ways of living in the material world "versus" a more adaptationist accounting of ancient behavioral repertoires. The now classic Bordes/ Binford debate concerning the behavioral significance of Middle Paleolithic interassemblage variability in lithic artifacts (colloquially known as the "form vs. function" debate) is the best exemplar of the differences inherent in these two theoretical perspectives. It is also a stellar example of how researchers are taught to see and make sense of artifact variability through different paradigmatic lenses. As several chapters in this volume show, causal accounts of artifact variability can take different forms, depending in large measure on the theoretical persuasions of the analysts and how they are taught to see and think about such things. Importantly, learning to see does not come "naturally"—it takes practice and guidance (Berger 1973; Forge 1970). Thus, it follows that even seeing empirical variability in the archaeological record (as well as the "norm" around which it is supposed to hover) is a learned skill. The trick, however, is that once learned it is often

difficult to see any other way (Fyfe and Law 1988; Margolis 1993). My concerns in this chapter are threefold: (1) to examine how, in one particular instance, artifact variability has been seen and dealt with by two different intellectual paradigms; (2) to consider their recent and compromised way of seeing; and (3) to explore how thinking and seeing differently can lead to potentially different empirical findings and even alternative understandings of the past. In this essay I argue that when the dynamics of human agency are taken seriously—when people matter—it does make a difference, not only to the study of artifact variability but to methodology and interpretation more generally.

I divide my argument into three parts: section 1 provides a synopsis of one archaeological culture, The Magdalenian, in order to show how artifact variability was seen and interpreted through the different lenses of French normativism and Anglo-American processualism prior to the 1980s. Section 2 outlines the convergent approach, recently forged between these explanatory models, to demonstrate how their compromised way of seeing still neglects potentially important analytic scales of empirical variability. Section 3 offers some methodological alternatives for the study of artifact variability grounded in an explicit concern with the people who created it. My goal here is to suggest that at least one key reason why certain kinds of empirical variability have not been given more analytic attention is because the way we currently see Magdalenian material culture, from both sides of the Atlantic, fails to take the dynamics of human agency and interpersonal relations as legitimate causal processes. What the third part of this chapter offers is an alternative way to think about, and see, artifact variability "as if people mattered" (after Vinsrygg 1988).

My intent is not to critique the earlier and distinct normative and processual perspectives for the study of Magdalenian artifact variability nor their contemporary alliance. Rather, my goal in this exercise is to analyze their research emphases in order to demonstrate by example how a credible focus on agency and interpersonal social dynamics (such as gender) demands different research methodologies and leads to new empirical findings and different understandings. It is my hope that the reader agrees there are larger lessons to be learned from this exercise than to wallow in the curious intellectual history of research on the Magdalenian.

SECTION 1: FRENCH NORMATIVISM AND ANGLO-AMERICAN PROCESSUALISM, PRE-1980

Archaeological culture: an arbitrary division of the space-time cultural continuum defined by reference to its imperishable content and whatever "common social tradition" can be inferred therefrom.

—Phillips and Willey 1953:617

Once called the Golden Age of Prehistory (Méroc 1953:45), The Magdalenian has captured the minds and imaginations of prehistorians for well over a century. In many ways its earliest descriptions remain strongly imprinted on contemporary research. We still think of this period as the sine qua non of Pleistocene cultural development and art. The Magdalenian (especially in France) is often still thought of as the origins point for modern Western (representational) art (Collins and Onians 1978). Characterized more than a century ago as the Reindeer Age, the conventional model has changed very little since the late 1880s. The Magdalenian is still

thought of as an "Eskimo way of life" (Sollas 1911; see also Binford 1978, 1980), characterized by nomadic hunter-gatherers in tune with the seasonal movements of wild reindeer migrating over a tundra-like landscape, by the practice of a primitive religion dominated by animistic art and totemism (Reinach 1903), and by a veritable explosion of lithic and organic technological innovations (see summaries as diverse as Bahn 1984; Breuil 1912; Clottes 1989; de Mortillet 1869; Méroc 1953; Peyrony 1950). In what follows I purposefully capitalize The Magdalenian to underscore the normative way we have long thought about (and seen the empirical remains of) this archaeological culture.

As an archaeological construct The Magdalenian (ca. 15,000–10,500 B.P.) is characterized by a widely recognized body of temporally discrete artifact patterns and "type fossils" that make it, to the trained eye, a generally homogenous cultural unit, materially and behaviorally distinct from other archaeological cultures. Although widely distributed in space (Figure 2.1), Magdalenian artifacts exhibit distinctive regional variations in composition and style. Variants of The Magdalenian are found in the Paris Basin, Périgord, French Pyrénées, Cantabrian Spain, Central Belgium, southwestern and central Germany, and Poland (Figure 2.2). A traditional and typologically oriented view of what an archaeological culture "looks like" on the ground has led most researchers, Anglo-American and French alike, to argue that on a regional basis different so-called ethnic groups of Magdalenians lived apart, although they sometimes exchanged source-specific objects or intruded into each others' territories with artifact "styles" coming from far away (Audouze 1992:345; Bahn 1982; Rozoy 1992:70; Straus 1990–91:19; on various limitations of typological approaches for understanding the dynamics of prehistoric social identity, see Arnold, Chilton, and Stark, this volume).

Today, The Magdalenian is simultaneously (1) a temporal period of cultural development; (2) a suite of distinctive archaeological materials (e.g., antler harpoons, certain

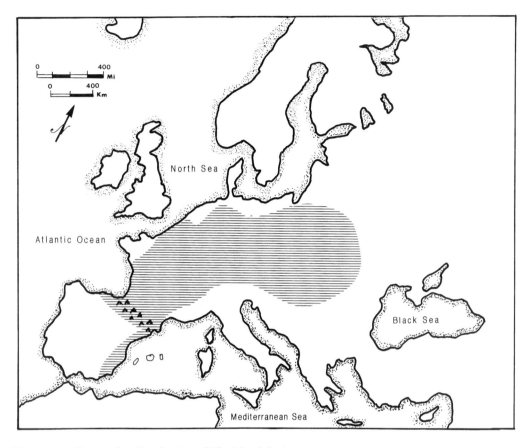

Figure 2.1. Geographic distribution of The Magdalenian, ca. 15,000–10,500 B.P.

kinds of spear throwers, backed blades, an abundance of wall and portable visual imagery) uniquely situated in time; and (3) a late Pleistocene "way of life" characterized by complex, seasonal patterns of resource exploitation and transhumance. In the following synopsis I refer to each of these three emphases, and I continue to employ "The Magdalenian" (hereafter "TM") as a shorthand for the time, objects, material patterns, and inferred lifeways of the people who left these material traces behind. I do not, however, refer to the people themselves as Magdalenians, for that is an inappropriate compounding of object and subject (Conkey 1989). The generations of agents who made and used material culture "in the style" of TM should not be associated with those objects nor with their patterned traces.

What follows is a characterization of TM as a temporally discrete body of artifacts, material patterns, and lifeways. With this as a general background, in the following section I outline the pre-1980s normative and processual frameworks differently employed to explain TM's temporal and spatial variability. Section 2 then discusses the convergent explanatory framework in use today. What can be seen from this review is that the contemporary paradigm has been applied atop a preexisting normative baseline and, thus, has unwittingly failed to investigate an important degree of artifact variability empirically evident in the archaeological record. As I go on to argue in section 3, when the dynamics of social agency (and especially gender relations) are taken as legitimate research questions, we are able to *see* material variability previously overlooked or discounted. More than this, we put ourselves in a credible

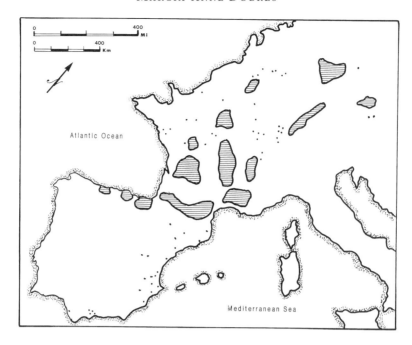

Figure 2.2. Regional zones of ethnic Magdalenian groups in western Europe (note the extent of un-marked areas and interspersed single sites between each hatch-marked region).

position to make reasonable inferences to ex-plain this variability.

THE MAGDALENIAN (15,000–10,500 B.P.)

The Magdalenian is not a temporal period within which to locate significant macro-evolutionary change in material repertoires or behaviors. Throughout most of France during this 4,500-year period, and in the French Midi-Pyrénées in particular, the over-all resource base available to Magdalenian hunter-gatherers remained rich and diverse. Compared with the significant behavioral shifts between the Middle and Upper Paleo-lithic, and between the Upper Paleolithic and subsequent Mesolithic, there is broad con-sensus that TM was a period of cultural sta-bility. Especially in the French Pyrénées, Clottes (1989:286, 1990) argues for general continuity between the middle and later phases. In fact, there is far more regional variation *within* TM (for example between the Paris Basin and the French Pyrénées) than there is temporal variation among its earlier and later phases.

These were the quintessential logistically organized mobile hunter-gatherers of prehis-tory. They made strategic use of varied land-scapes, taking advantage of the natural pro-tection of rock shelters and caves but also creating highly structured open-air camps (especially in the Paris Basin). They enjoyed controlled access to migratory land and wa-ter resources by making sophisticated use of topographic features, for example, situating open-air sites on or very near river con-fluences (Bahn 1984; White 1985). In the Ariège (Midi-Pyrénées), sites found at the highest elevations (< 1000 m) seem to be pri-marily short-term extraction locales for the specialized hunting of upland game such as mountain goat (ibex) and ptarmigan. In the Pyrénées, faunal exploitation centered pri-marily on large-scale migratory herd ani-mals, most especially reindeer but also horse, bison, wild cattle, red deer, and ibex. Limited osteological remains and indirect evidence suggest the large-scale exploitation of salmon, pike, and other fresh- and saltwater fish, as well as the use of traps to procure birds, especially ptarmigan, but also rabbit, hare, and other small game.

Current thought is that TM settlement system was one of periodic aggregations of typically dispersed "family" groups (averaging perhaps 10–30 individuals; Straus 1986: 342; Sturdy and Webley 1988). These gatherings appear to have served multiple social purposes, as well as to have exploited seasonally available resources best captured by group effort, such as migratory reindeer or salmon (Celerier 1992; Conkey 1980, 1992b). In the course of intra- and interregional transhumance these communities pursued a variety of everyday and specialized activities, and both Anglo-American and French researchers have focused special attention on identifying functionally different "types" of occupation sites. These include both *simple* and *complex base camps* (or what Straus [1990–1991] generally calls residential sites). Base camps typically yield evidence of multiple and overlapping daily sorts of activities: butchering; hide tanning; producing, using, and repairing lithic and organic artifacts; constructing flat stone "pavements"; creating hearths and pits; and so forth. There are also *special-purpose sites*, where more circumscribed (often shortduration) activities took place: lithic procurement at quarries, specialized artifact production or repair at "workshops," hunting and fishing (especially at river confluences and in the uplands), and even artistic endeavors at so-called art sanctuaries.

As with lithic manufacture (Pelegrin 1985; Pigeot 1987), sequential techniques for crafting, using, and repairing organic artifacts (such as bone needles, spear throwers, double-beveled bone points, and antler harpoons) were highly and recognizably rulebound (Dobres 1995a, 1996). The overall level of craft and skill demonstrated in the fabrication and morphology of Magdalenian material culture attests not only to a sophisticated level of manual dexterity but to a long tradition of working with the naturalmaterial world in contexts promoting social solidarity (I return to this point below). Of course, TM is perhaps best known for the sophisticated technical skills and artistry with which portable and wall imagery, such as at

Lascaux and Niaux, was created from an extraordinarily broad array of stone, mineral, and organic resources.

In sum, from the deeply stratified nature of cave sites (in particular), the abundance and diversity of remains in many Magdalenian assemblages, the redundant patterning of settlement and economic practices, the stylistic integrity of the visual imagery, and the recognizably rule-bound nature of their material technologies, it is clear that these communities shared basic adaptations such that their tangible remains are recognizable as Magdalenian. The fundamentally normative nature of this particular archaeological culture is contested neither by a processual way of seeing (discussed below) nor by the alternative that follows. The question remains, however: what is the degree of variability and divergence from these materially recognizable norms, and how can we best account for them as if people mattered?

WAYS OF SEEING MAGDALENIAN VARIABILITY: NORMATIVE AND PROCESSUAL GLASSES

What I have just presented is the general view of Magdalenian material traits—a suite of surficial, normative, artifact patterns circumscribed in time and subtly varying from region to region within and outside the boundaries of modern-day France. Until recently, even at the physical scale of site-specific research, most French-trained archaeologists worked to identify the typical and the average. In doing so they tended to see the atypical as indicating the presence of "other" groups from somewhere else simply practicing their own variant of TM (Bordes 1961, 1972; Robert et al. 1953; but also more recently Clottes and Rouzaud 1983; Rozoy 1992). As once practiced by generations of European-trained archaeologists in the first half of the twentieth century, the general goal of culture history research was to identify, describe, and then compare temporal trends by determining regional norms "built up" from site-specific findings. With time the goal was to develop even larger-scale spatiotemporal models of entire culture complexes, such as The Magdalenian. This culture history emphasis on building up regional-scale spatiotemporal frameworks from site-specific findings is in no way unique to French researchers studying the Upper Paleolithic. Indeed, the goal of identifying, describing, and tracking both regional and extraregional culture complexes through typological studies characterizes the explicit goal of most early and mid-century New and Old World archaeologists alike (Trigger 1989). As G. Clark (1991:84–85) and Kuhn (1991: 248–249), both American-trained processual archaeologists, have rightly argued for TM in particular, it is precisely because of the normative interest in time-space systematics through an almost exclusive focus on artifact typology that intraregional variability was not considered an important research question. As we can see, then, a particular way of thinking (normativism) structured a particular way of seeing (regional and extraregional empirical variability in morphological attributes), and together these processes structured on-the-ground analytic methodologies (typology and time-space systematics).

In comparison, first-generation processualists working on the European Middle and Upper Paleolithic were concerned with developing causal accounts for the most ubiquitous and recurrent patterning of material culture in terms of an adaptationist paradigm (classic statements include Binford 1968; Binford and Binford 1968; Clark 1953; Clarke 1968; Higgs 1972). According to the processual view of things, temporal and/or spatial variability in artifact patterning, either within or beyond circumscribed geographic regions, was explained as functionally specific behavioral adaptations to particular material conditions. For example, observed differences in the typological composition of lithic assemblages (and associated faunal remains) were explained as functional variants of logistical economic strategies differentially practiced by mobile hunter-gatherers (Binford 1966, 1972, 1973). Put another way, the remains of a butchery site should not look like those from a hide-processing site, and neither should look the same as a special-purpose hunting camp.

Like it or not, however, the normative looms large in this processual perspective. After all, a widely shared cultural paradigm of functionally variable "tricks of the trade" for coping with the environment is what enabled adaptation to, and survival within, the particular material conditions people faced during the Paleolithic. With the processualists' homeostatic view of things—with Culture as a self-regulating system sensitive and responsive to changes in the external conditions to which it must adapt—too much variability (or difference of opinion about how to get a job done) might "rock the boat." We see here, again, how a particular way of thinking (this time processualism) structured a particular way of seeing (intraregional empirical variability in morphological and functional attributes) and how together they structured on-the-ground analytic methodologies (functional studies, discussed below).

Nonetheless, the introduction of so-called man-land studies to causally account for the once dynamic behaviors of now static archaeological remains constituted a major shift in how researchers thought about the archaeological record (see personal reflections in G. Clark 1991; Straus 1991). Culture (past and present) was now seen as "man's extrasomatic means of adaptation" (Binford 1965:209). Coupled with the idea that widely shared cultural practices were played out differently on the physical landscape as people moved about doing different sorts of economic things, this new way of thinking led to a significantly different reason to focus on regional-scale variability in material behaviors and to start taking intraregional variability seriously. Where normative culture historians were interested in regional-scale typological norms to identify ethnic variants of prehistoric culture complexes, processualists argued that a focus on regional patterning in economic behaviors was the logical scale at which to model ancient settlement systems. The study of regional-scale variability made sense to processualists precisely because people "differentially participate in culture," and for mobile hunter-gatherers in particular, no single site could possibly represent the entirety of their adaptations (Binford 1965; Clarke 1972). As a combined way to think and see, this explicit focus on functional aspects of material culture variability is surely one of the most significant contributions the processual paradigm made to archaeological method, theory, and model building.

DISCUSSION

There is a curious paradox illustrated by these different ways of thinking about and seeing artifact variability. In this particular instance both normative and processual views of TM fixed their gaze on the same analytic scale, the region, and employed site-specific findings to further other research interests. Normative researchers put site-specific patterns of artifact variability to use in describing regional (ethnic) Magdalenian lifeways; processualists looked at individual sites as little more than points on the ground but as functionally differentiated locales where subsistence strategies making up the regional settlement system were variously played out. In both cases, however, "the region" was the physical and phenomenological scale at which site-specific variability was explained (or described). Site-specific finds were clearly necessary to further their different goals: for culture historians they were useful in describing the variety of things people did within their ethnic territories (as well as for placing them in chronostratigraphic order), and for processualists site-specific patterns were necessary to model regional subsistence behaviors. In both cases site-specific variability was seen as a means to an end rather than as meaningful in its own right.

SECTION 2: A CONVERGENCE OF NORMATIVE AND FUNCTIONAL MODELS, THE LAST 20 YEARS

In the past two decades normative and processually trained archaeologists have forged a compromise out of their different ways of thinking about and seeing TM. Today most research centers on the question of settlement systems, subsistence practices,

and the nature of resource exploitation and group mobility. Although at first glance it would appear that the processual lens has carried the day, in truth the contemporary paradigm has more of a bifocal appearance.

In the 1970s it was coincidence that the French appeal to Lapp reindeer economies as analogs for Magdalenian reindeer economies (Leroi-Gourhan and Brézillion 1972) overlapped with the processual ethnoarchaeology of Alaskan and Canadian Eskimo subsistence practices (pioneered by Binford 1977a, 1978, 1980, 1983; discussion in Dobres 1995b:86–100, 193–201). The fortuitous result of this convergence, however, was that today Anglo-American and French researchers are interested in describing and explaining regionally specific resource exploitation and seasonal mobility practices through the study of the spatial distribution of sites and their functional activities across the landscape. This combined framework fits well within the rubric of optimal foraging theory, and its goal is to articulate causal explanations of Magdalenian subsistence practices in terms of economic adaptations to the movement and distribution of seasonally available resources, especially reindeer (Spiess 1979; Sturdy and Webley 1988). For example, at the suite of interrelated Magdalenian open-air sites in the Paris Basin (Pincevent, Vérberie, Marsangy, and Etiolles), researchers are modeling the seasonally based aggregation-dispersion settlement pattern and use of sporadically available resources for the region as a whole (Alix et al. 1993; Audouze 1987; David and Enloe 1993). Three primary research questions in this regard are (1) the nature of the regional settlement system and intersite relationships (David and Enloe 1992; David et al. 1994), (2) site functions (Audouze 1988), and (3) delimiting intrasite activity areas (Enloe et al. 1994; Olive 1992; Olive and Pigeot 1992; Pigeot 1987; Simek 1984). In each instance the cross-fertilization of ideas (and labor) is noteworthy.

Because of Leroi-Gourhan's influence over his students working in the Paris Basin, as well as the infusion of Binford's ethnoarchaeological interest in the material patterning of hunter-gatherer logistical subsistence strategies, the past 20 years have witnessed a special momentum and coherence of regional-scale settlement research on TM in the Paris Basin (also on the Dordogne, further south). Unfortunately, the same cannot be said of the French Midi-Pyrénées, where, with the exception of Bahn (1977, 1984) and Sieveking (1976), a processual interest in subsistence strategies has not developed at the same pace. Archaeological research on TM in the Pyrénées is (still) primarily descriptive, focused separately on (1) empirically rigorous typology and technology studies, (2) identifying and describing various hunting techniques, (3) identifying seasons of occupation from detailed pollen and faunal studies, and (4) delineating site-types. Also unlike work in the Paris Basin, there has been scant interest in the intrasite spatial patterning of artifact remains and activity areas until quite recently. This lack of concern with horizontal spatial distribution patterns is perhaps the single best example to show how important Leroi-Gourhan's and Binford's influence was further north. In the Midi-Pyrénées, only at sites excavated in the past 15 years or so has the spatial patterning of artifact distributions become of interest. However, because there is (still) no explicit interpretive desire to make sense of intrasite activity zones as functional variants in a regional subsistence system, this work remains primarily descriptive (e.g., Bégouën and Clottes 1981; Clottes and Rouzaud 1984; but also see Nougier 1968; Nougier and Robert 1956).

THE CONTEMPORARY NORMATIVE-PROCESSUAL COMPROMISE, OR THE CAKE AND ITS ICING

The paradox in this processual-looking compromise is that although contemporary research into the functional differentiation of seasonally occupied sites and activity areas has introduced far more rigor into understandings of TM material record (and has given the semblance of an anthropological framework to Magdalenian time-space systematics), these concerns have been no more than applied on top of the typological framework in place since the turn of the century. By this I mean that contemporary paleoeconomic questions related to the seasonal use of the landscape and its resources, and how these (literally) map out at the scale of individual sites, are still undertaken in order to type sites, hunting strategies, butchery practices, activity areas, and even flint-knapping techniques. Importantly, the focus here is not on sites as meaningful locales where people interacted with each other while "taking care of business" but as geographically distributed locations forming a regional settlement system. Now, I do not contest that this regional perspective has led to a richer and far more nuanced picture of the morphological contours of The Magdalenian. Indeed, because of this focus we better understand when and for how long people occupied various sites, the way site activities were partitioned across space and on a seasonal basis, how the rewards of the hunt were variously butchered and shared, the intrasite movement of lithic material during the sequence of operations by which tools were manufactured, and so forth. Nonetheless, these processual and functionally oriented studies are driven by classificatory—typological—interests. What a processual lens has provided Magdalenian prehistory is a typology of seasonal land use, explaining it by virtue of macroscale behavioral adaptations to specific environmental conditions. Once sites are dated and regional trends identified, contemporary research focuses almost exclusively on developing a typology of site function and explaining subsistence behaviors in this light. The apparent lack of interest in moving beyond a typological way of thinking about and seeing Magdalenian material variability attests to the staying power of the midcentury ways of thinking and seeing. *Plus ça change, la plus c'est la même chose.*

Because of its descriptive nature, contemporary research is intent on identifying the normative Magdalenian subsistence system from region to region and from season to season. This decidedly normative way of seeing artifact variability, whether functional or ethnic, only "dips" down to site-specific material patterning in order to "build up" to regional generalizations. As currently practiced, this Eskimo paradigm—this "Nunamuitization of the Upper Palaeolithic" (Enloe et al. 1994:111)—is employed to aid what the French call *paléoethnique* descriptions of economic practices. As but one telling example of this lingering typological view of TM, consider how Straus, a self-avowed processualist (1991), describes TM in the Pyrénées:

> While it is unlikely that whole human groups moved the entire length of the Pyrénées during an annual round, individual bands may have followed or at least intercepted reindeer herds in different parts of their movements between upland and lowland pastures.... In short, the Pyrenean evidence suggests substantial residential mobility on a seasonal schedule and on an altitudinal axis, combined with logistical mobility to exploit particular resources (e.g., ibex, salmon, ptarmigan) in a seasonal direction opposite to the fundamental rhythm of the reindeer migrations. (Straus 1990–91:19)

WHAT'S MISSING?

Proposing (macro)scale explanatory models of artifact patterning in terms of regional adaptations to environmental conditions and fluctuating resource availability has never made it necessary, or behaviorally meaningful, to think about material variability in terms of interpersonal social dynamics nor to see interacting social agents as the explanatory culprits (Brumfiel 1991; Cowgill 1993; Dobres and Hoffman 1994; Hodder 1986). Contemporary models of Magdalenian material life provide little room for an explicit consideration of the *people* who variously hunted reindeer, the *people* who variously moved around their subsistence territory, or the *people* who variously organized their functionally adaptive activities from site to site. Although processual archaeology has long been premised on understanding not

only behavioral norms but functional variability around them, it is surprising that there has been so little explicit concern with artifact variability at microanalytic scales, such as at the physical scale of the site.

I take my cue from Marquardt (1992) and suggest that if we want to understand The Magdalenian not only as a systemically integrated suite of functionally differentiated adaptive behaviors that varied across space, but also at the phenomenological scale at which life was meaningful to the agents involved, then we need to pay explicit theoretical and analytic attention to microscale variability in their material repertoires. More than this, we must consider explicitly what flexibility around that idealized norm implies about the dynamics of interpersonal social and material action in which these people engaged (Dobres 1995b; Dobres and Hoffman 1994; see also Wobst, this volume). According to some, only macroscale material variability is behaviorally relevant, and "arbitrary cultural choices" that vary from site to site are little more than deviations, or "noise," of no particular functional or adaptive import (in particular, see Gallay 1992: 119–120). A look at contemporary research on TM demonstrates the extent to which a seemingly processual way of seeing suppresses certain scales of artifact variability in much the same way that normative research suppressed intraregional variability in favor of extraregional patterning. In contrast to this rather extrasocial view of the prehistoric world, I argue below that because the site is the scale at which prehistoric agents meaningfully and materially interacted with each other while "taking care of business," site-specific material variability is anthropologically important.

SECTION 3: ANOTHER WAY OF SEEING: PEOPLE *DO* MAKE A DIFFERENCE

What concerns me about the contemporary compromise implicitly worked out between once distinct normative and processual views of Magdalenian artifact variability is that site-specific data seem to be relevant only as they help elucidate regional trends of one sort or another. But what of the dynamic nature of social engagement in and through which economic and ethnic behaviors were learned, taught, expressed materially, and thus made part of everyday life? How such intersubjective dynamics played out among people engaged in social and material activities that varied from site to site and the role these agential dynamics played in creating the material variability on which we place so much importance are never considered causal factors of anthropological relevance. In decided contrast, when we approach our archaeological object matter (artifact patterning) as if people were the explicit subject of interest, then our approach to studying TM should change (Dobres 1995c). In what follows I use my own work on TM in the French Midi-Pyrénées as an exemplar to explore the more general methodological question of what material and interpretive difference it makes for understanding artifact variability if we take human agency as a potentially significant anthropological dynamic in prehistory.

Since publication of Conkey and Spector's (1984) pivotal essay, archaeology has enjoyed a veritable explosion of critically sensitive research exploring how to approach the question of ancient gender processes through the study of material culture (an excellent and rather thorough overview can be found in Nelson 1997). No matter how successful or overextended these studies have been to date, gender research has probably done more to put a human face to a peopled past (Tringham 1991) than just about any other research agenda this century. Across the breadth of the discipline tightly focused work is beginning to generate insights that are proving especially useful. It is worth pausing to consider two general processual dynamics this body of research has begun to illuminate: (1) gender processes, as a fundamental anthropological dynamic of identity and as an institutionalized system of values, and (2) the inseparability of agency, gender, and technology.

THE SIMULTANEITY OF THE PERSONAL AND POLITICAL: GENDER AS A MULTISCALAR AND PROCESSUAL DYNAMIC

Among other things, gender theory is premised on the ontological standpoint that biological sex and gender, although embodied in the same instant, are not synonymous. Gender, as a salient category of social identity, is a nexus of socially circumscribed meanings, roles, expectations, and values applied to differently sexed individuals and the things they do. Although today we recognize two distinct biological sexes (but see Laqueur 1990; Jordanova 1980, 1993; and Schiebinger 1993 for the history of changing views on the facts of biological sex in Western medicine), there is, in fact, no limit to the variety of genders a society can define, enjoy, or disparage. Importantly, however, gender never stands alone. It blends seamlessly with other salient social markings, such as kin, class, race, age, ethnicity, moieties, and religion (to name but a few). Through these complex blendings of identity, gender provides individuals with much of their rank and standing in the community. Gender also serves to define and regulate the associated privileges, rights, obligations, expectations, and work roles individuals undertake in various contexts (Goucher and Herbert 1996: 54). As such, gender is a more processual, variable, and ambiguous social dynamic than the static concept "identity" typically allows. To my way of thinking, gender is best thought of as a *verb* of enactment and the *processing* of identity over the course of one's life rather than a noun (or thing) to possess (after de Lauretis 1987). That is, precisely because gender blends with time-factored processes such as age, sexual maturity, and work roles, and because its meanings are sensitive to the contexts in which identities are expressed and contested, gender necessarily encompasses the changing place(s) individuals may have in society (Dobres 1998). Throughout the life cycle, and depending on context, an individual's gender is mutable.

At the same time that gender concerns identities and actions processed over time, it is also a collective set of institutional, symbolic, economic, political, and ideological value systems continually played out, reaffirmed, and contested in and through daily routines of sociomaterial interaction. The inevitable tensions and day-to-day negotiation of self and collective interests are very often played out against and through ideologies and actions of a particularly gendered sort. As such, gender is concomitantly "at work" at multiple phenomenological scales, from the personal to the political. Importantly, cultural attitudes about gendered individuals and the collective actions these ideals invoke are inscribed onto the material world in which people live, just as they are inscribed in systems of power afforded by the control of material objects, their production, and technological knowledge (McGaw 1989, 1996). As well, gender and material culture intersect in the symbolic and economic values people give to the material world around them. The role the material world plays both in marking gendered identities and in challenging gendered expectations and rules is something to which students of contemporary and ancient material culture have devoted much attention in recent years (e.g., essays in Gero and Conkey 1991; Wright 1996). And although few today are ready to propose detailed theories to explicate the inseparability of agency and gender at their multiple phenomenological "sites" of interaction with material culture, a compendium of empirical studies across the social sciences demonstrates that they are of undeniable importance to the general human condition and of a single, inseparable piece (for especially compelling studies, see MacKenzie 1991; Moore 1986; Schwartz Cowan 1983; a more comprehensive discussion of these points is found in Dobres 1998).

THE INSEPARABILITY OF AGENCY, GENDER, AND TECHNOLOGY

Material objects, techniques, and production-related tasks are inevitably blended with perceptions of and proscriptions about gender, most obviously because gendered individuals are what make technologies happen (Cockburn and Ormrod 1993). But more than the gendered divisions of labor that help make organized production possible, gender ideologies are part and parcel of material making and use more generally. For example, in western industrial societies, hard and utilitarian materials, technical gadgets, and a particular range of technical activities are stereotypically associated with men, whereas soft, supposedly nontechnical activities are associated with women (for extraordinarily detailed considerations of some of the many ways gendered ideologies can structure material technologies see Bodenhorn 1990; Childs 1998; Cockburn 1985; Herbert 1993; Pacey 1983; Sharp 1991). Now at hand is a decidedly human-centered understanding of the dialectic of agency, gender, and technology that is set in motion during the everyday reproduction of social collectivities. This focus on the seamless web of agency, gender, and technology is also allowing more nuanced understandings of the processual dynamics of macroscale culture change (e.g., David and Robertson 1996; Drygulski Wright et al. 1987; Hastorf 1991; Silverblatt 1988; Trescott 1979; Watson and Kennedy 1991), showing yet again that agency and gender are about far more than issues of personhood. Thus, we can add the gendered dynamics of technology, artifact use, and the cultural values afforded to material objects made by gendered agents (both individual and collective) as key factors contributing to that tightly woven web of meaningful and peopled structures through which the prehistoric material world was both mediated and manipulated by agents "differentially participating in it" (after Binford 1965).

AS IF PEOPLE MATTERED: SOME METHODOLOGICAL IMPLICATIONS FOR THE STUDY OF ARTIFACT VARIABILITY

With the above premises in mind I now turn to a more personal account of the impact this human-centered way of thinking about prehistori culture has had on my analytic methodology for studying Magdalenian technology and, in particular, how I have dealt with the question of artifact variability. Although an engendered approach to the study of the past through the medium of the archaeological record has been shown to demand major conceptual shifts (Conkey 1991; Conkey and Gero 1991; Tringham 1994), it has also been argued that to take prehistoric gender (and, by extension, agency) seriously does not require a methodological "breakthrough." In subtly different ways, and with each emphasizing different aspects of the argument, Conkey and Gero (1991), Wylie (1991), and Costin (1996) suggest that to think about the past as peopled by gendered agents, and accept that such interpersonal dynamics were a significant anthropological process, much less to propose causal inferences about particular genders from the study of material patterns, is more a conceptual and (epistemo)logical problem than a methodological one.

Part of their argument, that methodological breakthroughs are not the solution to the very real difficulties faced in attempts to engender the past, may have to do with their reticence to repeat history. That is, there was a time when processualists placed almost blind faith in methodological solutions to resolving issues of plausibility, testability, and the difficulty of linking material statics with cultural dynamics (e.g., Binford 1981; Raab and Goodyear 1984; Schiffer 1972, 1983; Watson et al. 1971). To this day, of course, there are precious few methodological solutions to what are essentially epistemological issues of interpretation. Thus, I agree with the argument that analytic methods are not the solution to interpretation. At the same time, however, I maintain that shifts in thinking do require shifts in doing and that both can lead to different ways of seeing.

There is no doubt that engendering the past requires significant shifts in how to imagine and think through the archaeological record. I contend that these shifts in thinking differently about the past require us to rethink the significance of what counts as relevant material data, how best to collect and study them, and to evaluate how they

may (or may not) be of relevance to the intangible social process in question. Although this may not require a methodological "breakthrough" (a far too strong and argumentative label for my tastes), my own experience in studying TM as if people mattered suggests that when the specific question of human agency is a privileged research problem, then how we deal with empirical data does indeed change. To give some empirical grounding to this rather abstract claim, in what follows I discuss two methodological strategies that are making a significant difference in how I search for and study Magdalenian artifact patterning: (1) a shift in analytical scale(s) and (2) an explicit focus on site-specific composite assemblages.

SOME CAVEATS

The reader should keep in mind that my particular methodological approach (not solution) to the credible study of prehistoric agency and gender is situated against a concrete archaeological problem I define for TM, just as it is also structured by my thinking about this question in explicitly human terms. The analytic scales on which I focus attention (individual sites juxtaposed to "the region") and how I choose to organize my observations (working against typology by studying composite assemblages) make sense for these interests. As such, they may be of general guidance to researchers with similar concerns. At the same time one must always tailor his or her choice of analytic strategies by taking into consideration the antecedent history of the particular research question (which may be very unlike TM), the state of that art (which may be superior to what is known of TM), and the material contours of the prehistory in question. It is also important to distinguish between analytic *methods* (such as microscopic use-wear analysis, replicative studies, typological seriations, GIS, and so forth) and a research *methodology* (which is a suite of particularly chosen analytic methods combined for a specific research problem; after Harding 1987). Analytic methods common to practically all archaeological research can be combined in any number of ways to create significantly different research methodologies, each suited to the particular questions at hand and the interpretive or explanatory interests of the researcher.

To briefly return to my previous comparative discussion, with the advent of processual archaeology in the mid to late 1960s, both analytic and inferential methodologies for studying the archaeological record changed significantly. This new way of thinking about ancient cultures, as functionally differentially adaptive behaviors, led (in due course) to new methods of research and analysis. These new approaches included regional settlement systems analysis, functional and resource utilization studies, and a long-overdue concern with site-formation processes. Even new methods of analogical reasoning were explored (Binford 1978; Gould 1978). New ways of thinking also led to new methods of excavation. More to the point, the very definition of what now constituted relevant material data changed considerably with the advent of a processual way of thinking. For example, just in terms of the study of technology there was a significant shift away from the collection of whole and near-complete specimens (desired to identify temporal and spatial patterning in artifact morphology). In its stead developed a range of new interests in studying artifact function and the mechanical properties of raw materials. In time this led to the realization that debitage and broken specimens were more valuable kinds of data than typologically diagnostic formal tools (for an in-depth consideration of normative and processual methods for studying prehistoric technology, see Dobres 1995b:75–81). With the shift from studies of form to the study of function, whole new sets of empirical data were "discovered," and some long-standing kinds of data no longer provided information deemed useful for the questions at hand.

Given the inseparable relationship between thinking and doing, or more properly between theory and practice, how can we expect to take questions of prehistoric agency and gender seriously, change our ways of

thinking to accommodate such interests, and not also alter our methodologies for the study of the archaeological record? Using my research on organic technology in the Ariège and Haute-Garonne (French Midi-Pyrénées) as an exemplar, I briefly discuss two methodological strategies I am employing to make sense of Magdalenian artifact variability as if people mattered.

SHIFTS IN ANALYTICAL SCALES: FROM MACRO TO MICRO AND BACK AGAIN

If we can accept the argument that the processual dynamics of interpersonal social relationships mattered to prehistoric lifeways and culture change, it seems to me that the phenomenological scale(s) at which social agents interacted with each other while taking care of material matters should be of explicit interest. Marquardt (1992) has made the case that there are many phenomenological, analytic, and interpretive scales useful for investigating the past. Different scales "make sense" depending on the nature of one's questions and the theoretical perspectives guiding that research. There is no one "best" scale at which to investigate a particular ancient dynamic, nor is there a particular class of data best suited to that work. Inasmuch as no single analytic scale can meet all research needs, and because empirical observations vary from scale to scale to inform differently on one's question, Marquardt argues for the value of juxtaposing findings and interpretations across scales, even if they do not form a single coherent whole. For lack of a better definition, I call the *microscale* that phenomenological level at which people engage with one another while making sense of and acting upon their sociomaterial world (Cross 1990; Dobres and Hoffman 1994; Tringham 1994).

The microscale is not the only best scale at which to study people, but it is a phenomenological scale long sidelined in mainstream research on TM. Recall that research on TM has focused primarily on regional-scale variability. In the process, material attributes patterning out at the physical scale of "the site" have not been considered in terms of the people who produced them but in terms of something else: functional variants of the regional adaptive system, ethnic variations in traditional lifeways, or something in between. In contrast, because my interest in Magdalenian artifact variability concerns the dynamic nature of social interaction during technological activities of artifact manufacture, use, repair, and discard, it makes analytic sense to focus on a physical scale experienced by the agents themselves while occupied with these tasks. Toward that end I have highlighted the site for its own sake, because that is where people interacted with each other while going about their daily technological activities.

Perhaps of surprise to some, although my research question is decidedly intangible and concerns the social dynamics of Magdalenian technical agency, to further that interpretive end I have paid extraordinary attention to empirical detail, collecting data on some 90 different technical attributes per artifact. Beyond description for its own sake, this explicit attention to empirical detail has allowed for a more rigorous identification of the specific activities practiced at each of the eight sites in my study area (Dobres 1996). With such empirical information at my disposal I have been in a far more credible position to identify the nature, degree, and intensity of intangible social interaction likely to have been going on at each site.

When I took site-specific artifact patterning seriously, as a static link to ancient social dynamics, I found a fascinating set of empirical patterns in technical attributes that did not simply replicate TM regional norm for making harpoons, bone needles, spear points, and awls. However, although I placed special analytic attention on the microscale, I simultaneously recognized that people living during TM were highly mobile. Thus, it was necessary to juxtapose site-specific findings, for it is likely that "the same" people visited many different sites in the region. Following Marquardt's suggestion, then, for my particular research interests it made sense to work simultaneously at more than one analytic scale (micro and macro) and to juxtapose my

findings along several different axes (e.g., according to typology, by function, by raw material, etc.) as suited my interpretive goals. Importantly, my decision to compare and contrast technical patterns across eight separate sites was not done in order to "build up" to a regional understanding of differential land and resource-use in the Ariège and Haute-Garonne. Rather, with people in mind I wanted to see how technological activities varied from locale to locale and use these data to pinpoint the specific activities undertaken at each site and the intensity with which each activity was practiced.

I discovered through these means a wealth of data on the variety of technical strategies carried out across the region to make, use, and repair the most ubiquitous of Magdalenian material culture. These site-specific strategies "hovered" around TM norm, but on a site-by-site basis that norm played out very differently. Importantly, by taking the site as a meaningful scale of study (and as meaningfully experienced by the people visiting it), I found that even when they undertook the same basic activities (e.g., hunting and butchering mountain goat at small upland sites) and used the same equipment (e.g., harpoons and spear points), their technical strategies and gestural techniques varied. Choice in barb designs on harpoons, strategies for hafting spear points to a shaft, even decisions about when and how to repair or recycle broken artifacts varied among sites where the same functional activities were pursued by "the same" people (Dobres 1996).

However, because I started this research with the premise that people differentially participate in culture (especially as gendered individuals with possibly different agential interests), and that this matters to seeking out and understanding artifact variability, I was not satisfied to brush aside my findings as merely the idiosyncratic vagaries of individual hands. Because of the particular paradigmatic glasses I wore for this work (ground by theories of agency and gender), what I saw in these patterns of technical variability were traces of individual agents interacting with each other through and during their everyday material activities, such as ibex hunting (Dobres 1995b, 1998). Because of the implicitly normative underpinnings of contemporary research on TM, what is characteristically "left out" of consideration as a causal explanation for observed material differences in special-purpose (ibex hunting) sites is the possibility that variability in technical strategies might relate to the nature of the social interaction between the agents who visited these sites while they prepared for, hunted, and processed game and maintained their tool kits. But without an explicit concern with making sense of artifact variability in terms of the people responsible for it, such low-level variability in ibex hunting activities would probably never have been discerned. Even if it were, however, it would most likely be called "noise" and considered all but irrelevant to settlement system analyses. In an argument too involved to rehearse here, I prefer to think of the "noise" of technical variability at the microscale as related to the "babble of technological voices" (Dobres 1998).

ON THE STUDY OF COMPOSITE ASSEMBLAGES: AGAINST THE TYPOLOGICAL GRAIN

As discussed previously, the contemporary convergence of French and Anglo-American interests in TM has a strong typological bent. Although interest in discerning the function of sites, or site types, prevails, researchers from both sides of the Atlantic favor studies of individual classes of artifacts (such as harpoons, bone points, burins, needles, awls, and so forth). The goal of such an approach is to delineate broad temporal and/or spatial distribution patterns. Even on a site-specific basis the methodological strategy is to separate whole assemblages into type-specific artifact categories then conduct detailed study of each separately. Especially in the Pyrénées it is rare to find technical studies that work on integrated assemblages as site-specific "wholes." Yet from a people-centered point of view, a focus on composite assemblages (made up of a variety of artifact types) better approximates the lived experience of the

people who in their daily lives made and did more than one thing at a time.

How can we possibly understand the complexity of technical decisions and productive strategies practiced at individual sites if we continue to segment "for heuristic purposes" the material traces of once overlapping material activities? In other words, can we understand what structured technical decisions as to when, how, and why to cut harpoon barbs in a certain way, whether to repair a broken point, or how many preforms to sketch out for later use if we do not think of them as choices balanced against each other and against a host of other material activities also making demands on these people's attention, skills, labor, and resources? According to this logic, it clearly makes a methodological difference to study artifact variability as if people mattered. By making agency and gender my explicit research question, it makes more methodological "sense" to work against a typological orientation— for the simple fact is that during TM (as with most any other time, I suspect) people did more than one thing at a time.

I have called my focus on the study of Magdalenian composite assemblages a "Humpty Dumpty" methodology (not method) because from the start it takes as the object of study an integrated assemblage of typologically discrete artifacts. By making the *assemblage* the object of study, not separate classes of artifacts to be "put back together" afterward, and by working on more than one class of artifacts at a time, I am able to counter the conventional, piecemeal approach to TM. For example, for the eight individual assemblages in my study this means investigating and recording observations using a series of cross-cutting empirical axes: typological category (of course), but also raw material, function, and even physical segment (proximal, medial, and distal). As well, I am able to investigate variability at multiple physical scales: microscopic, macroscopic, parts of objects, entire specimens. Coupled with my overall focus on composite assemblages, this juxtaposition of physical scales allows me to garner a wide variety of comparative observations: (1) on the composite assemblage as an integrated "whole"; (2) on morphologically similar segments of typologically different sorts of objects (e.g., technical treatments of points and hafted bases on antler harpoons and bone points; techniques to manufacture and/or repair pierced eyes on bone needles and horse teeth; shafts of bone points, harpoons, needles, awls, and so forth); (3) on different or similar treatments correlated to raw material (specifically bone, antler, ivory, teeth); (4) on differences in technical treatments of similarly used artifacts; (5) on similarities in technical treatments of differently used objects; and finally, (6) all these empirical observations on a comparative interassemblage basis.

The main objectives of this analytic methodology are (1) to counter typological research that segments the material remains of past webs of technological actions into discrete units, (2) to better discern empirical variability at multiple physical scales, and most important, (3) to organize my findings in such a way as to be relevant to the questions driving this research—understanding the nature of social interaction by people of various genders making and using these objects during TM. Because my subject matter is people I approach my object matter differently from researchers whose interest is regional resource procurement strategies.

To summarize my findings briefly, what this multiscalar "Humpty Dumpty" methodology has allowed me to *see* are significantly different technical strategies of artifact manufacture, use, and repair played out differently at each of my eight sites. Because I am working under the premise that site-specific material variability in the structure of technological activities was part of the agential dynamics by which people negotiated social relationships while taking care of business, my findings suggest that the basis of Magdalenian social organization in productive activities was *flexibility* (Dobres 1995a, 1995b). The phenomenological scale at which I have found technical choice hovering around TM norm is "the site," and from site to site choice was clearly not structured by

blind submission to normative rules, functional need, typology, or even raw material. To me this implies that for TM (in the Pyrénées at least), normative technical rules of conduct were made to be broken. Why people made the specific choices they did at different sites where the same (or different) activities were pursued is a fascinating anthropological question. Classic sorts of pragmatic and efficiency-minded explanations will not suffice, nor will appeal to artifact physics. People made these choices, people pursued these activities, and people must be the explanatory culprits. At higher-order phenomenological scales, it is easy to lose sight of this fact.

SOME SUMMARY REMARKS

Thinking Differently. Because I take seriously the dynamics of interpersonal social agency as a possible causal factor structuring material variability in Magdalenian technology, several methodological strategies make logical sense if I am to operationalize this (post)processual question and not simply tell tall tales. Specifically, a phenomenological focus on everyday social interaction leads me to privilege research at the physical and analytic (micro)scale of "the site." At the same time, because people living during TM were highly mobile, it makes sense to juxtapose micro- and macroscale findings by comparing and contrasting intra- and intersite patterns—in effect, playing one off the other.

Doing Differently. Given the specific history of research on TM in particular, a concern with site-specific variability juxtaposed to regional patterns leads me to think about and treat the archaeological record differently. It has led to my explicit concern with composite assemblages and to developing a Humpty Dumpty strategy for data collection and analysis.

Seeing Differently. In turn (and as with any happy ending) this multiscalar methodology has enabled me to identify hitherto unknown but interesting patterns of artifact variability that challenge conventional wisdom on the normative and rule-bound structure of TM. Rather than practicing the same

Magdalenian way of life from site to site to site, differentiated only by functional activity or ethnicity, I have found data to suggest that these people knew but stretched, broke, or changed the rules depending on where they were, what they were doing, and with whom they were doing it. More than simply uncovering different and more rigorously controlled artifact patterns, the particular empirical findings that have resulted from this theory-driven methodology have allowed me to propose credible and anthropologically relevant inferences about the meaningful lives of people living during TM.

It is not the purpose of this discussion to evaluate the appropriateness or efficacy of my methodological strategy for artifact analysis as if people mattered by judging the interpretive ends to which my particular findings have been put. Ends do not justify means. Thus, even if my particular interpretation of artifact variability turns out to be wrong-headed, it does not follow that the methodological means to get me there are also invalid. From the outset I have taken the position that to think about The Magdalenian as if people mattered required me to study the material remains of TM differently. Thus, it may well be that the means of study do matter at least as much as the ends to which they are put. In archaeology, having worthy anthropological, processual, and interpretive goals is clearly not enough anymore. If we are ever to put a meaningful face

on prehistory that is more rigorous than ad hoc accommodation and post hoc reasoning, we must concentrate more attention on the means and not just the ends. Nor can we continue to use methodologies designed for other questions and simply "add people and stir." The advent of a processual way of thinking taught us that thinking, doing, and seeing—that theory, methodology, and explanation—were interconnected endeavors. As we continue to change the way we think about the past, so too must we change the way we study and see the archaeological record. I hope to have made here some headway with the idea that seeing artifact variability as if people mattered does, after all, make a difference.

Acknowledgments. This essay was written while I was in residence at the School of American Research (1996–1997), and I admit to playing hooky from the real purpose of my tenure there by taking the time to pull these thoughts together. I was further supported in this bit of procrastination by a fellowship from the National Endowment for the Humanities, to whom I also apologize for detouring ever so slightly from my proposed plan of action. I appreciate Elizabeth Chilton's providing me the opportunity to present these ideas here and thank her for helpful comments on a previous (and terribly rough) draft.

3

Social Dimensions of Technical Choice in Kalinga Ceramic Traditions

Miriam T. Stark

In the late nineteenth and early twentieth centuries material culture studies formed the foundation of cultural anthropological research in North America. Although museum anthropology is now subordinate to academic anthropology, material culture studies were a central force behind the establishment of major museum collections and the employment of anthropologists throughout North America until the middle of this century (Miller 1987:110–112; Pfaffenberger 1992; Wright 1996:81–85). This material culture focus in North American anthropology also shaped the development of early culture theory: culture areas, theories of style, and models of diffusion and migration were all conceptualized through a material culture lens. With the Boasian shift toward historical particularism, interest in material culture studies by cultural anthropologists waned. For many decades that followed, material culture studies were relegated to the research domains of "primitive" art and "primitive" technology (Conkey 1989; Miller 1987; Stark 1998).

In contrast, of course, archaeologists have maintained an active interest in material culture from the mid-nineteenth century to the present. The nature of our database has encouraged archaeologists to study material culture continuously since the inception of the discipline as a recognized profession. Archaeologists describe, illustrate, excavate, record, organize, and seriate material culture; little else unifies archaeological practice

today beyond our shared focus on physical, durable remains of the past. What is perhaps surprising is that archaeologists only began to develop comprehensive theoretical frameworks for understanding material culture in the last 20 years. Some approaches work from the bottom up, using case studies to illustrate principles of an emerging behavioral theory (e.g., Schiffer 1995; Schiffer and Skibo 1997). Others have worked from the top down, applying evolutionary theory to selected artifact classes (e.g., Neiman 1995; Teltser, ed. 1995). Until recently, however, material culture studies in anthropology have been dominated either by narrow discussions of style (e.g., Carr and Neitzel 1995a; Hegmon 1992) or by postmodern approaches (e.g., Dobres and Hoffman 1994; Hodder 1982b; Hodder, ed. 1989; Leone 1992; Shanks and Tilley 1987a; Tilley 1993).

The irony of this situation is not lost on most archaeologists: we all use material culture in our analyses, but most recent efforts to develop a comprehensive material culture theory in our field derive from a postmodernist school of thought. Most of us also agree that in traditional societies today and in the historic past people manipulate(d) material culture through social acts: goods are (and were) used to create cultural categories, to straddle social and cultural boundaries, and to construct social frames (Goodby 1998; Little 1992). The consequences of these individual acts often appear in aggregate as material culture patterning, which is the primary domain of archaeological interpretation.

This narrow scope of material-culture theory in archaeology—which has been dominated recently by postmodern approaches—has alienated many archaeologists who might otherwise be interested in material-culture studies. One important exception to this pattern is found in studies of material culture and technology, an area of research that has grown as rapidly as new techniques are introduced into the field of archaeology. Great advances in archaeological science, in ethnoarchaeological studies of production, and in experimental archaeology have expanded the range of questions that we can ask of material culture. A great deal of ethnoarchaeological research in recent decades has also concentrated on issues germane to material-culture theory. Even there, however, a glaring problem remains: the sophistication of our analytic techniques outstrips the sophistication of our explanatory (or theoretical) frameworks.

The goal of this chapter is to discuss new approaches for understanding social boundaries in the archaeological record. Two questions structure the discussion. First, how are social boundaries reflected in material-culture patterning? Second, what is the nature of these boundaries in nonstate societies? I employ methods from two different schools of thought: one European and one North American. One approach, inspired by the French *techniques et culture* school, explores links among cognition, technical choice, and material culture patterning (see Cresswell 1990; Gosselain 1992a; Lemonnier 1986, 1992, 1993; Leroi-Gourhan 1993). Although initially focused on production sequences (see discussion in Sellet 1993), this approach has now been applied in studies of organizational dynamics in prestate and state societies from the Old World (e.g., Bernbeck 1995; Vidale et al. 1992). Related research has also been carried out recently in the United States as part of an "anthropology of technology" (see, for example, Pfaffenberger 1992) but largely in industrial settings.

A second, Americanist approach (e.g., Childs 1991; Lechtman 1977; Sackett 1985, 1986, 1990) examines formal variation as it is expressed in the goods of everyday life. One of the greatest contributions of this approach is that it challenges the style-function dichotomy that archaeologists commonly use to examine formal variability in artifacts. This analytical division of variability into style and function has its roots in the earliest publications of Lewis Binford (e.g., 1962, 1965). In this technology-oriented approach, which focuses on the production process, functional and stylistic considerations are intertwined. James Sackett introduced the term *isochrestic variation* (1985, 1986) to capture this different picture of variability, and Heather Lechtman's (1977) notion of "technological style" seems closely related.

Despite active discussions of technology and culture in European circles, North Americanists have restricted most discussion of the subject to debates over the precise meanings of "isochrestic variation" (Sackett 1990) and "technological style" (Childs 1991; Lechtman 1977). Other archaeologists who study style ignore these approaches altogether. This is unfortunate because each perspective focuses on a type of variation that expands the scope of traditional conceptions of style in archaeology (Dietler and Herbich 1998; Hegmon 1992, 1998; Wiessner 1983; Wobst 1977, and this volume). Although these two technologically oriented approaches from opposite sides of the Atlantic seem complementary, little synthetic research has been done to date. This paper attempts such a synthesis.

SOCIAL BOUNDARIES, ETHNICITY, AND THE ARCHAEOLOGICAL RECORD

The identification of social groups has been a perennial concern throughout the history of archaeology. Archaeologists have identified groups in material-culture patterning from scales that range from household and sodality to ethnic group, regional system, and culture area. Not surprisingly, many archaeologists continue to equate stylistic boundaries with ethnic boundaries in their study of nonstate societies (MacEachern 1998). Group boundaries for these social units are generally identified using trait distributions of key artifact types, selected practices and customs that leave physical traces, and architectural traditions. Of course, many archaeologists now acknowledge problems inherent in equating "ethnic groups" with such distributional boundaries in nonstate societies (e.g., Cordell and Yannie 1991; Hodder 1979; Shennan 1989a). Neither the meaning of "ethnicity" as a social phenomenon nor the significance of stylistic variation as an archaeological pattern is adequately understood (Carr and Neitzel 1995a; Stark, ed. 1998; Terrell et al. 1997). Yet persistent questions related to long-term change in social process hinge on identifying such groups.

Ethnicity in Cultural Anthropology

The notion of ethnicity in cultural anthropology is problematic for those wishing to import theoretical frameworks into their interpretations of the archaeological record. Many anthropologists believe that ethnicity is situational, that ethnic boundaries are inescapably fluid, and that the relationship between ethnic and sociolinguistic boundaries is constantly in flux. Many cultural anthropologists now maintain that "ethnicity" is not a relevant framework for analysis: it is a product of ethnographic field strategies, of European contact, or of a theoretical obsession with finding tribal formations (e.g., Alonso 1994; Lewis 1991). In Asia and the Pacific, for example, some scholars muse that the idea of ethnicity is no more than "western ethnotheory" (Linnekin and Poyer 1990:10), with few referents in societies under study.

"Ethnicity" in Archaeology

Many cultural anthropologists tell us that our focus on ethnicity in the past is impractical and unfeasible. Yet many archaeologists believe that ethnicity structured ancient social identity, both in nonstate and state societies, but that we cannot identify ethnic boundaries in the archaeological record (e.g., Ferguson 1992; Hill 1989; Jones 1997; Shennan 1989a). Are we relying on flawed conceptual frameworks when we seek ethnicity in the archaeological record? The answer to this question may be yes—and, perhaps, no. The search for ethnicity per se seems unproductive (if not tautological) for archaeologists who study nonstate societies. Yet efforts to understand patterns of cultural variation, and to identify and explore social boundaries in the material record, are not.

Despite myriad attempts, archaeologists continue to experience difficulties in developing an archaeology of ethnicity (Hodder 1979; Shennan 1989a). One reason, perhaps, lies in our general resistance to using terminology that is still associated with culture historians, terms such as *ethnic group, culture area*, and *migration*. The search for cultural difference is a legitimate (if difficult) task in nonstate societies, which commonly have rich traditions of cultural diversity and little evidence for formalized ethnic groups. In the archaeology of nonstate societies, analytical problems that center on two related issues plague this search for ethnic groups (and/or tribes). The first concerns how archaeologists identify these social units in the material record. The second issue concerns how we define relevant units of analysis in studying social formations among nonstate societies. Let us first examine some archaeological approaches to the study of social boundaries.

STYLE AND TECHNOLOGY IN THE ARCHAEOLOGICAL STUDY OF SOCIAL BOUNDARIES

Discussions that explore the types and functions of style in archaeology are numerous (e.g., Conkey and Hastorf 1990; Dietler and Herbich 1998; Hegmon 1992, 1998; Wobst, this volume). However, few discussions provide satisfactory definitions of key concepts such as stylistic and isochrestic variation or active and passive styles (e.g., Hegmon 1992:522–529; Sackett 1985, 1990; Wiessner 1985). Stylistic variability, a favorite topic of archaeological ceramicists, is a fickle signature of group membership. In traditional societies we see that stylistic expressions vary according to the media (e.g., ceramics, textiles, baskets, house walls) on which stylistic information is inscribed, the level of antagonism and interaction between neighboring groups, economic conditions in a local area, and (perhaps) the sociopolitical structure of the society (Dietler and Herbich 1989, 1998; Hegmon 1992:527–528; Hodder 1979; Stark 1995). The relationship between style and social boundaries is highly contextualized (Hodder 1979; Lechtman 1977; Lemonnier 1986; Wiessner 1983), and which (if any) category of material culture marks these boundaries varies from one society to the next. Iconography that expresses aspects of social identity in certain situations may in other cases merge social boundaries to convey information about broader patterns of interregional interaction.

Stylistic studies in archaeology generally focus on active and consciously manipulated aspects of material-culture variability. Style thus has functions, a point made effectively by H. Martin Wobst (1977) in his "information-exchange" model. The approach used in the present study differs from the information-exchange model in its focus and theoretical framework and is inspired by work on an "anthropology of technology" (see Pfaffenberger 1992). In such an approach all goods (not simply those with decoration, as many inferred from Wobst [1977]) convey information about behavior. This technological patterning both embodies and generates meaning in different cultural traditions. Spatial discontinuities in technological traditions—which include but are broader than simply stylistic traditions—should reflect social boundaries in the material record.

Perhaps one reason it is so difficult to find "ethnicity" in the archaeological record of nonstate societies is that we are looking for the wrong kinds of social units. Examination of archaeological materials from these societies confirms the existence of differences in manufacturing techniques and reveals boundaries in distributional patterning. Adopting a technological approach to understanding material culture provides a more holistic perspective than do conventional stylistic frameworks used in archaeology. These goods, precisely because of their ver-

nacular qualities (see Conkey 1989:21), may be more indicative of some types of prehistoric social boundaries than goods that people consciously manipulate for conveying social information, the content of which the archaeologist can only approximate.

A TECHNOLOGICAL APPROACH

How do we go about identifying technological boundaries in the archaeological record? One way is through systematic analysis of how artisans make goods; we can do this by examining the steps involved in manufacture. The sum of these technical choices (embodied in production steps), following Heather Lechtman (1977), is called "technological style." Childs (1991:332) defines *technological style* as the "formal integration of the behaviors performed during the manufacture and use of material culture, which expresses social information." It represents the outcome of repetitive and mundane activities associated with everyday life; artisans often conceptualize technological style as "the way things are always done" (Wiessner 1984: 161, 195). Artisans make technical choices at most stages of the production sequence, from materials procurement to final decoration, and these choices constitute knowledge of a manufacturing tradition that is passed from one generation to the next (Gosselain 1992a, 1998; Lechtman 1977:15; Mahias 1993; Sackett 1986:268–269, 1990:33, 37). Technological styles thus represent the sum of the technical process: raw materials, sources of energy, tools, and scheduling (Lemonnier 1993:4; van der Leeuw 1993).

In this approach, then, formal variability in manufactured goods reflects a series of technical choices that are largely shaped by tradition and constrained by environmental factors. Disagreement exists among archaeologists regarding the relationship between style and intentionality in the manufacturing process. Some archaeologists contend that producers consciously use manufacturing methods to signal group identity (e.g., P. Arnold, this volume; Goodby 1998; Hodder 1982b; Hodder, ed. 1989; Wobst 1977, this volume). Others believe that much of this social information is encoded unconsciously and that producers are largely unaware of the social signature that their goods bear (e.g., Leroi-Gourhan 1993; Sackett 1985, 1986, 1990). A growing literature on the relationship between human agency and technology reminds us of the complexity of this issue (e.g., Cresswell 1990; Pfaffenberger 1992; see discussion in Jones 1997:116–127).

Because all manufactured objects reflect technological styles, technological variation also characterizes objects laden with symbolic content. These include architecture, clothing, portable and mural art, body tattooing, and, of course, pottery. Understanding the technological styles of goods laden with iconographic complexity, however, is difficult. Let us take the case of decorated ceramics as one example (see also Costin, this volume). Differences in vessel function and value, the addition of production steps to the decorated pottery manufacturing process, and the implicit stylistic information that accompanies the production of decorated ceramics render their variation more enigmatic than are differences among the goods of everyday life.

Technological styles vary across media within a production community (DeBoer 1990; Hodder 1979). Commonly, technological style boundaries are isomorphic with community boundaries. Luo potters of Kenya, for example, employ a "sort of intuitive multi-variant analysis" in assigning pots to a particular technological tradition (Dietler and Herbich 1989:157). Attributes may include the color of fired clay, the shape of the rim, the general vessel shape, and morphological proportions (Gosselain 1992a: 572). Attributes that reflect technological styles are influenced by many factors, including technofunctional considerations, strategies of affiliation (Miller 1986), caste, and dietary preference. For example, the distribution of water jar shapes in Guatemala conforms to geographically discrete methods for carrying jars. These differences reflect distinct cultural values across regions regarding how women, who are the water jar carriers, comport themselves in public (Reina and Hill 1978:238–243). Vessels used to prepare ethnic specialty foods might also have characteristic vessel forms.

RELATED CONCEPTS IN CULTURAL
ANTHROPOLOGY

This archaeological notion of technological style is closely related to notions introduced by cultural anthropologists. Foremost among these is Pierre Bourdieu (1977) and his concept of "habitus" (Dietler and Herbich 1998; Hegmon 1998; Miller 1987). Habitus consists of sets of learned behaviors that can be expressed, consciously or unconsciously, in material ways. Whether learned through formal education or through acculturation in daily life, habitus is reflected in the goods that people make. Parallels to the concept of technological style are also found in ethnological studies of Pacific societies. In his research in highland New Guinea, James Watson (1990) has also formulated a similar notion, which he calls "cultural diacritics." These cultural diacritics "reflect familiarity, custom, habituation, and an acquired accommodation to the creatures, things, spirits, and…powers of a particular locale, aided by the instruction and the ritual and magical proclivities of parents and other elders of a community" (Watson 1990:38).

Some of these diacritics have material correlates, either as places or as goods that are essential elements in a particular culture. Habituation, familiarity, and repetition: these concepts inhere in notions of technological style, habitus, and cultural diacritics. The similarities found among these three discrete concepts suggest the possibility of synthesis in the development of material-culture theory. Whether one prefers to describe habitus, cultural diacritics, or technological style, each idea refers to conscious and unconscious elements of technical choices. Some of these choices are explicit; others are considered too trivial for comment.

All manufactured goods contain formal variability that reflects technical choices involved in the manufacturing process. However, studying meaningful patterns in such variability is easier with utilitarian goods than with highly decorative items. Utilitarian goods may be more sensitive to cultural boundaries, which vary in their degree of closure (e.g., Hodder 1979, 1982b). Cross-cultural research suggests that social boundaries for fineware ceramics and other non-utilitarian commodities are often permeable because such goods circulate widely and, thus, reach a wide range of consumers (e.g., Larick 1987; Lyons 1987; Sterner 1989). Perhaps contrasting contexts of production and distribution account for scalar differences in how these categories mark boundaries: where artisans make goods for a consumer market, the goods may reveal more about the identity of their producers than about their consumers (Dietler and Herbich 1994).

Utilitarian goods for which technological style is most easily studied include ground-stone tools, chipped-stone tools (e.g., projectile points), and pottery (Chilton 1998a; Dean 1988; Goodby 1998; Sackett 1985; Stark 1995; Stark et al. 1995; Sterner 1989). Extensive recent research by ethnoarchaeologists (e.g., Kramer 1985; Longacre 1991) has shown that utilitarian pottery is a particularly sensitive medium. Vernacular architecture, the most complex and least portable of all artifacts, can be another sensitive indicator of social affiliation (e.g., Baker 1980; Baldwin 1987; Cameron 1998; Ferguson 1992; Stark et al. 1995).

STABILITY AND CHANGE IN TECHNOLOGICAL STYLES

Change in technological style occurs on different temporal and geographic scales than does iconological style. Whereas iconological style often exhibits extensive distributions (or horizons) in the archaeological record, technological styles commonly have restricted distributions that reflect local technical systems and their populations of human producers. Boundaries of these technical systems conform to local communities, an important and previously overlooked social scale of analysis for those who study iconological style. Two qualities of technological variability are thus important: (1) its inherent stability through time and (2) its potential role in differentiating groups from one another in the archaeological record.

Ethnoarchaeological research has shown that technological styles are more resistant to change than are decorative aspects of material culture because change in technological style requires a change in the manufacturing process (Gosselain 1992a:582–583; Rice 1984:252; Wiessner 1985). Because technological styles tend to be conservative, they are ideal for studying social boundaries in the archaeological record. One example from the American Southwest illustrates this point. When Tohono O'odham potters were asked why they did not adopt flat bases for their cooking pots (which could then be used on modern stoves), "the universal answer was laughter, as if doing it any other way would be ludicrously unthinkable....[They] made convex-based pottery because that is the way their cultural dictates would have it" (Fontana et al. 1962:49).

Both the types of goods used (Welsch and Terrell 1991, 1998; Wiessner 1983) and variation in the styles of widely used goods may reflect social boundaries (Sackett 1986:270). Examination of a specific class of material culture provides clues regarding a particular technological style. Spatial variability should be evident, then, at two scales: in the technological style that shapes each artifact class and in the suite of technological styles that constitute a culture's technical system.

Although technological styles are generally stable, changes do occur within the bounds of a particular technological tradition. Producers may manipulate technological styles in conscious attempts to instigate change, or external forces may compel them to change aspects of their manufacturing technology (Childs 1991:337; Roe 1980; Stark and Longacre 1993). Understanding differences in manufacturing techniques offers a means to reconstruct the technical choices made during the manufacturing process. Factors that affect vessel forms in each functional category are many and include socioeconomic considerations and also individual idiosyncrasies. Changing subsistence strategies and the subsequent demand for different functional categories, demographic changes that lead to the establishment of aggregated communities with many mouths to feed, and changing patterns of social interaction and social integration may affect the forms that potters produce. These factors (as well as others) influence the forms of variation that are expressed as a technological style.

Change in technological style may be rapid or gradual. Unique technological styles develop and change in response to local influences on technical choices by individuals or groups. Individual expressions of technological style may change when potters are adopted (Lathrap 1983), married (Miller 1985), or even abducted (DeBoer 1986) into new communities. Groups may change in response to colonization (Ferguson 1992:38–41) or in response to consumer demand for new products (Annis 1985; Glick 1977; Hallifax 1894:40; Mossman and Selsor 1988:221). When change occurs in response to external pressures, the nature of this external influence determines the tempo of change.

EXAMINING TECHNOLOGICAL STYLE IN ARCHAEOLOGICAL CERAMICS

The Operational Sequence

Cross-cultural research on technology helps bridge the analytic gap between ethnoarchaeological and archaeological ceramic studies. For various reasons ceramic manufacturing traditions have been studied more extensively than other categories of material culture. The "operational sequence" or *chaîne opératoire* (Lemonnier 1986) of ceramic manufacture involves multiple technical steps, each of which poses problems that artisans can resolve in many ways (Gosselain 1992a, 1998; Leroi-Gourhan 1993; Mahias 1993:165; van der Leeuw 1993:243). As noted previously, this arbitrariness in some technological steps generates variability in material culture patterning.

Previous approaches have examined the operational sequence to compare production complexity across different ceramic traditions (Feinman et al. 1981; Hagstrum 1988). Production steps structure the ceramic man-

ufacturing sequence from materials procurement onward, and many steps are sensitive to local variations in how goods are made. Parameters of this technical variability can be compared by examining operational sequences among technological traditions. The task is to identify steps in the operational sequence of ceramic manufacture and then to evaluate which of these steps display variability that is visible on archaeological ceramics.

The ceramic manufacturing sequence for hand-built technologies is divided into seven tasks, which are summarized in Table 3.1 (Rice 1987; Rye 1981). Materials procurement and preparation are the first two tasks. The third and fourth tasks are forming processes: vessels are shaped using primary forming techniques, and vessel proportions are refined using secondary forming techniques (Rye 1981:62). The fifth task, the decorative forming process, modifies the vessel's surface, often through changes in texture. Drying and firing processes, included in the sixth task, affect shrinkage rates (and susceptibility to cracking), as well as relative vessel strength and hardness. Postfiring techniques, such as smudging, are the final steps in the manufacturing sequence.

Factors That Affect Technical Choices in Ceramic Manufacture

Because production technologies often involve compound manufacturing techniques (Rice 1987:124; Rye 1981), potters may use multiple production steps in some tasks, such as materials procurement, forming, and decoration. Some of these steps are more sensitive to the local manufacturing idiom than are others (Table 3.1). Factors that influence the potter's decision-making process are complex, and ceramic ecological studies (e.g., Arnold 1985) tend to privilege ecological and functional considerations over the influence of local manufacturing traditions. Ecological factors include the nature and accessibility of raw materials, climatic regime, and the intended vessel function. However, the relationship between these functional/environmental considerations and the local

TABLE 3.1.
Steps in the Operational Sequence of Hand-built Utilitarian Ceramic Manufacture

Operational Task	Production Step	Determinants in Relative Order of Importance
Materials procurement	Collection of raw materials (clay, temper, slips, paints, glaze)	Local environment, local manufacturing tradition
Materials preparation	Crushing (clay, temper, or both)	Materials, local environment
	Cleaning (clay) and/or size sorting (temper)	Materials, local environment
	Blending (clay and temper)	Materials, local environment, local manufacturing tradition
	Kneading (combination of clays or clay and temper mixture)	Materials, local environment, local manufacturing tradition
Primary forming techniques	Pinching and drawing	Materials, local manufacturing tradition
	Coiling	Materials, local manufacturing tradition
Secondary forming techniques	Beating/Paddling	Materials, local manufacturing tradition
	Scraping	Materials, local manufacturing tradition
Decorative forming techniques	Smoothing—polishing	Local manufacturing tradition, materials
	Slipping	Local manufacturing tradition, environment
	Texturing (includes corrugation and incising)	Local manufacturing tradition
	Painting or glazing	Local manufacturing tradition, materials
Drying and firing	Creation of fire clouds	Local manufacturing tradition
	Use of reducing atmosphere	Local manufacturing tradition, environment
Postfiring treatments	Smudging	Local manufacturing tradition, materials, environment

manufacturing traditions is complex and understudied.

In some cases the range of locally available resources largely determines the procurement of ceramic production materials among sedentary groups, whereas other factors, such as local manufacturing tradition and social considerations, may be secondary determinants (see Arnold, this volume; Mahias 1993). Exceptions to this generalization include societies that rely on water transport and those that use pack animals for transport. Likewise, drying and firing decisions are affected by climate and available fuels (Arnold 1985). In each case environmental factors play an important role in constraining the technological choices that producers make.

Production steps in other parts of the manufacturing sequence have more freedom to vary. There is a certain element of arbitrariness in how the potter selects among several equivalent technical choices during the manufacturing sequence (Table 3.2). Clearly, production steps reflect a combination of local tradition and environmentally constrained considerations. For example, postfiring treatments to decrease permeability in vessels might be restricted to certain types of clays found in a narrow range of ecological zones (especially the tropics). As another example, raw materials used for hand-built pottery are often inappropriate for making wheel-thrown pottery. Yet the decision to use certain types of hand-building techniques—and the resistance that producers show toward

TABLE 3.2.
Technical Variation in Utilitarian Ceramic Manufacture:
Some Examples of Production Steps and Vessel Attributes

Operational Task	Production Step	Vessel Attribute
Primary and secondary forming techniques	Coiling and scraping Beating/paddling	Temper orientation Vessel form Rim shape Angle of eversion
Decorative forming techniques	Smoothing/burnishing Texturing	Degree of luster Corrugation Corrugation with obliteration
Postfiring techniques	Smudging Application of organic materials	Blackened surface

adopting alternative techniques—reflects the idiomatic nature of forming techniques.

A wide range of decorative forming techniques also reflects technological styles. Although surface treatments such as painting and glazing are generally considered decorative, other forms of surface treatment are also informative. Smoothing—particularly when it involves lustrous burnishing—and texturing are two examples of decorative forming techniques. One of the most common types of texturing in the prehistoric Southwest, for example, is corrugation, but other types, such as carving, incising, stamping, rouletting, and sprigging, are used worldwide (Rice 1987:140–141; Rye 1981: 90–92). Additive techniques, such as appliqué or inlay (Rice 1987:148), also distinguish various ceramic technological traditions from each other.

MATERIAL PATTERNING AND TECHNOLOGICAL STYLE

The collective material outcome of these production steps throughout the operational sequence constitutes a technological style. Which production steps are most free from constraints imposed by the local environment, including raw material composition? Ethnographic case studies (DeBoer 1990; Dietler and Herbich 1989; Gosselain 1992a; Reina and Hill 1978; van der Leeuw 1993) suggest that particular vessel forms within a functional class of pottery may be hallmarks of a technological style. Vessel forms also reflect mechanical agencies, ideographic requirements, and aesthetic forces (Holmes 1903:61). The use of specific decorative forming techniques, such as corrugation, might also provide technological markers. Technological styles, rather than ceramic subvarieties, may become evident when we view ceramics as combinations of technological attributes rather than simply as types (see also Wobst, this volume).

Can researchers identify ceramic attributes in archaeological assemblages that reflect these production steps in a consistent fashion? Measurement of such attributes should entail low-cost but accurate techniques to ensure that variability is examined across large samples. Table 3.2 lists some relevant production steps and potential material correlates for the analysis of utilitarian ceramics in archaeological contexts. What remains unclear is how well these attributes can be used to identify technological styles in traditional societies. Technological traditions among the Kalinga of the northern Philippines provide a case study in which social and material boundaries can be compared. In the ethnoarchaeological case study reported here, patterns of social affiliation are reflected in utilitarian ceramic traditions of neighboring Kalinga communities.

BACKGROUND TO THE KALINGA AREA
Nearly one million people live in small villages (and an occasional town) in the Philippine Cordilleras, which is the highest moun-

tain range on the island of Luzon (Figure 3.1). This area consists of rugged mountain valleys with steep slopes that Cordillera populations use for terraced irrigation agriculture. The absence of paved roads in much of this region limits contact among areas, and lingering intertribal animosity (which formerly involved headhunting) hampers efforts to establish stronger communication networks. The Cordillera Central (approximately 20,000 km² in area) houses a diverse population that has remained culturally and socially distinct from the surrounding lowlands. Lowlanders and colonial administrators in the last three centuries have subsumed all highland peoples under the single (previously pejorative) label of *Igorot* (for history of the term, see Scott 1969:154–172).

ETHNICITY AND SOCIAL BOUNDARIES IN THE CORDILLERAS

For decades ethnographers and historians have commented on similarities among various groups who occupy the Philippine highlands. The integrity of these groups is reflected in the fact that less than 10 percent of Cordillera residents today are Ilocano immigrants from the lowlands (De Raedt 1991: 355). Cordillera populations have a long tradition of resisting outside influence. From the sixteenth through nineteenth centuries all highland groups were formidable opponents to the Spanish colonial administration (Scott 1977). Not until the 1880s, after the introduction of the bolt-action repeating rifle, did the Spaniards establish permanent garrisons in the area (Scott 1977: 274). Lowland travelers in the Cordillera Mountains were thus not guaranteed protection until the very end of the Spanish colonial period. Efforts to incorporate the Igorot populations into the domain of American colonial administration relied on traditional economic and social institutions, and the Americans encouraged Philippine highlanders to participate in this development (Magannon 1984:254; Wilson 1956).

Great cultural diversity also characterizes this aggregate of separate linguistic groups. The region houses seven major ethnolinguistic groups (Ifugao, Kalinga, Tingguian, Isneg, Bontok, Kankaney, and Ibaloy), each of which speaks a distinctive language. The area also contains many minor language groups and closely related local dialects (Reid 1994). Major differences exist in economic strategies (e.g., shifting cultivation, wet-rice farming, commercial vegetable cropping), as they do in social structures and settlement patterns. By the eighteenth century, Spanish accounts identified subareas of the Cordilleras by their settlement names rather than by ethnonyms (Keesing 1962: 224, 234; Scott 1969:161–162); this pattern hardly changed for 200 years.

Cordillerans were known first in a generic sense as "Igorottes" or "Igorots" (by the Spanish) and then as "Non-Christian Tribes" (by the Americans). American administrator Dean Worcester divided the Cordilleras into seven tribal groups using ethnolinguistic boundaries when the Philippines came under American colonial control (Scott 1969:165–166; Worcester 1906). This administrative policy of assigning ethnonyms where none had existed previously was common throughout colonial Southeast Asia (Anderson 1991: 163–178; Hutterer 1991). Ironically, these political subdivisions contributed to a new "tribal" consciousness among Cordillerans by the 1930s (e.g., Keesing and Keesing 1934:130) that was absent before the twentieth century. These groupings were problematic and ill founded (Lewis 1991:616–617); even provincial names used by the American administration lacked indigenous referents (Scott 1969:157–165).

Recognized recently as "cultural minorities," many Cordillerans actively maintain their highland traditions and beliefs. With this maintenance comes a sort of pan-Cordilleran solidarity, and recent incursions by the Philippine government and by zealous clergy have strengthened this sentiment (De Raedt 1991:356; Drucker 1977; Rood 1991). However, notions of pan-Cordilleran identity, and of coherent ethnic boundaries among the five provinces in this mountain chain, remain vague (Lewis 1991:618–619; Rood 1991).

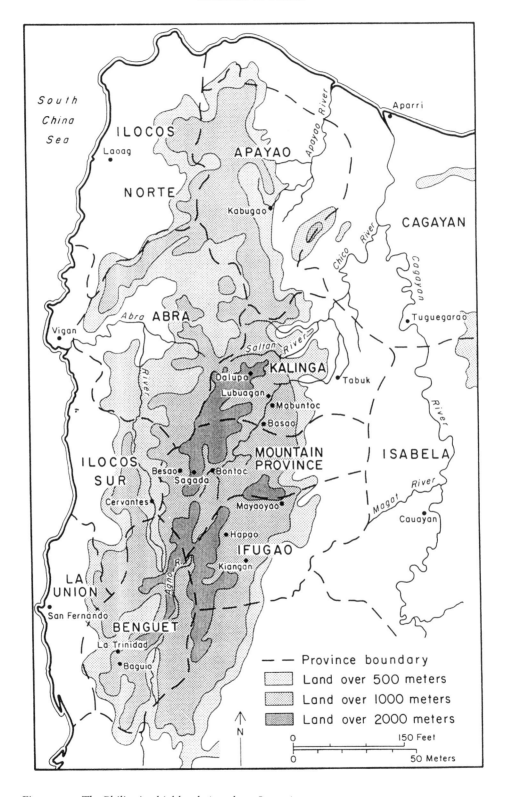

Figure 3.1. The Philippine highlands (northern Luzon).

Although ethnic boundaries are fuzzy in and across Cordilleran provinces, social boundaries are remarkably distinct at the local and regional levels; even more remarkable is the tenacity of Cordillerans within these boundaries throughout the twentieth century. The history of tribal wars and subsequent peace pacts among villages is kept alive by elders of each village and extends back several generations (e.g., Dozier 1966:Appendix IV). Until recently, Kalingas reckoned identity at multiple levels, from the household and village to the drainage system (see Jenks 1905:65; Kroeber 1943:68; Lewis [1991:618] describes a Kankaney-speaking area of the Cordilleras). This pattern, in which social characterization focused on the settlement and community rather than on a larger grouping that anthropologists often associate with ethnicity, was common throughout the Cordilleras (Hutterer 1991:21).

Even 60 years ago the Kalingas used more localized group names to describe populations living in separate drainage systems (Dozier 1966:240; Keesing 1962:221–224). Of the Kalinga, Kroeber observed differences in custom and idiom from one river valley to the next (Kroeber 1943:68). Fortunately for ethnoarchaeologists, these earlier ethnologists established a precedent for studying social boundaries with respect to earthenware pottery. They observed that "a great diversity in the pattern of such material objects exists, and even in the same culture area there are all kinds of minor variations between the work of different communities and family craftworkers, over which they have a kind of tacitly recognized patent right" (Keesing and Keesing 1934:202).

Kalinga communities continue to engage in community-based craft specialization in a variety of goods, from manufactured crafts to forest resources (Stark 1991). Complex trading relationships link individuals and communities to one another within regional networks in contiguous river valleys (Stark 1994). Many items circulate through this elaborate exchange network, which we can divide grossly into two spheres. The prestige-goods exchange sphere involves water buffalo, heirloom porcelain, and gold jewelry; these goods are costly, move vast distances, and carry with them symbolic and social status (e.g., Takaki 1977). The utilitarian-goods exchange sphere involves pottery, baskets, raw materials, and foodstuffs; these goods circulate in limited distribution networks and (although essential) lack the cachet associated with prestige goods (Stark 1993a). Utilitarian goods also have either short use lives or low visibility: foodstuffs are quickly consumed, and pots and baskets obtained through trade rarely stray far from their consumers' homes (see Sterner 1989 for an African parallel on pottery).

My research during the 1980s confirmed that regional traditions observed by the Keesings six decades earlier are still alive and well. From one river valley to the next, utilitarian goods are sensitive to local social boundaries; one reason for this, perhaps, lies in their restricted circulation networks. Do such boundaries reflect Bourdieu's (1977) habitus and Watson's (1990) cultural diacritics? To what extent are these consciously maintained boundaries? Although differences in regional traditions may appear subtle to the archaeologist, producers and consumers of these goods clearly recognize technical differences in their goods. In fact, neighboring groups are generally well aware of each other's technological practices and occasionally copy neighboring traditions. Terms such as *habitus, cultural diacritics,* and *technological style* begin to converge when we examine spatial patterning of this technological variability in southern Kalinga.

KALINGA SOCIAL BOUNDARIES AND MATERIAL CULTURE PATTERNING

This research focuses on Kalinga communities in the southern portion of Kalinga province (e.g., Stark 1991, 1993a, 1994; Stark and Longacre 1993). The most important social unit in Kalinga is what Dozier (1966:65–70) called the kinship circle or kindred, which consists of a bilateral grouping of family. A broader effective social unit in Kalinga is a multisettlement, an autonomous territorial unit or region (following Takaki

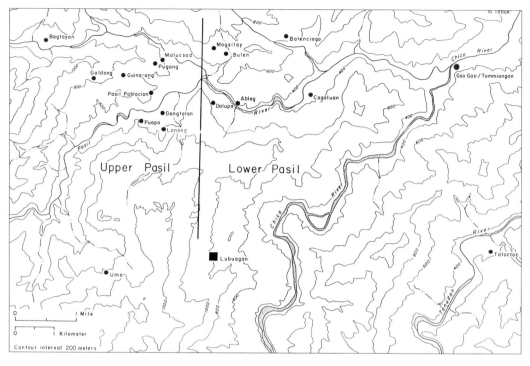

Figure 3.2. Upper Pasil vs. Lower Pasil.

1977) that consists of one or more villages and satellite settlements. Languages throughout the northern Philippines, including the Kalinga dialect, share the same term, *ili,* for this concept of community (also see Reid 1972). The Kalinga *ili* involves one or several settlements and local groups of kinsmen rather than simply a localized kin group and was traditionally endogamous (Dozier 1966: 66–70). Kalingas equate each *ili* (or local system) with a collection of extended kin groups that must bond together for protection against enemies.

Webs of social relations, such as marriage, tie each local system to some of its neighbors in a broader social network. Today local systems are laced together at a broader level into a web of obligation, custom, and familiarity that crosscuts kin ties. Contemporary tribal warfare commonly involves two warring local systems from different river valleys, and neighbors to each adversary join in the conflict as tensions mount through time. Kalingas maintain a complicated system of peace

pacts, inherited from one generation to the next, to minimize and resolve intergroup conflict (Bacdayan 1967; Barton 1949; Dozier 1966).

In the Pasil municipality (where I conducted my research) the river's settlement system is split into two roughly equal parts: Lower Pasil and Upper Pasil (Figure 3.2). Social and economic interactions are more intense within each of these sections than between them, as was clear from the voting patterns for municipal offices during 1988. Residents of Lower Pasil tended to vote as a bloc for Lower Pasil candidates, whereas residents of Upper Pasil voted for candidates from their section of the drainage system. In Kalinga, then, affiliation is reckoned at the kindred level, the village level, and then at the level of the interaction network. Although people in the study area occasionally called themselves *I-Pasil* (or members of the Pasil system), their primary allegiance is to their kindred and local systems.

Pasil residents are not alone in reckoning

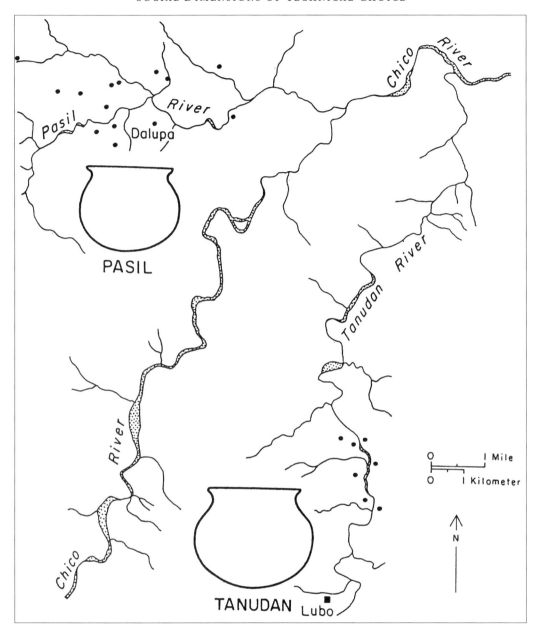

Figure 3.3. Variation in water jar profiles from neighboring river valleys in southern Kalinga.

their social affiliation to their drainage system; this is clear not only from daily behavior and interactions but also from Kalinga material culture. In several river valleys of southern Kalinga (Figure 3.3), the distribution of one technological style, utilitarian ceramics, largely corresponds with differences in regional economic networks. Kalingas interact socially and economically with other members of their regional system; members of local systems throughout the region attend celebrations and funerals for others in the general area. Marriages tie together kindred from different local systems, and a continuous stream of exchange transactions (e.g., gift giving, barter) reinforce these intercommunity links. Most individuals in each regional network share a similar accent and use colloquialisms that may not be understood outside their area. They joke about differences in dialect and custom that distinguish neighboring networks from their own.

Regional boundaries today correspond roughly to externally imposed municipal boundaries. Within each regional network is at least one pottery-making village, which supplies the needs of most consumers (Stark 1994); consumers on each system's periphery are an exception because they may sample products from multiple systems. The products of each network exhibit the "tacitly recognized patent right" (Keesing and Keesing 1934:202) that the Keesings noted half a century before in the region. These are subtle differences that characterize the technological styles of goods made by potters from different villages in the same network (e.g., Graves 1985, 1994; Stark 1993a). Most potters know, and manipulate, these differences through the manufacturing process.

THE OPERATIONAL SEQUENCE OF KALINGA POTTERY MANUFACTURE

Let us turn to the earthenware pottery of the Pasil River valley. It is simply decorated with incised patterns; traditional Pasil cooking pots lack appliqué decorations, appendages, elaborate vessel forms, or elaborate painted designs. This valley contains two pottery-making communities: Dalupa and Dangtalan (see Longacre 1981, 1991). Cooking pots and water-storage containers are made in each village. Construction steps in the manufacturing process are similar in these two villages and involve a combination of paddle-and-anvil and coil-and-scrape techniques. The potter first shapes a lump of clay into a cylinder. To form the vessel the potter pulls the clay away from the cylinder's center to begin the building process. She then adds a series of coils to the vessel, and when it reaches a sufficient height, she scrapes it smooth using a piece of bamboo. The neck and rim are shaped using a wet cloth to produce an everted rim. The potter sets the vessel out to dry; when the clay is leather hard, she scrapes

excess clay from the vessel's interior, paddles the base into a globular shape, and applies ocher. She incises a simple decoration around the vessel's neck, which ranges from one to three bands in width (Graves 1985).

Dalupa and Dangtalan potters use different techniques to paint and water-seal their vessels. For cooking pots Dalupa potters use ocher around the perimeter of the exterior and interior surfaces of the vessel's lip (Stark 1991). Dangtalan potters decorate their cooking pots with ocher around the perimeter of the exterior and interior surfaces of the vessel's lip in combination with a band of red immediately below the neck (Longacre 1991). Dalupa potters decorate the exterior surfaces of their water storage jars with elaborate ocher designs and only coat the interior surface with resin (Stark 1991). Dangtalan potters cover their water jars' exterior surface with ocher first and then with resin. Both Dalupa and Dangtalan vessels are dried and fired in an open setting for no longer than an hour (also see Aronson et al. 1994).

Although Dalupa and Dangtalan pots are similar in general morphology (Graves 1994:158), their basic dimensions are significantly different (Stark 1993a). Dalupa pots are taller and lighter than Dangtalan pots. Producers and consumers alike recognize these differences, and Pasil consumers occasionally express preferences for products of one village based on these morphological differences (Aronson et al. 1994). Slightly different technological traditions thus characterize Dalupa and Dangtalan (Graves 1985, 1994; Stark 1993a), differences which might be described simply as stylistic (e.g., Longacre 1991) in form. However, each requires different manufacturing technologies to obtain the end products.

Kalinga potters peddle most of their pots in consumer villages that they can reach by foot, and most of their bartering destinations are found within a day's journey. As recently as the 1970s Dangtalan supplied several Pasil villages with most of their utilitarian pottery (Graves 1991). Since the mid-1980s Dalupa has become the ceramic production center in the Pasil economic network (Stark 1993a,

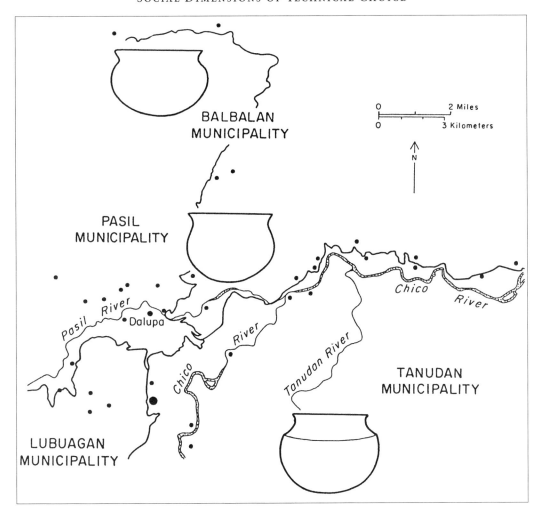

Figure 3.4. Vessel profiles of cooking pots from three different river valleys (municipalities) in southern Kalinga.

1994). Dalupa potters today peddle their wares by foot and by truck and often travel beyond the boundaries of their own municipality to seek customers for their goods.

FACTORS THAT AFFECT TECHNOLOGICAL TRADITIONS AND THE ISSUE OF TECHNOLOGICAL CHANGE

When we expand this technological perspective beyond Pasil to encompass river valleys across the southern portion of Kalinga, patterned differences in vessel form become even clearer. Variation in ceramic morphology in cooking pots and water jars is isomorphic with variation in subdialect and politi-

cal affiliation. We can see this clearly by examining cooking vessels from two neighboring drainage systems: the Pasil River valley and the Balbalan municipality. To producers and consumers from each network the differences are sufficiently distinct to be discussed and debated among consumers. Potters from some areas occasionally emulate the traditions of potters in neighboring regions but always revert to the technological style that characterizes their own area.

Potters from one regional economic network occasionally bring their goods on visits to settlements in other regional networks. Most consumers recognize the technological

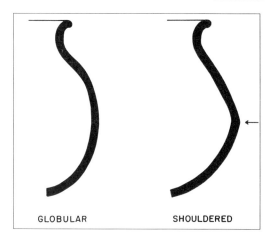

GLOBULAR   SHOULDERED

Figure 3.5. Vessel profile of Binontoc style shoulder that some Dalupa potters adopted.

styles of pottery from neighboring networks (Figure 3.4). Profiles shown here from three Kalinga river valleys illustrate morphological differences in cooking pots that reflect distinct shaping techniques. Balbalan pots are more squat than Pasil or Tanudan pots; the height of the vessel is determined during the primary forming process (through coiling and scraping) and through the secondary forming process (through paddle-and-anvil techniques). Tanudan pots have a pronounced shoulder that Pasil and Balbalan pots lack. To make a Pasil-style pot, the potter paddles the semidried vessel into a globular shape. To make a Tanudan style pot, the potter retains a pronounced shoulder during the paddling process.

These technological differences do not result from isolation and divergent evolution in the pottery manufacturing traditions. No long-standing animosity has prevented Pasil and Balbalan Kalingas from traveling between their respective river valleys; in fact, Dalupa potters regularly barter their goods in some Balbalan municipality villages that lie farthest from the Balbalan pottery-making villages (Stark 1994). Tanudan potters live at a greater distance from Pasil, and warfare sporadically rages between intervening communities that prevents Pasil-Tanudan travel. However, marriage ties between the two communities have brought Tanudan people (and, occasionally, their pots) into

Dalupa in recent decades, and Dalupa potters are familiar with Tanudan-style pots. Subsistence regimes are nearly identical in these three areas, so we cannot attribute the differences to diet.

One hallmark of technological traditions, mentioned previously, is their inherent stability (e.g., Rice 1984); such stability in utilitarian pottery from different Kalinga river valleys is evident through comparisons with Eduardo Masferré's photographs from the 1940s (housed in the National Anthropological Archive, Smithsonian Institution). Some of these photographs, taken in southern Kalinga villages, illustrate morphological characteristics in pottery that parallel differences seen today.

Even technological traditions are subject to change, and some steps of the operational sequence are more sensitive to innovation than are others. Changes in some production steps do not affect the success of the production process or require the development of qualitatively different motor habits (Gosselain 1992a:582). We can see such change as it occurred in the village of Dalupa. In the early 1980s enterprising potters added a pronounced shoulder to the water jar's previously globular shape. Dalupa potters call this style *Binontoc,* and it emulates ceramic morphology in the Bontoc community just south of the provincial boundary (Figure 3.5). Dalupa potters had also begun to decorate the exterior surfaces of water jars with geometric and floral designs in ocher. At the same time, a Dalupa potter whose father was from the Tanudan River valley (13 to 14 km southeast of Pasil) introduced a carinated (or ridged) Tanudan-style shoulder for cooking pots to Dalupa potters (Longacre 1991:107–108). Several other potters experimented with this carinated Lubo style, so named for the Tanudan pottery production center where such carinated shoulders are found (Figure 3.4). Dalupa potters who make the Lubo-style shoulder do not wholly replicate the Tanudan technology, but the vessel shape they produce looks more like Tanudan pots than Pasil pots.

Both the shouldered-water-jar form and

the carinated-cooking-pot form were introduced after Dalupa potters had encountered foreign potters and their goods. Dalupa potters observed Bontoc potters' styles during visits to the former provincial capital of Lubuagan. Alterations in the operational sequence required for shaping a Bontoc-style shoulder are minor, and many potters make this *Binontoc*-style water jar. Making a Lubo-style carinated cooking pot requires changes in the shaping process and additional incised decoration on the vessel's exterior. Although the pots are harder to scrape, they are easier to paddle.

These two technological innovations have fared quite differently in the Dalupa manufacturing tradition: shouldered, decorated water jars are extremely popular among consumers, whereas potters have abandoned the Lubo-style carinated shoulder. The different success rates of innovations in certain production steps is intriguing. Why were shouldered water jars embraced but carinated pots rejected? Dalupa potters provided some answers. First, the long-term success of these stylistic innovations depended on their marketability (Gosselain 1992a:176). Experimentation with new forms is a hallmark of Dalupa pottery production today (Stark 1991; Stark and Longacre 1993) as potters test new products for a wider consumer market. Painted, shouldered water jars proved popular with consumers throughout the exchange network and are now entrenched in the Dalupa technological style. On the other hand, carinated Lubo-style cooking pots captured only a small consumer market. Few Dalupa potters continue to make the Tanudan-style carinated shoulder because this innovation proved to be just a passing fancy.

I was able to visit an enclave of Lubo (Tanudan) potters in the provincial capital of Tabuk before my departure from the area in 1988. In this Tanudan enclave transplanted potters continue to make Lubo-style pots. Lubo potters in this enclave are not only familiar with the Dalupa technological style, but they showed me experimental versions of the globular (or "Pasil") shape. When questioned, Lubo potters observed that Dalupa-style pots were easier to scrape and faster to manufacture because this style of pottery requires less incised decoration. I asked them why they did not abandon their Tanudan style for the easier Dalupa style; the Tanudan potters laughed and responded that being from Tanudan, they must make Lubo-style pots. These potters held strong cultural sanctions against changing a particular technological style (see also Mahias 1993 concerning India). Kalinga potters from various regions share different ideas about technical process, and these ideas figure into their wider symbolic systems (see also Lemonnier 1993:4).

SCALES OF SOCIAL BOUNDARIES AND THEIR MATERIAL REFLECTIONS

This discussion of social identity and social boundaries began by asking how we define relevant units of analysis in the study of social formations among nonstate societies. In the Cordillera highlands of the northern Philippines, households are linked into village wards or divisions, which are then linked into villages and local systems or peace-pact-holding units. The local system is the integral social unit in Kalinga beyond the family. However, local systems occasionally unite at a broader level to lend political support for an insider or to wager political opposition against an antagonistic outsider. These levels of social identity characterize every Cordilleran group that has been studied, be it Ifugao, Kalinga, Tingguian, Bontok, or Kankaney (e.g., De Raedt 1991; Dozier 1966; Jenks 1905; Keesing 1962; Kroeber 1943; Lawless 1978; Lewis 1991; Takaki 1977). It is reasonable to suggest that similar social units are found in small-scale societies today in Southeast Asia and, perhaps, in the Pacific.

In the Kalinga area and throughout the Cordillera highlands, then, at least two levels of social identity exist beyond the household: the local system and the broader network. The fact that these scalar units are not synonymous with ethnic groups may frustrate more traditional anthropologists: these boundaries circumscribe smaller demographic units and subdivide ethnolinguistic groups. Individuals identify with this nested hierarchy of affiliation in everyday discourse and maintain these boundaries through everyday acts. The prominence of kin and kin-like relations in these boundaries provides them with some temporal stability. Temporal stability is what archaeologists crave, of course, because our diachronic perspective is notably different from the synchronic (or snapshot) view that most cultural anthropologists employ.

Recall that the second concern here is with methods for identifying these social units in the material record. Social boundaries demarcate local systems and regions and are frequently exhibited as boundaries in material culture, although this is unintentional and asymmetrical. Archaeologists would be most delighted, of course, if stylistic boundaries (inscribed in painted pottery, monumental architecture, and other emblemic forms of material culture) conformed to these social boundaries in some neat, Wobstian arrangement (at least as Wobst has been commonly interpreted; see Wobst, this volume). Cases in which they do not are indeed intriguing. Yet we see boundaries become evident when analytical concepts are applied to the patterning from an anthropology of technology (Pfaffenberger 1992). The next section of this paper illustrates ways in which social and material culture boundaries, at the levels of local system and region, coincide in the Philippine highlands.

The notion of technical choices as maintaining social boundaries is not simply an archaeological phenomenon. Ethnologists working in the Pacific and in Southeast Asia have also observed that social boundaries are linked to material culture differences. Lemonnier's (1986) research in the central New Guinea highlands identifies localized technical systems in architecture and wild animal procurement with clearly maintained social boundaries. Watson (1990) describes cultural diacritics that mark different social groups in the eastern New Guinea highlands that include (but are not limited to) produc-

tive specialties and distinctive local artifacts (reed bustle skirts, bark cooking drums, carved tree-fern figurines). Rosaldo (1988: 163–164), for example, concludes his examination of social boundaries by noting that cultural practices (such as agricultural techniques) define and sustain Ilongot identity from one generation to the next.

Artisans express technical choices through their selection of particular raw materials and through variation in the manufacturing process. Technical choices that Kalinga potters make reflect an internalized understanding that they pass on (with or without modification) to the next generation. These technical behaviors are not passive responses to environmental or functional pressures, nor are they entirely unconscious. Kalinga potters observe and occasionally imitate neighboring styles of pottery technology. Yet even the innovations that they impute to neighboring styles have a distinctly local imprint. To be a Pasil potter, one must make pots according to Pasil methods.

CONCLUSIONS

I have stepped outside various theoretically opposed positions to focus on technology with respect to material culture. The examination of technical choices provides insights for archaeologists who study many topics in a wide variety of settings and periods. One insight from the Kalinga case study is that dichotomies blur between style and function, and between the technological and the social. In many traditional societies these qualities are contextually and analytically intertwined. We must move beyond heuristic divisions between style and function to gain a more nuanced understanding of the social dimensions of material culture (see also Schiffer and Skibo 1997).

Another insight from the Kalinga vessel form study is that technological styles provide more stable and resilient patterning of social boundaries than does iconological style, which archaeologists commonly study. Kalinga culture does not lack media that carry iconological style: traditional techniques of weaving and tattooing both involve intricate designs, for example. In this ethnoarchaeological study we see that everyday goods inform on social boundaries in different ways than do iconologically complex materials. The study also suggests that use of technological approaches has potential for progress in the study of the archaeological record.

It should be clear from this exercise that developing material-culture theory in archaeology requires a great deal of hard work. We need to concentrate more ethnoarchaeological research on two areas to understand the meaning of multiple social boundaries that are present in the archaeological record. The first involves detailed studies that examine the relationship among contexts of production, distribution, and use. The second area involves systematic, long-term research on spatial scales of social boundaries and their material expressions. We can extend our time depth through longitudinal ethnoarchaeological research in particular societies. Long-term field projects in Central America (e.g., Arnold 1985; Arnold and Nieves 1992; Arnold et al., this volume), West Africa (David and Hennig 1972; David and MacEachern 1988; MacEachern 1992, 1998; Sterner 1989), and Southeast Asia (Longacre 1981, 1991; Stark 1991, 1993a, 1994) have begun to yield insights on technological and organizational change at scales that approach that of archaeological time. Research that combines old museum collections with contemporary field research (e.g., Welsch and Terrell 1991, 1998) extends our time depth even further.

In this era of rapidly expanding theoretical approaches we are learning that deference to social theory from outside our discipline's confines is rarely adequate for interpreting archaeological data. It is time for us to develop an explicit material-culture theory from the vantage point of archaeology. The approach discussed here is unique and timely in its attempt to bridge divergent approaches from North American and European archaeology and to build a unified study of material culture. European research on technical choices still occupies a marginal place in North Americanist archaeology, largely because of the lack of European literature in English translation. Use of innovative methods—and an emphasis on understanding how technological behavior generates and reflects social boundaries—is critical to our continuing efforts to build a uniquely archaeological theory of material culture.

Acknowledgments. Funding for research reported in this study was provided by the National Science Foundation BNS 87–10275 to William Longacre; the Arizona-Nevada Academy of Sciences; the University of Arizona Graduate College; Desert Archaeology, Inc.; and a postdoctoral fellowship at the Conservation Analytical Laboratory, Smithsonian Institution. I thank Josephine Bommogas for assistance in data collection and for her patience with my persistent questions. I also thank Bill Longacre, for his guidance, generosity, and good humor throughout my Kalinga research. Portions of this paper were presented at the 1993 American Anthropological Meetings; many thanks go to Elizabeth Chilton for inviting me to present a revised version of this paper in her 1996 SAA symposium. The following individuals also provided thoughtful comments on previous drafts and/or engaged in valuable discussions with me on this topic: James Bayman, Elizabeth Chilton, James Heidke, and Ben Nelson. Ronald Beckwith drafted all figures in this chapter. I accept full responsibility for remaining weaknesses of the study.

4

One Size Fits All

Typology and Alternatives for Ceramic Research

ELIZABETH S. CHILTON

[T]ypologies are tools made for a purpose, and as long as they can be shown to work for that purpose they require no more abstract justification than does a crowbar.

—Adams and Adams 1991:8

Typologies and classifications of material culture form the core of archaeological interpretation; they facilitate communication by providing a kind of shorthand for description. Typologies also provide a means of expressing time-space relationships in material culture, which leads to the formulation of cultural chronologies (Wright 1967:99). Despite the popularity and clear advantages to the use of typology, however, there are potential drawbacks.

First, by assuming continuity *within* and discontinuity *between* types, and by assuming the relationship between attributes of material culture to be static through time, the typological process masks a certain amount of diversity in material culture—the same diversity archaeologists often seek to understand (see Wobst, this volume).

Second, in discussions of typology there is often a conflation between *empirical* units—"real" or "natural" groupings of artifacts to be discovered by the researcher—and *theoretical* units, which are the result of the scales and tools of measurement (Dunnell 1986: 154). There was, and still is, an "opposition between those who believe that types are arbitrarily 'designed' by the classifier and those who think that types exist in nature and the classifier 'discovers' them" (Willey and Phillips 1958:13).

Hill and Evans (1972) attribute much of the "typological debate" in archaeology to this basic epistemological difference between what they call the *empiricist* and the *positivist* models of classification. In the empiricist model, which they consider to be the traditional archaeological model, one looks for the "best" typology possible, given the nature of the materials. This approach "works" in the sense that there *are* nonrandom associations of attributes in material culture that can be discovered either intuitively or statistically (Spaulding 1953, 1954). The problem with this empiricist epistemology is that it "often leads the archaeologist into viewing his types as *the types*...[and] his types become...canonized in the literature as 'truth'" (Hill and Evans 1972:235).

Contrary to the empiricist model, in the positivist view objects do not have inherent or primary meanings—they are assigned meanings by the human mind (Hill and Evans 1972). The positivist begins with certain research questions or hypotheses and then selects the appropriate attributes of material culture to examine. Therefore, decisions about which attributes of material culture to examine—and whether or not to attempt to synthesize the attributes into types or other classes—depend on specific and well-defined research questions. Important to this model is the understanding that by using different criteria, the researcher can create different groupings of objects. As Adams and Adams (1991:4–5) put it: "There is no right or wrong way to classify anything, but there are better or worse ways of achieving purposes, once we have decided what those purposes are."

In this chapter I apply Hill and Evans's positivist model of variation in material culture to a specific archaeological case: the New England interior during the Late Woodland period (A.D. 1000–1600). In this region a strictly typological, culture-historical approach to archaeological ceramics has inhibited our ability to understand the broader technical system. I discuss how typologies have been used and misused in the region and present an alternative method of ceramic analysis that focuses on production context and technical choices.

THE LIMITATIONS OF CERAMIC TYPOLO- GIES IN NEW ENGLAND

Archaeologists in the northeastern United States rely on stylistic ceramic typologies in order to infer ethnicity and chronology (e.g., Engelbrecht 1978; MacNeish 1952; Ritchie and MacNeish 1949; Rouse 1947; Smith 1947). The view of typology in the region is decidedly empirical. For example, Ritchie and MacNeish explain in their seminal paper *Pre-Iroquoian Pottery of New York State* (1949:98): "We believe that, at least to a certain degree, our types reflect aesthetic and utilitarian standards of value which operated as cultural compulsives on the minds of the artisans, and, therefore, they possess some genuine measure of intrinsic validity."

This position is similar to the views expressed by MacNeish (1952) concerning Iroquoian pottery types in New York and implied by Lavin (1986), Rouse (1947), and Smith (1947) for New England. Often stylistic types in the region are taken to be a direct reflection of group affiliation or ethnicity: for example, when a certain "type" of ceramic is found outside of its "homeland," it is often interpreted as either stylistic copying, trade, or "female capture" (see Engelbrecht 1972 and Latta 1991).

The way that ceramic typologies are used by Northeast archaeologists is problematic for three primary reasons. First, in the quest for empirical, cultural-historical types, New England archaeologists have for the most part discounted nondecorative attributes of ceramics. A focus on culture history and chronology—"who, where, and when?"— has led archaeologists to focus on the aspects of artifacts that vary the most through time and are the easiest to recognize and code. For ceramics, this amounts to decorative technique and motif, and rim shape. As a result, there has been relatively little research on nondecorative attributes of ceramics (e.g., paste characteristics, vessel size and shape, and firing conditions). Thus, questions concerning ceramic technology, production, and use have been largely ignored.

A second problem with the current use of Northeast ceramic classifications is that the type names developed for *one* region are often imported into *another* without any demonstration that they apply. More specifically, the uncritical borrowing of typologies from New York (Iroquois) and coastal New England has caused much confusion in the archaeology of the New England interior. It is often assumed that New England peoples were greatly influenced by groups to the south and west (e.g., Byers and Rouse 1960; Lavin and Miroff 1992:50; Snow 1980:308). However, the origin of culture change is rarely tested, and the putative direction of cultural influence in prehistory is clearly determined by *where the type names were first defined by archaeologists* (for a more detailed discussion of this problem see Chilton 1996).

Last, the ceramic classifications used in the region are either implicitly (e.g., Ritchie and MacNeish 1949; Whallon 1972) or explicitly (e.g., Rouse 1947; Lavin 1986) taxonomic. In New England ceramics are first sorted into traditions, then types, then subtypes, based on oppositions in attributes such as paste, vessel form, surface treatment, and decoration. Each of these oppositions requires a set of assumptions about the relative importance of various attributes; many of these assumptions are implicit. If these assumptions were treated instead as hypotheses to be tested, then taxonomy would be a parsimonious means of classification because it can potentially express more complex relationships between attributes than can other kinds of classification (Dunnell 1971: 82). However, the assumptions and oppositions are rarely tested, which leads to the "intuitive qualities" often attributed to taxonomy in New England and elsewhere (Dunnell 1971: 82; see also Goodby [1998] for a critique of New England ceramic typologies).

CERAMIC PRODUCTION IN NEW ENGLAND

Ceramic classifications have not been developed specifically for the New England interior. As mentioned above, type names are often borrowed from New York and coastal New England. In these latter regions the typologies were created to answer very specific questions: What is the age of these ceramic sherds, and which cultural group produced them? In this study I am not concerned with analyzing ceramics for the purpose of creating culture-historical types. My questions are, perhaps, more fundamental: What are some of the choices made by the potter during the production sequence? How are these choices manifested in the finished vessel or vessel fragments? How can these choices be understood in terms of—and inform us about—cultural context?

To address these questions I conducted an attribute analysis of ceramics from three Late Woodland sites: two in western Massachusetts (Guida Farm in Westfield and Pine Hill in Deerfield) and one from the Mohawk Valley in New York (the Klock site in Ephratah, approximately 80 km west of Albany) (Figure 4.1). The two Massachusetts sites were inhabited by Algonquian-speaking peoples of the Connecticut Valley (most likely the Pocumtuck at Pine Hill and the Woronoco at Guida Farm). The Klock site has been interpreted by Kuhn and Funk (1994) as an "early protohistoric period Iroquois settlement" and was most likely occupied by a Mohawk community. All three sites date to the latter part of the Late Woodland period (ca. A.D. 1300–1600). These particular Connecticut Valley sites were chosen because they represent the best excavated and documented Late Woodland sites in the middle valley (see By-

ers and Rouse [1960] for a discussion of the Guida Farm site and Chilton [1996] for a discussion of the Pine Hill site). Because the study of Late Woodland ceramics in New England is strongly influenced by typologies created for the New York Iroquois, it was important to choose an Iroquois site for comparison. Thus, the Klock site was chosen because it was one of the best documented Mohawk sites from the latter part of the Late Woodland period.

In the method of analysis used here, what I term an *attribute analysis of technical choice,* the goal is to look for variation *and* co-variation across objects—not between groups of objects. Thus, vessel lots are the units of analysis. Attribute analysis is used increasingly in the Northeast as a means to record a range of potentially relevant variables, without making judgments a priori as to which variables are the most important for pattern recognition (see Goodby 1998). In New England Dincauze (1975) and Kenyon (1979) paved the way for analyses of physical attributes of ceramics, such as characteristics of clay, nonplastic inclusions (which include temper), and the effects of firing.

Because I am interested in the decisions made by potters along the production sequence (e.g., paste preparation, vessel forming techniques, wall thickness, vessel size and shape, and surface treatment), the variables used in this analysis reflect these decisions: the type of inclusions in the clay, inclusion density, wall thickness, vessel size, surface treatment (including decoration), and color (Table 4.1; for a detailed discussion of methods see Chilton 1996).

The term *attribute* requires some definition: in this analysis I define an attribute as *one variable of a ceramic vessel,* such as surface treatment, color, temper type, or rim shape. An *attribute state* is one of many possible values or states for that variable, such as "cord-marked," "quartz," or "23 mm." Thus, each attribute has an infinite number of possible attribute states. This is consistent with Clarke's (1968:139) use of the term *attribute:* "a logically irreducible and independent

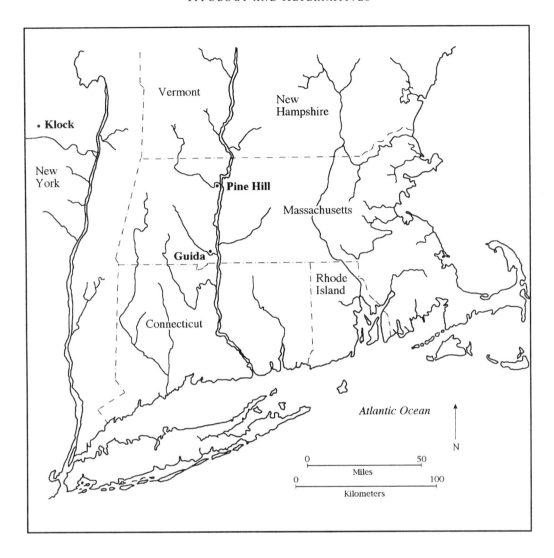

Figure 4.1. Map of southern New England and eastern New York, showing the location of key sites.

variable within a specific frame of reference...[having] two or more states" (cf. Adams and Adams 1991:169; Cowgill 1982; Krieger 1944; and Rouse 1960, 1964). I have chosen the definition of *attribute* most consistent with other New England researchers (e.g., Dincauze 1975; *contra* Petersen and Sanger 1991).

Although attribute analysis has often been used to create typologies in New England (e.g., Lavin 1986; Rouse 1947; Smith 1947), the goal of this study is to interpret the pat-

terns *within each attribute*. Even if one isolates individual attributes of ceramics, the selection and interpretation of the distribution of those attributes depends very much on the researcher's perspective and objectives (see Dobres, this volume). In the research presented here my interpretation of ceramic variability is very much influenced by my perspective on the concept of *technological style* (see Chilton 1998a). Thus, in the next section I present a theoretical background for my approach to technical systems.

TABLE 4.1.
Sample Data from the Attribute Analysis of the Pine Hill Assemblage

Vessel lot	Catalog Number	No. of Sherds	Thickness	Incl 1	Grit Comp	Grit Comp 2	Grit Comp 3	Incl Min	Incl Max	Incl Density	Interior Color	Exterior Color	Surface Treatment	Surface Treatment 2	Surface Portion	Rim Form	Lip Form	Orifice	Collar Width	Residues
2	93.1275	1	5	GR	QT	FE	MI	VF	C	7	10YR52	10YR52	WI		N	NA	NA	0	0	N
2	93.1781	2	4	GR	FE	QT	MI	VF	C	5	10YR52	10YR52	IN	SM	R	CL	FL	12	33	N
2	93.1811	1	6	GR	FE	QT	MI	VF	C	5	10YR52	10YR52	IN	SM	N	NA	NA	0	0	N
2	93.1815	1	4	GR	QT	FE	MI	VF	C	7	10YR41	10YR52	SM		N	NA	NA	0	0	N
2	93.1823	1	4	GR	QT	FE	MI	VF	C	7	10YR52	10YR52	WI		N	NA	NA	0	0	N
2	93.1862	1	4	GR	QT	FE	MI	VF	C	7	10YR52	10YR31	WI	SM	B	NA	NA	0	0	N
2	93.1964	2	4	GR	QT	FE	MI	VF	C	7	10YR41	10YR52	SM	WI	N	NA	NA	0	0	Y
2	93.205	1	5	GR	FE	QT	MI	VF	C	5	10YR52	10YR52	IN	WI	N	NA	NA	0	0	N
2	93.2057	1	6	GR	FE	QT	MI	VF	C	5	10YR52	10YR52	IN	WI	N	NA	NA	0	0	N
2	93.2139	1	5	GR	QT	FE	MI	VF	C	7	10YR52	10YR52	WI	SM	S	NA	NA	0	0	N
2	93.2195	1	5	GR	QT	FE	MI	VF	C	7	10YR52	10YR52	WI	SM	N	NA	NA	0	0	N
3	91.376	1	5	MS	NA	NA	NA	VF	VC	15	10YR41	10YR52	SM		B	NA	NA	0	0	N
3	91.38	1	6	MS	NA	NA	NA	VF	VC	15	10YR31	10YR63	SM		B	NA	NA	0	0	N
3	91.38	1	5	MS	NA	NA	NA	VF	VC	15	10YR31	10YR63	SM		N	NA	NA	0	0	N
3	91.396	1	6	MS	NA	NA	NA	VF	G	15	10YR52	10YR63	WI		B	NA	NA	0	0	N
3	91.396	2	6	MS	NA	NA	NA	VF	VC	15	10YR62	10YR63	WI	SM	B	NA	NA	0	0	N
3	91.421	1	5	MS	NA	NA	NA	VF	VC	15	10YR31	10YR63	SM		B	NA	NA	0	0	N
3	91.423	1	5	MS	NA	NA	NA	VF	VC	15	10YR41	10YR41	SM		B	NA	NA	0	0	N
3	91.429	1	6	MS	NA	NA	NA	VF	G	15	10YR31	10YR63	SM		B	NA	NA	0	0	N
3	91.431	3	5	MS	NA	NA	NA	VF	G	15	10YR31	10YR63	SM		B	NA	NA	0	0	N
3	91.435	2	5	MS	NA	NA	NA	VF	VC	15	10YR41	10YR63	WI		B	NA	NA	0	0	N
3	91.435	1	5	MS	NA	NA	NA	VF	G	15	10YR41	10YR63	SM		B	NA	NA	0	0	N
3	93.1266	2	5	MS	NA	NA	NA	VF	P	15	10YR31	10YR63	SM		B	NA	NA	0	0	N

Vessel lot	Catalog Number	No. of Sherds	Thickness	Incl 1	Grit Comp	Grit Comp 2	Grit Comp 3	Incl Min	Incl Max	Incl Density	Interior Color	Exterior Color	Surface Treatment	Surface Treatment 2	Portion	Rim Form	Lip Form	Orifice	Collar Width	Residues
4	91.53	1	8	GR	QT	QZ	FE	VF	G	7	7.5YR52	7.5YR53	RD	SM	N	NA	NA	0	0	N
4	91.951	1	12	GR	QT	QZ	FE	VF	G	7	7.5YR53	7.5YR53	SM		B	NA	NA	0	0	N
4	93.1136	1	9	GR	QT	QZ	FE	VF	G	7	7.5YR42	7.5YR53	RD	SM	N	NA	NA	0	0	N
4	93.1139	1	8	GR	QT	QZ	FE	VF	G	7	10YR52	7.5YR54	RD	SM	N	NA	NA	0	0	N
4	93.1144	1	8	GR	QT	QZ	FE	VF	G	7	7.5YR53	7.5YR52	RD	SM	N	NA	NA	0	0	N
4	93.1324	1	8	GR	QT	QZ	FE	VF	G	7	7.5Y453	7.5YR53	RD	SM	N	NA	NA	0	0	N
4	93.1324	1	8	GR	QT	QZ	FE	VF	G	7	7.5YR53	7.5YR53	RD	SM	N	NA	NA	0	0	N
4	93.1324	1	8	GR	QT	QZ	FE	VF	G	7	7.5YR53	7.5YR53	RD	SM	N	NA	NA	0	0	N
4	93.1327	1	8	GR	QT	QZ	FE	VF	G	7	10YR52	7.5YR54	RD	SM	R	EV	FL	10	0	N
4	93.1334	1	9	GR	QT	QZ	FE	VF	G	7	7.5YR42	7.5YR53	RD	SM	N	NA	NA	0	0	N

Key for Table 4.1

Inclusions (Incl 1, Grit Comp, Grit Comp 2, Grit Comp 3):
AR = Arcose
BA = Basalt
BI = Biotite
CH = Chert
FE = Feldspar
GR = Grit
HO = Hornblende
LM = Limestone
MI = Muscovite
MS = Missing
NA = Not applicable
QT = Quart
QZ = Quartzite
SA = Sand
SH = Shell

Size (Incl Min, Incl Max):
VF = Very fine ($\frac{1}{16}$–$\frac{1}{8}$ mm)
F = Fine ($\frac{1}{8}$–$\frac{1}{4}$ mm)
M = Medium ($\frac{1}{4}$–$\frac{1}{2}$ mm)
C = Coarse ($\frac{1}{2}$–1 mm)
VC = Very coarse (1–2 mm)
G = Granule (2–4 mm)
P = Pebble (4–6 mm)

Surface Treatment:
CM = Cord-marked
DE = Dentate-stamped
FA = Fabric-impressed
LP = Linear-punctate
NO = Notched
PU = Punctate
RD = Rocker-dentate
SC = Scraped
SL = Scallop
SM = Smooth
WI = Wiped

Portion:
B = Body
C = Collar
N = Neck
R = Rim
S = Shoulder

Rim Form:
CC = Collared/Castellated
CL = Collared
CS = Castellated
EV = Everted
FL = Flat
IN = Inverted
NA = Not available

Lip Form:
EV = Everted
FL = Flat
IN = Inverted
NA = Not available
PT = Pointed
RO = Rounded
TH = Thickened

TECHNOLOGICAL STYLE AND
TECHNICAL CHOICE

In this chapter I define *style* as the *way* an artifact is made, which includes but is not limited to the way it is decorated (see Stark 1998, and this volume). Further, I suggest that it is neither possible nor desirable to separate "style" from "function" or decoration from technology (see also Stark and Wobst, this volume). Style, as the "characteristic manner of expression, execution, construction or design" (Hill 1985:374), permeates all aspects of variation in material culture.

This all-encompassing definition of style informs research on "technical" or "technological style," which focuses on the relationship between techniques and society (Lechtman 1977; van der Leeuw 1993:240). Much of the research on technological style is grounded in ethnography and focuses on the techniques and choices that underlay variation in the finished products that archaeologists analyze.

Although most artifact typologies give primacy to decoration or shape, research in the realm of technological style has shown that in certain contexts decorative style may be less indicative of social identities than are technological traditions (see Childs 1991; Dietler and Herbich 1989; Gosselain 1992a; Lechtman 1977; Pfaffenberger 1992; Stark, this volume; Steinberg 1977:78; Sterner 1989). For example, both Gosselain (1992a) and Stark (this volume) have shown in ethnographic contexts that the vessel shaping *process* reflects social boundaries more than the look of the finished vessels. Likewise, Miller (1985) suggests in his ethnographic study of pottery manufacture in central India that shaping techniques reflect social divisions of caste. In these ethnographic examples the emphasis is on *choice*—rather than the materials or tools—as critical in determining the final product (van der Leeuw 1993:241). Thus, models that emphasize technical choice underscore social agency as critical in "defining, determining, and articulating particular technologies and…operational sequences" (Dobres and Hoffman 1991:231).

At the core of theories of technological style is the understanding that given a technical problem, artifact producers choose among a number of viable options, such that choices transcend mere material efficacy or technical logic (Lemonnier 1989:156, 1993: 16; Mahias 1993:177; Sackett 1990). These choices are then linked through "operational sequences" or the series of steps taken in artifact production (Mahias 1993:162). Decisions or choices made at one point in the sequence will thus affect decisions made later in the production process. Thus, the nature of the technological or social problem, access to knowledge and raw materials, and social- or self-censure all play a part in the material product of technical choice. An individual artifact producer may not consciously be aware of the existence of choices per se, but "neither are these ever totally hidden" (Mahias 1993: 177). Individuals within a particular society simply come to rely on a particular technique, even though other viable options are potentially available (Lemonnier 1992:17). Although it may be useful to look for cross-cultural patterning in technical choices, it is clear that for each society attention must be paid to the particular environmental, historical, and social parameters (contexts) of choice.

By emphasizing technological style in this analysis I do not intend to replace an overemphasis on decoration with an overemphasis on technology or "function." Decoration is seen simply as one attribute of technical choice. Therefore, style is viewed not as something added on to objects but as the "result of alternative technical and design choices" (Dietler and Herbich 1989:159).

THE LATE PREHISTORIC PERIOD:
ETHNOHISTORIC AND
ARCHAEOLOGICAL EVIDENCE

In the last section I underscored the importance of cultural context for interpreting variation in material culture. Therefore, as a backdrop for the ceramic analysis, in this section I summarize what is known of the latter part of the Late Woodland period in the Connecticut and Mohawk valleys (A.D. 1300–1600).

Ethnohistoric and linguistic evidence indicates that at the time of contact native peoples of southern New England spoke dialects belonging to the Algonquian language family, whereas Iroquoian tribal groups in central and western New York (Mohawk Valley) spoke dialects belonging to the Iroquoian language family. Aside from linguistic differences, Algonquians of southern New England and the New York Iroquois differed with respect to settlement patterns, subsistence, and political organization. I briefly summarize these differences below.

New England Algonquians

Towns they have none, being always removing from one place to another for conveniency of food.... I have seen half a hundred of their Wigwams together in a piece of ground and they shew prettily, within a day or two, or a week they have all been dispersed.

—Josselyn 1988:91 [1674]

The latter part of the Late Woodland is thought to have been culturally dynamic in central and western New York: agriculture became important for subsistence, communities became more sedentary, population increased, and warfare was on the rise (Fenton 1978). However, in southern New England, unlike areas to the south and west, there is no evidence for large, permanent, fortified settlements and intensive agriculture during the Late Woodland period (Thorbahn 1988; cf. Bendremer and Dewar 1994; Bragdon 1996; Lavin 1988a).

Archaeological evidence indicates that maize horticulture was present in the greater New England area by A.D. 1000 but not to the same degree across the region (George and Bendremer 1995:14; see also Cassedy et al. 1993, Chilton 1996, and Heckenberger et al. 1992). The consensus in the published literature is that intensive maize horticulture was *not* practiced on the coast until the contact period or just before (Bernstein 1992; Little and Schoeninger 1995). Others assert that inland peoples practiced intensive horticulture (Bendremer 1993; Lavin 1988a). Although the degree of reliance on maize horticulture by Native Americans in the region is controversial, there is currently insufficient evidence to support the claim that maize was anything more than a dietary supplement in the New England interior prior to European settlement (Chilton 1998b; cf. Bendremer and Dewar 1994; Bragdon 1996; Ceci 1979, 1990; Demerritt 1991; Dincauze 1990:30; McBride 1984:144; and Silver 1980).

Most of the seventeenth century accounts of Native American subsistence in southern New England do not support claims of maize specialization. Instead, it is likely that the hunting and gathering of a variety of plants and animals formed the core of the New England diet (see Josselyn 1988:93 [1674]; Jameson 1909:105–107; Williams 1963 [1643]; and Wood 1977:86 [1634]). For example, Wood (1977:86 [1634]) records the following about the peoples of the Massachusetts Bay: "In wintertime they have all manner of fowls of the water and of the land, and the beasts of the land and water, pond-fish, with catharres and other roots, Indian beans and clams. In the summer they have all manner of shellfish, with all sorts of berries." Although most of the ethnohistoric evidence for this period pertains to the New England coast, there is also evidence that hunting and gathering were equally important in the New England interior. In a letter from the seventeenth century, Isaack Rasieres (in Jameson 1909:105–107) states that Hudson Valley peoples "support themselves with hunting and fishing, and the sowing of maize and beans."

Thus, although we know that maize horticulture was practiced by the New England Indians, it may not have consumed much of their time or energy. Cronon (1983:45) indicates that after planting maize native peoples would disperse for two to three months, as the maize ripened, to plant and gather elsewhere. Thus, the Algonquians of the region may be seen as mobile farmers, a category for which we currently lack sufficient archaeological understanding (see Graham 1994).

There is little evidence for settled village life in the interior of New England prior to European contact. Concerning the lack of evidence for large Late Woodland villages in the region, archaeologists used to claim that such sites had not yet been found or, as Ritchie claimed for the Hudson Valley, that they had been obliterated by the large-scale destruction of sites as a result of Euro-American settlement and digging by amateurs (Ritchie 1958:7; see also Snow 1980: 320). Certainly, the looting of sites has had a serious impact on the visibility of sites in the Connecticut Valley (Jordan 1975). Also, because of the large, dynamic floodplain of the Connecticut River valley, sites may have been buried or destroyed. Nevertheless, at this point archaeologists must base their interpretations on available evidence. The relative invisibility of Late Woodland villages in New England is most likely due to a high degree of mobility for the small groups that resided in the valleys of the interior (Ritchie 1958:108). I explore this last point further below.

Although settlement pattern data are not plentiful in New England, especially in the interior, it is clear that the large, semipermanent settlements characteristic of the Late Woodland period elsewhere in the deciduous Woodlands are absent. The basic population unit in southern New England was apparently the village (Johnson 1993), which consisted of a few hundred inhabitants related through extended kin networks (Cronon 1983:37–38). New England villages differed from those of the Iroquois in that the inhabitants were often widely dispersed within a "homeland" (Handsman 1991; Johnson 1993:30). Settlement patterns were thus "characterized by a high degree of individual and community dispersion and mobility" (Johnson 1993:246). Mobility may have been a strategy to maintain the environmental diversity on which these communities depended.

Ethnohistoric and archaeological evidence suggests that the traditional dwelling throughout New England was the wigwam. The size of wigwams was usually small; Williams (1963:121 [1643]) describes a dwelling for two families as "a little round house of some fourteen or fifteen foot over." Each house was likely shared by one or two related families (Morgan 1965:124; Williams 1963: 61 [1643]). Johan de Laet (ca. 1625–1640 in Jameson [1909:57]) notes that whereas some native peoples in western New England led a "wandering life in the open aire," others had "fixed places of abode." Thus, it is clear that there was diversity in Algonquian settlement practices. For some groups the size and shape of dwellings would change, depending on population density and the season (Cronon 1983:38).

Although there is some archaeological evidence for larger population aggregations in the lower Connecticut Valley during the Late Woodland period (Bendremer and Dewar 1994; Lavin 1988b), the situation is less clear for the rest of southern New England. Ceci (1979) reports that there is *no* evidence of prehistoric village-based settlement patterns on Long Island prior to European contact; this is also the case in the middle Connecticut Valley in Massachusetts (Chilton 1996). As Dincauze (1990:30) points out for southern New England in general, "We cannot clearly see any dramatic changes in settlement distribution or size coincident with the adoption of maize horticulture" (see also Chilton 1998b).

In terms of political organization, Algonquians of New England can best be described as "loosely organized" (Fenton 1940: 162). No political unit was larger than the village, and there was no central authority able to force political conformity (Thomas 1979: 400). Because groups were fissioning and fusing seasonally, patterns of residence and the reckoning of kin were quite flexible. Johnson (1993) suggests that mobility may have been a political strategy of resistance to authority—that is, the authority of certain native political leaders and, later, the English. By maintaining flexibility and mobility in their settlement practices the Algonquians of the interior could literally "vote with their feet," which accounts for the infrequent occurrence of warfare prior to European contact.

THE IROQUOIS OF UPSTATE NEW YORK

In contrast to the evidence we currently have for New England Algonquians, the New York Iroquois clearly devoted much time to cultivating, harvesting, storing, and preparing maize (see Parker 1968). The type of maize cultivated by the Iroquois was Northern Flint or closely related varieties (Fenton 1978:325). This type of maize is unlike modern sweet corn in that to be palatable it needs to be either cooked intensively or ground into a flour. According to Parker (1968:9), maize was so important to the Iroquois "that they called it by a name meaning 'our life' or 'it sustains us.'"

The New York Iroquois resided in large, semipermanent villages during the Late Woodland period. These villages comprised multiroomed longhouses that ranged in length from 30 to 150 feet (Fenton 1978: 306). Villages were often maintained for up to 100 years (Snow 1994:36), depending on the availability of arable land and firewood. Longhouses would have accommodated up to 20 families of matrilineal kin, each in their own room/compartment (Morgan 1965:64).

During the Late Woodland period, intercommunity conflict increased dramatically as a result of sedentism and intensive horticulture (Hasenstab 1990:1; see also Morgan 1901:306). As a result many of the Iroquois villages of the Late Woodland period were palisaded for defense, sometimes with double or triple palisades (Snow 1994:36). In contrast to the overlapping and shallow nature of postmolds on New England sites, Iroquois longhouse structures are easily identified archaeologically. The houses in some Iroquois villages were apparently arranged in somewhat orderly rows (Tuck 1971:2); Chaumont recorded that he found the "streets cleaned" when he visited Onondaga in 1654 (Thwaites 1896–1901:42:87), which indicates the structured nature of village layout.

Unlike the relatively flexible and fluid so-cial organization of Algonquian society, the five, and later six, nations (tribes) of the Iroquois shared a structured and clearly defined sociopolitical organization (Niemczycki 1984:3). Matrilineages were the building blocks of the Iroquoian social system; a clan comprised one or more maternal families or lineages (Fenton 1978:309). Two or more of these clans constituted a moiety. Each tribe was divided into two of these moieties, as well as being divided into villages (Fenton 1978:309). Each clan had its own titled offices in the General Council of the League of the Iroquois; these offices were inherited matrilineally (Fenton 1978:314). According to Whallon (1968), as a result of population growth during the Late Woodland period, the size, power, and rigidity of matrilineal groups increased as a means of controlling intergroup relations.

ALGONQUIAN-IROQUOIS INTERACTIONS

Although I have emphasized cultural dissimilarities for the purpose of discussing ceramic variation, differences between Algonquian and Iroquoian societies are for the most part in degree and not in kind. Also, there is clear evidence of interaction between the Mohawk Valley and Connecticut Valley groups in the early historic period (Haefeli and Sweeney 1993; Salisbury 1993). There is also archaeological evidence for prehistoric contact and trade across what is now the New York–Massachusetts border; for example, throughout prehistory chert artifacts from New York are found on archaeological sites in New England. Although these "exotic" materials are more numerous in certain periods (ca. 5000–3000 years before present), they were clearly present throughout prehistory.

CERAMIC ANALYSIS RESULTS

Based on the cultural differences between New England Algonquians and Mohawk Valley Iroquoians discussed in the previous section, at the outset of this research some of my expectations for ceramic variation were that Algonquian ceramics would (1) exhibit more stylistic and technological heterogeneity within and between vessels than do

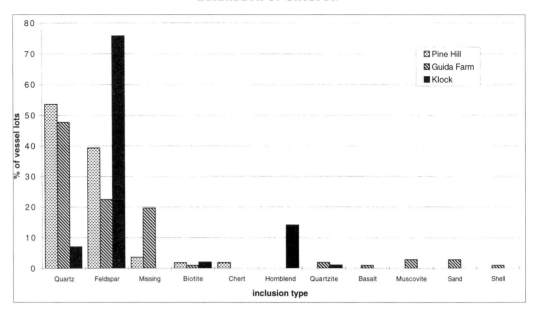

Figure 4.2. Primary inclusion type by site.

Iroquoian ceramics (reflecting social, subsistence, and settlement flexibility/variability), (2) have technological attributes that suggest a wide variety of intended uses, and (3) demonstrate a selection for mechanical strength over thermal shock resistance, because they would more likely have been used for transport than for the intensive cooking of maize.

Although there are some notable differences between the Algonquian assemblages from Pine Hill and Guida Farm, in the following summary I emphasize their similarities in order to compare them to the ceramics from the Mohawk–Iroquoian Klock site (for a further exposition of the ceramic analysis see Chilton 1996, 1998a).

ALGONQUIAN/CONNECTICUT VALLEY VESSELS
Ceramic vessels from the Pine Hill and Guida Farm sites have dense inclusions and exhibit a wide variety of inclusion types; the most common inclusion type is quartz (Figures 4.2 and 4.3). Vessel walls are consistently thick with respect to vessel size, and overall vessel size is significantly smaller in comparison to vessels from the Klock site. Algonquian ceramics appear to be predominantly coil made and show a great diversity in interior and ex-

terior color. Rim and lip forms indicate the presence of both collared and uncollared vessels, and surface treatments demonstrate a preference for roughened surfaces. Vessel shape ranged from conical to globular. In virtually all attributes analyzed the Connecticut Valley assemblages show a great deal of diversity in attribute states, and very few specimens approximate known ceramic types from New York or coastal New England (Figure 4.4).

IROQUOIAN/KLOCK VESSELS
Klock vessels show less diversity in inclusion type and have on average a lower inclusion density than the Connecticut Valley assemblages. Klock vessels also have relatively thinner walls than the Connecticut Valley pots (when vessel size is taken into account). The average maximum diameter for Klock site vessels is 58 percent larger than for Connecticut Valley vessels (the median greatest vessel diameter based on body sherd curvature for Pine Hill and Guida was 18 and 16 cm, respectively, whereas for Klock it was 29 cm). Pots from the Klock site were likely either drawn or slab built; there is no clear evidence of coiling. Generally, vessels from the Iroquoian Klock site were smooth bodied,

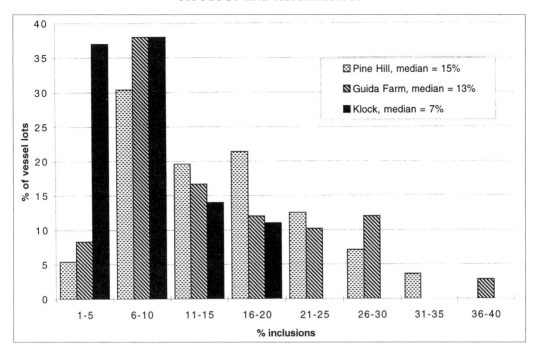

Figure 4.3. Inclusion density by site.

DIFFERENCES IN INTENDED FUNCTION

How might these differences be interpreted with respect to vessel function? First, I would like to make it clear that I am referring to *intended* vessel function (and only the widest parameters of vessel function, at that). Ceramic use-wear studies and residue analyses are not well developed in New England. With respect to the parameters of *intended* use, in his analysis of midwestern ceramics David Braun (1983, 1987) proposed that during the Late Woodland period the change from thick-walled, densely tempered vessels to thin-walled, less densely tempered vessels represented a transition in the intended uses of pots. Pots with larger, denser temper and thicker walls (like the Algonquian pots analyzed here) are generally more resistant to

globular in shape, and had incised, notched, and castellated rims. Overall, the assemblage is quite homogeneous. Decorated sherds (all rimsherds) fit neatly into the established ceramic typologies for the Mohawk Valley (Figure 4.5; see Lenig 1965 and MacNeish 1952).

mechanical stress but are more prone to crack initiation as a result of thermal stress (Braun 1983; Rice 1987). This is very much contingent on the type of temper used, however. For example, quartz (the predominant temper type in the Algonquian vessels), with a large coefficient of expansion, appears to be poorly suited for use in cooking vessels (Rye 1976:118). Conversely, pots with thinner walls and less dense temper (like the Iroquois vessels discussed here) may be less apt to crack when heated but are more likely to break as a result of mechanical stress. Braun proposed that Woodland peoples made choices that affected the performance characteristics of ceramic vessels in response to an increasing reliance on seed crops: through time potters added less temper to ceramic pastes and produced pots with thinner walls so that the vessels could better withstand the repeated thermal stresses of cooking.

I propose a similar scenario for the Northeast, except I focus here on synchronic differences rather than diachronic change. On the basis of attributes of vessel wall thickness, inclusion type, and inclusion density, it appears

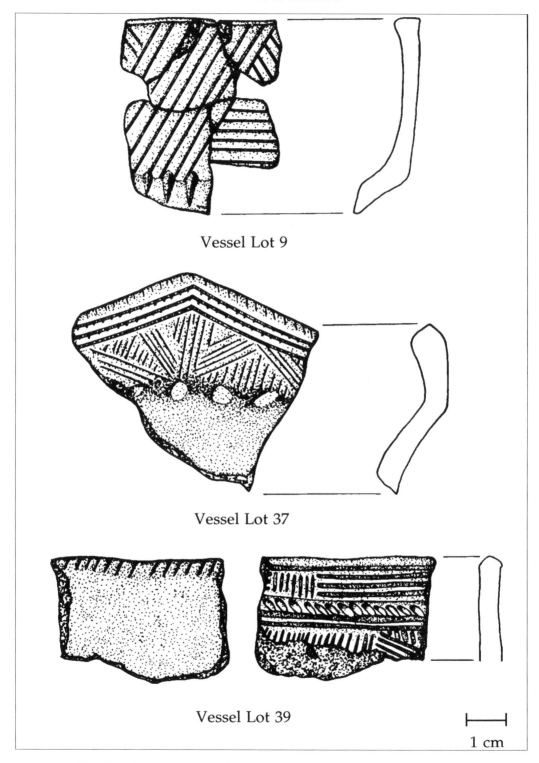

Figure 4.4. Vessel lots from the Pine Hill site.

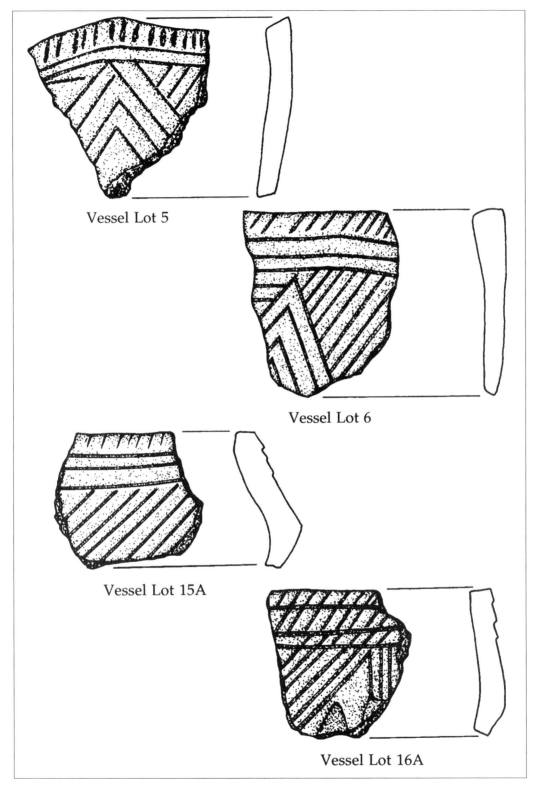

Vessel Lot 5

Vessel Lot 6

Vessel Lot 15A

Vessel Lot 16A

Figure 4.5. Vessel lots from the Klock site.

that Iroquois vessels would have been well suited for cooking (Chilton 1996, 1998a). In contrast, I suggest that Algonquian potters were producing pots *intended* to withstand mechanical stress, even at the expense of vulnerability to thermal stress. Algonquian pots may have performed well in the transport and storage of food and water, but they would not have performed as well as Iroquois pots for intensive cooking.

Vessel size also provides a clue to the intended use of a vessel. As mentioned above, Iroquois pots in this study were, on average, 58 percent larger than Algonquian pots. This difference in size may indicate their use for cooking and serving relatively large amounts of food and, perhaps, communal dining by extended family groups (Snow 1994:13). Mohawk pots were apparently designed to stay in one place for most of their use lives; because the Klock vessels have thinner walls and are generally much larger than Algonquian pots, they would not have been easily transported.

In contrast, Algonquian potters produced relatively small pots that would have been easily transported. Also, the degree of attribute diversity in Algonquian pots may reflect the diverse diet of New England Algonquians; pots may have been used to collect, transport, prepare, serve, and store a wide variety of animal and plant foods, as well as for sporadic cooking.

Thus far I have focused on utilitarian reasons for technical choices made by native potters—of explanations for "pots as tools" (Braun 1983). How can we explain the overall greater diversity of Algonquian vessels in nearly *all* of the attributes examined?

CONTEXTS AND SCALES OF PRODUCTION

The great diversity in Algonquian ceramics may be accounted for in part by the high degree of mobility and small group size of Late Woodland Algonquian groups in the New England interior. If, as I have suggested elsewhere (Chilton 1996), the Connecticut Valley Algonquians were highly mobile, with fluid social boundaries, then the social contexts of ceramic manufacture were variable—pots were made in a wide variety of environmental contexts. Potters would choose from a diverse range of nearby clay and temper resources, depending on their seasonal location. Thus, if pots were made at various locations throughout the year, different ceramic pastes were selected, prepared, and used. Accordingly, we would expect the Late Woodland ceramics of the Connecticut Valley to show a significant degree of variability in paste characteristics (e.g., kinds of inclusions).

In contrast to the mobile farmers of the middle Connecticut Valley, as discussed above, the Iroquois were semisedentary, intensive farmers. Under these circumstances I would expect pots to have been made under more consistent and predictable social circumstances and ecological contexts. In accordance with this expectation the Iroquoian ceramics analyzed in this study show much more uniformity than Algonquian ceramics. The uniformity in ceramic pastes may be a result of (1) part-time specialists using a narrow range of clay and temper resources and/or (2) a more sedentary lifestyle (affording access to a limited number of resources). Also, a standardization in certain attributes may be the result of a certain amount of repetition and routinization of the production process (Rice 1991:268).

Algonquian and Iroquoian ceramics apparently differ not only in their intended use and production contexts but also in production scale. For New England Algonquians ceramics were likely produced by the nuclear or small extended family—what is termed *household production* (Arnold 1985:225). Variability in ceramics may have been constituted by (1) the infrequency of pottery production, (2) the low number of producers involved, (3) the lack of restriction to resources and information (Rice 1991:273), and/or (4) the small, family groups producing pottery with disparate technologies and norms.

For the Iroquois the pottery producers were most likely groups of related women (Engelbrecht 1978:141). As in other examples of "household industry," production would have been conducted more frequently than for New England Algonquians, and the amount of pottery produced was greater (see Arnold 1991:92). A change from household production to household industry in pre-industrial societies is expected to correlate with population increase when there is an increase in demand for ceramics (Arnold 1985: 226). In accordance with this expectation, archaeological evidence for the Iroquois supports a population nucleation and increased pottery production during the Late Woodland period (Tuck 1978).

TECHNICAL STYLE

Diversity and uniformity in ceramic assemblages may also reflect different aspects of social messaging as defined by Wobst (1977). For example, Brumbach (1975:27) suggests in her analysis of ceramics in the Hudson Valley that greater heterogeneity of Algonquian ceramics as compared to Iroquoian ceramics indicates relatively small social groups; her conclusion is based on the assumption that large social groups need to integrate themselves with consistency in material culture or social signaling. This is consistent with McPherron's (1967:101) observation for the Iroquois that ceramic similarity correlates with larger group and house size. How does group size relate to social integration and information exchange within groups?

SOCIAL INTEGRATION IN IROQUOIS SOCIETY

Iroquois population size apparently grew during the Late Woodland period, and settlements became more nucleated (Tuck 1978: 333). With a greater reliance on cultigens and with increasing population density, social and economic ties may have proliferated; these ties may have led to the development of regional networks that were signaled stylistically (Hargrave et al. 1991; Tuck 1971:219). Wobst (1977:329) suggests that "those sets of material culture which potentially are visible to all members of a given social group are much more likely to show...expression of stylistic form." Pots were used for cooking on the hearth in the center of each longhouse

compartment and were visible to everyone on a daily basis. Because maize stews were cooked for long periods of time, pots would often sit on the hearth for many hours. With the base of the pots either sitting in or dangling over the fire, the pronounced, geometrically incised collars on the vessels were a prominent, central icon for anyone entering the longhouse compartment.

Although the potential for social messaging is clear in this case, style is not simply encoded in or tacked on to finished products (Dietler and Herbich 1989:157). It is also encoded in the operational sequence of manufacture or technical style (Mahias 1993). For example, it is likely that stylistic information was exchanged not only when pots were sitting in the hearth but when groups of women gathered to make pots. The slab-building of pots of consistent size and shape and the repetitive incising of decorations on collars provide the potential for pots to embody messages about group membership, the role of women, social integration, and the egalitarian ideal of Iroquois society. Thus, pots, as a central and visible output of the joint effort of women within the matrilineage, had the potential for carrying social messages in both manufacture and use.

THE MUTABILITY OF ALGONQUIAN SOCIETY

Just as stylistic messages encode information about group membership—matrilineal or tribal group membership for the Iroquois—they can also encode messages about the fluidity of social boundaries. As previously discussed, Connecticut Valley Algonquians were mobile farmers who used a wide variety of plants and animals on a seasonal basis. Aside from reasons of subsistence, there may also have been social reasons to maintain mobility. Eric Johnson (1993) suggests that mobility was a strategy of resistance to the authority of political leaders by the Algonquians of southern New England. This flexibility in social relations distinguishes the egalitarian Algonquians of the New England interior from the "tribal" Iroquois.

Social explanations for the maintenance of variability in Algonquian ceramics include

(1) no felt need for social signaling (at least in ceramics), (2) competition for "power in the public, symbolic domain" via individual expression (Goodby 1992:14), and (3) the expression of nonconformity as both a reflection and precedent of Algonquian society. The symbolic expression of the individual potter as exhibited in the entire production process was free to vary such that pots both represented and constituted fluidity, individual expression, movement, and change.

DISCUSSION

The Law of the Hammer suggests that, although the methods we use are often appropriate to the task, too frequently a given method is used simply because it is the tool currently in hand.

—Moore and Keene 1983:3

To return to the discussion at the beginning of this chapter, the tools of research, whether typological or otherwise, should be determined by the specific research questions being asked. Whether a "crowbar" or a "hammer" works or not, the same tool cannot and should not be used for every task.

The empirical typologies used in the Northeast have long served as the only valid methods of analysis for ceramics. Iroquoian and New England Algonquian pottery typologies have been used indiscriminately across cultural boundaries. As this study has shown, there is a marked contrast between Iroquoian and Algonquian ceramics with respect to the scale and contexts of production, intended uses, and the social roots of technical choices. The means and meanings of stylistic signaling are obviously quite different for Algonquian and Iroquoian societies (although the differences evident in my attribute analysis may or may not have been significant to the makers and users of these vessels). It is clear that, because there is so much diversity in the ceramics of the New England interior, *a typological approach is simply not useful in this context.* Certainly there are *general trends* in ceramics that prove useful for the relative dating of a given archaeological site. For example, cord/fabric-marked, conical shaped vessels predominate in the Early and Middle Woodland periods (A.D. 0–1000), whereas collared, incised, globular-shaped vessels are more common in the Late Woodland period. However, these trends are not linear, nor are they absolute.

I suggest that the kind of analysis undertaken here—an attribute analysis of technical choice—is an important first step in understanding some of the axes of choice for potters in New England and elsewhere. An awareness of the many agents of ceramic variability—knowledge, tradition, ability, production scale, intended use, ideology—will help archaeologists to formulate means of analysis that will allow them to ask questions that go beyond culture history into the realm of social and technical choice.

Acknowledgments. Many thanks to Dena F. Dincauze and H. Martin Wobst for inspiration, brainstorming sessions, and editorial comments throughout the term of the research presented here. I also wish to thank Charles Kolb and Louana Lackey for bringing me into the ceramic ecology fold and Miriam Stark for introducing me to technological style. This research was funded in part by a Grant-in-Aid from Sigma Xi and a Graduate Research Award from the Department of Anthropology and a University Fellowship at the University of Massachusetts, Amherst. Pottery sherds were drawn by Maureen Manning-Bernatsky. Any flaws in this work are solely my responsibility.

5

Testing Interpretative Assumptions of Neutron Activation Analysis
Contemporary Pottery in Yucatán, 1964–1994

Dean E. Arnold, Hector A. Neff, Ronald L. Bishop, and Michael D. Glascoc

For the archaeologist concerned with interpreting the meaning of ancient artifacts, the techniques of the physical sciences appear to provide an easy solution. Not only do the "hard sciences" provide a rigorous set of analytical, scientific procedures that can be replicated, but they also provide quantitative data that may appear to be self-interpreting. As we know from the work of Kuhn (1962), Hanson (1958), and more recent interpretive approaches, however, there is no science without presuppositions (see Agger 1991), and scientific knowledge is contextualized by its historical and cultural nature. Archaeology as "science" takes place within a cultural, social (e.g., the "tradition" of archaeological training), and theoretical context. Because archaeology involves the study of human behavior, the study of the past is no better off with the physical sciences than without them unless the links between the data of the physical sciences and human behavior can be made explicit and tested empirically. One way to tie the data of the physical sciences to human behavior is to combine ethnography and the methods of the physical sciences to understand more precisely how known behavior is reflected in artifacts and artifactual distributions.

This relationship between behavior and physical science data is no less problematic in the neutron activation analysis (NAA) of pottery. NAA is a technique for characterizing the chemical composition of materials and is based on the counting of gamma rays emitted from a sample that has been exposed to a source of neutrons (usually in a nuclear reactor). Atoms of different elements are "activated" through the addition of a neutron to their nucleus, and these radioactive isotopes decay with characteristic half-lives and gamma-ray energies. The quantification of these energies yields an indication of the amount of the original element in the sample.

Neutron activation analysis has become much more routine in recent years. Because chemical constituents[1] are conceptually so far removed from the way that humans select and mix raw materials, however, it is important to refine, reexamine, and test the assumptions for interpreting chemical data from ancient pottery. One approach to this problem is to analyze ethnographic pottery from a location where the behavioral variables are known and then discover whether the chemical data co-vary with the actual behavior of potters.

This chapter explores the relationship between the behavior of contemporary potters and chemical patterning. Using pottery for which the behavioral variables and production locations are known, it focuses on several major research questions. First, what is the resolving power of NAA in the relatively homogeneous geological environment of northern Yucatán? Would the resolving

TABLE 5.1.
Details of Sample of Kiln Wasters Collected in Yucatán

Community	Date of Sample	Purpose of Sample	Number of Kilns Sampled	Number of Wasters Analyzed[a]
Ticul	1964	Longitudinal study	1	44
Ticul	1988	Longitudinal study and interhousehold variability	6	86
Ticul	1994	Longitudinal study and interhousehold variability	4	120
Mama	1994	Regional variability	2	44
Tepakan	1994	Regional variability	2	53
Akil	1994	Regional variability	1	28
			Total	375

a The number of sherds actually analyzed is less than the number of sherds collected (see text).

power of neutron activation analysis enable us to identify production communities as Arnold et al. (1991) did in contemporary Guatemala? Second, if NAA has sufficient resolution power to differentiate northern Yucatecan potting communities, can the products of individual households be identified within those communities? Finally, what is the effect of time on the elemental patterns? Do they change through time? If so, how? Why? To answer these questions, 375 wasters from contemporary Mexican kilns were collected between 1964 and 1994 and were analyzed using NAA. One set of data was collected in Ticul, Yucatán, in 1964; another was collected there in 1988; and a third set was collected from the communities of Ticul, Tepakan, Mama, and Akil, Yucatán, in 1994 (Table 5.1).

ETHNOGRAPHY AND
COMPOSITIONAL ANALYSIS

In the last decade great strides have been made in the compositional analyses of pottery. Building on the pioneering work of Anna O. Shepard of some 50 years ago (see Shepard 1956), it is now possible to understand more about the social, cultural, and historical significance of ancient ceramic pastes. Along with the refinement of neutron activation analysis and multivariate statistical techniques, research using ethnoarchaeo-

logical materials has greatly aided in clarifying the relationship between the chemical composition of ancient pottery and the behavior of ancient potters.

Because ancient potters obviously did not select their raw materials on the basis of their chemical composition, the relationship between the abundance of elemental constituents and human behavior is not only the most fundamental question about compositional studies of pottery but is also its most perplexing. It is particularly acute because pottery is a complex chemical and physical mixture. For years archaeologists and analysts have recognized that the chemical composition of pottery is influenced by a variety of factors: water, clay, natural nonplastic inclusions, and "temper" added by the potter (Arnold 1971:32–33, 1975; Arnold et al. 1978; Arnold et al. 1991; Rice 1978; Sayre and Dodson 1957; Shepard 1956). Although 25 years ago some analysts suggested that the "clay" was responsible for the observed chemical variability, one behaviorally valid way of regarding pottery was to recognize it as a composite of several different materials mixed by a particular community of potters in geographic space (Arnold 1981; Arnold et al. 1978; Arnold et al. 1991; Bishop 1975). This was an important change in the way archaeologists viewed pottery because some potters mix two or more clays together, and tempering materials may also contain clay minerals (see Arnold 1971, 1975). Potters may further modify the composition of clays and tempers by dry sieving or levigation. These activities alter the particle size distribution and can affect the chemical composition of the pottery. Although one might assume that firing may also affect the chemical composition, experiments by Cogswell et al. (1996) suggest that firing does not significantly affect the variability of any element routinely used in the neutron activation analysis of pottery. In addition to these factors are the possible effects that percolating groundwater might have on the composition of the pottery that has been buried in subsurface contexts (see Vitelli et al. 1987), but these effects are usually restricted to only a few of the elemental quantities usually determined in NAA (Bishop 1980).

Chemical analyses of contemporary pottery in Guatemala and its constituent raw materials have shown that ceramics can be matched to raw materials in a resource area if the contributions of all raw materials are taken into account (Arnold et al. 1991). Simulation studies by Neff et al. (1988, 1989), however, have revealed that immense amounts of temper have to be added to ceramic mixtures before chemically distinct clays begin to merge into a single chemical group and the elemental signature of each clay is lost. In these simulations the source locations of one temper group and two clay groups were held constant and only the temper-to-clay ratios were altered.

Apparently discrete compositional groups of ethnographic pottery, however, may be complicated by time. Potters may exploit multiple raw material sources, change source locations, and modify paste recipes over time, and these factors may confound efforts to characterize the products of a single production center.

Information has also accumulated about the meaning of "local" and "nonlocal" resources. Land-locked communities of potters[2] obtain their raw materials from a resource area that rarely has a radius exceeding 7 km and most often has a radius of 1 km or less (Arnold 1981, 1985:35–57, 1993:200–204). Although some communities obtain clays from land-based distances of greater than 7 km (Arnold 1981), most of these higher distances occur in communities where travel occurs via a twentieth-century transportation infrastructure. This fact renders it extremely improbable that potters in any ancient community would have obtained their clays and tempers at a land-based distance greater than 7 km. The small size of ceramic resource areas suggests that "sources" of pottery should be tied to a particular geographic area, called the "resource area," within which a particular community of potters exploits its resources (see Arnold 1980: 148–149, 1981, 1993:200–204; see also Rands and Bishop 1980).

The complexities of ceramic mixtures and the great potential variations of modifying ceramic raw materials suggest that inferring a specific geographical source location from ceramic data may be quite complicated. Although it is clear that chemical analyses do reveal the exploitation of resources within a geographical "resource area," it is less clear whether one or more communities are represented in the analyses of archaeological pottery, even though the size of resource areas of any one community is small. Furthermore, overlapping resource areas, and the variation of pastes in a community by physical modification (such as sieving and levigation), and changes in raw materials sources over time may render the identification of discrete production centers difficult.

BACKGROUND OF THE PROJECT

During 1969 and 1970 Dean Arnold initiated a study that would test the assumptions of neutron activation analysis by analyzing pottery and constituent raw materials from contemporary communities in Guatemala. The main task was to analyze clays and tempers from a community and compare these analyses with those of the fired pottery of that community. By controlling the behavioral variables of source location, potter, and community, he wanted to determine if neutron activation analysis could reveal the use of different clay sources (Perlman and Asaro 1969) or some other aspect of the potters' behavior.

In the summer of 1970 Arnold collected samples of clays, tempers, and pottery from pottery-making communities in the Valley of Guatemala. These materials were analyzed using neutron activation at the Brezeale Nuclear Reactor at Pennsylvania State University. Although the overall research design was sound, Arnold, his students, and his reactor colleagues had several difficulties with the presentation and analysis of the chemical data (Arnold et al. 1978; see Bishop et al. 1982). First, no analytical standards were employed so that the elemental data could be represented as actual concentrations of the elements in parts per million. As a result, the data were presented as ratios of the heights of the gamma ray peaks of each element to those of scandium. This solution, however, was problematic because without actual elemental concentrations the peak ratios did not take into account the variation in the reactor flux. As a result, the elemental data from different irradiation events (or "runs"), both in the same reactor and from different reactors, could not be compared easily. Consequently, such data could not be compared to future data analyzed from other reactors (see Bishop et al. 1982). Further, no multivariate statistical techniques were employed to summarize the structure of the data derived from the entire suite of elements analyzed. This problem made it impossible to describe and compare subsets of the data (e.g., clays, tempers, and pottery) because only one element was compared at a time. As a result, decisions of sameness or difference for comparing aggregate samples of clays, tempers, and pottery were somewhat arbitrary or, at best, ambiguous.

As a result of these problems and the criticisms of the Penn State procedures by Bishop (personal communication 1977; Bishop et al. 1982), Arnold turned the samples over to Bishop for reanalysis using the original 1970 research design. Fortunately, a large number of samples had been collected, and this permitted a statistical analysis of the resulting chemical data. This analysis revealed that pottery was a mixture that could be easily related to its constituent clays and tempers (Arnold et al. 1991). Furthermore, it was clear that the compositional profile of the pottery could be related to specific production communities that existed within particular "resource areas" exploited by the communities.

FIELDWORK AND DERIVATION OF THE CURRENT DATA SET

In a continuing effort to refine the methodology and interpretation of the chemical analysis of pottery, Arnold, Neff, and Bishop wanted to test the conclusions derived from the analyses of the contemporary Guatemala pottery and raw materials (Arnold et al. 1991). Were the Guatemala data unique? Would the analysis of pottery from another area support the conclusion from the Guatemala data?

Because Arnold had been engaged in the study of contemporary potters in Yucatán since 1965 and was familiar with the potters there, it was decided that his Yucatecan data could be used to advance the study of the link between behavior and compositional patterning. Arnold had made a long-term study of raw material preparation in Ticul and had collected many raw material samples there in the 1960s. Furthermore, he had visited briefly other communities of potters in Yucatán in 1967 and 1968 (with B. F. Bohor) for comparative purposes. Field research in Ticul in 1984 provided a rich source of data about changes in raw material procurement, craft organization, demand, and distribution since the 1960s. In all, during the 30-year period between 1965 and 1994, Arnold made nine trips to Yucatán, documenting the changes that had occurred in pottery production and in raw-material procurement. These data have provided a behavioral data set for undertaking a rather unique longitudinal study relating behavior and compositional variation.

In 1988 Arnold returned to Ticul to collect pottery from different households and assess the changes in the craft since his last visit in 1984. Arnold collected approximately 50 kiln wasters from each of six potters (Table 5.1).[3] At each kiln every effort was made to collect a sample that was as diverse as possible, selecting sherds from different shapes, wall thicknesses, kinds of slip, and degrees of firing.[4] The goal was to characterize the chemical patterning of each household's pottery across a broad range of vessel shapes, wares, and repeated firings.

Kiln wasters were used for the 1988 sample for several reasons. First, wasters were easy to sample because potters consider them useless. Adjacent to every active Ticul kiln is a waster pile that potters use as a source of kiln furniture. Some wasters are used as receptacles in which small vessels are placed; some are used as supports to raise pottery above the ground during firing, and others are used to stabilize the pottery to keep it from shifting during firing. A second reason for sampling wasters was to provide a specific household provenance without using unfired clay or whole vessels (fired or unfired). Third, wasters are abundant and provide a large sampling universe for a household producing a variety of different vessel shapes and thicknesses with potentially different degrees of firing. Fourth, kiln wasters change over time and represent a fair approximation of the raw materials used in pottery during a rather short period of time. Although this factor was not anticipated when the wasters were collected, it is now clear that wasters have a short life in their position next to the kiln. As larger wasters are broken and become smaller, they are discarded and ultimately end up as fill in low places in house lots and streets or are thrown into garbage middens away from the high-traffic areas. In some cases smaller sherds may be thrown into small mines in house lots that have been excavated to obtain building materials. Further evidence of the short life of wasters next to the kiln is that abandoned kilns have no waster piles. It is possible that wasters may also be moved away from kilns for more mundane reasons. For example, during ethnographic research with pottery production in highland Guatemala in 1970 Arnold was told by some informants that

sherds were often used to clean oneself after defecation. If this practice occurred in Yucatán, it would eventually move sherds away from the kilns into the rear of house lots. Finally, kiln waster piles are as close to an archaeological context as one can find in the present and still maintain precise social and spatial provenance.

At first we only envisioned a study of the intracommunity chemical variability in Ticul from the 1988 data. Then Arnold remembered that Duane Metzger had made a collection of wasters from a Ticul kiln in 1964 and had brought them to the Department of Anthropology at the University of Illinois in Urbana. Arnold was familiar with the kiln that Metzger had sampled and surmised that this collection would be a convenient baseline for comparison. The existence of this baseline stimulated a further question: Does the chemical composition of pottery change through time? If so, what factors might have affected this change? If not, why not? By sampling the wasters from the same household that Metzger sampled in 1964, one could examine the effect of time on the elemental patterning within the same provenance unit. The 1964 sherds thus provided data for a longitudinal study of compositional variation that supplemented the behavioral information about pottery production that Arnold has collected in Ticul during the last 30 years. Arnold sampled Metzger's sherds in March of 1990 using a strategy identical to that used to collect sherds during the 1988 field season. The goal was to have many different shapes, wall thicknesses, slip types, and degrees of firing represented in the sample in order to subsume any possible elemental variations resulting from behavioral factors, such as vessel shapes (shape and wall thickness), slips, and firing frequency within the household.

In 1994 Arnold returned to Yucatán for a brief study of the changes that had occurred in ceramic production since 1988. A secondary goal of this research was to discover if and how chemical patterns of the pottery reflected the evolution in production that had occurred since 1964 and 1988. In addition, it was important to test the resolving power of chemistry-based sourcing in a more challenging geological environment (relatively homogeneous bedrock) than occurred in Guatemala (see Arnold et al. 1991). Did the pottery from resource areas of other communities of potters in Yucatán have distinct chemical patterns like the communities did in Guatemala (Arnold et al. 1991)?

Approximately 30 sherds were collected from each of four kilns[5] in Ticul (Table 5.1). Three of these kilns had been sampled in 1988; the fourth had been newly built by a potter who had moved since 1988.[6] By 1994 he no longer made pottery himself and owned a store on the property. He had become a part-time firing specialist,[7] firing the pottery of others. Because the kiln was built after the 1988 collection, the waster sample from this kiln better reflected the composition of pottery made between 1988 and 1994. Because the purpose of the project was to ascertain the composition of the pottery in 1994 and compare it with the pottery collected in 1964 and 1988, samples from this new kiln biased the sample away from the 1988 and pre-1988 wasters. The kiln thus provided a more accurate behavioral picture of pottery made since the 1988 visit.

The same sampling procedures that were used with the previous collections were followed in 1994 with one significant exception: the 1994 collection was biased towards sherds made with a new clay from the State of Campeche. Beginning about January of 1992, clay mining at the traditional Ticul clay source (Hacienda Yo' K'at) was totally abandoned, after which clay was brought by truck from sources near Dzitbalché, more than 80 km away. In addition, two workshop owners each had their own private clay sources in the same region.[8] Because the fired paste of the Campeche clay was whiter than the pinkish color of the fired clay from Hacienda Yo' K'at, sherds of this new clay were easily identified by potters. As Arnold collected wasters, potters told him which sherds had been made with the Campeche clay. To obtain an adequate sample of sherds made with the new clays mined after the local clay

source was abandoned, Arnold collected sherds that were made with both the new clay and the old clay. This bias assured the inclusion of pottery produced since the 1988 visit and biased it against including wasters that had been made before the Ticul clay source had been abandoned.

Potters were also visited in the towns of Tepakan, Akil, and Mama (Figure 5.1; Table 5.1), and kiln wasters were collected in these communities. Like Ticul potters, Tepakan potters were both males and females. Four Tepakan potters were visited. Both sets of two potters were related, and each set shared one kiln. The firing technique used in Tepakan is different from that used in Ticul; there were no waster piles next to kilns used for kiln furniture. Some sherds were collected from inside the kilns, but the remainder were collected nearby, wherever sherds could be found. In one household was a large midden of discarded and fragmentary wasters near the kiln; this midden was sampled.[9] The other household kiln had few wasters near it, so most of the sherds were collected at the base of a nearby fence.

In Mama two potters were visited (Table 5.1). Potters were exclusively women, and production was seasonal. Pottery was not made during Arnold's visit (July 1994) but rather was produced only in the months preceding the Day of the Dead rituals in late October and early November. There were no waster piles next to the kilns, but in one case sherds occurred near the base of a nearby fence. At the other kiln wasters had been thrown over a fence into an adjacent pasture, where they were retrieved by the potter's husband. Because there was a limited range of shapes produced in Mama in 1994, any latent sampling bias of the potter's husband was not deemed significant.

In Akil only one potter was found.[10] She fired in the open at the rear of her house lot without using a kiln. There was no obvious firing area other than three rocks. Sherds were very small and fragmentary, and shape classes were impossible to identify. Sherds were collected intensively around the supposed firing area.

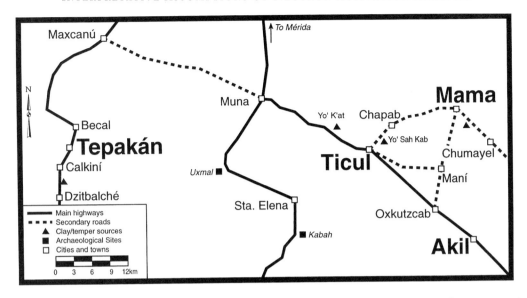

Figure 5.1. Map showing the relationship of the four communities in the States of Yucatán and Campeche, Mexico, in which potters were visited and kilns were sampled.

Some samples of clay and tempers were also collected in 1994. They will not be discussed here because their number is too small to make a significant comparison to the pottery analyzed in this study.

NEUTRON ACTIVATION ANALYSIS

Pottery specimens were prepared for neutron activation analysis using standard procedures at the Missouri University Research Reactor (MURR). Sherd surfaces and all adhering soil were removed with a tungsten carbide burr. Sherds were then washed with deionized water and allowed to air-dry. Part of each specimen was retained for the MURR archive of analyzed ceramic fabrics, and a portion of the remainder was crushed into a fine powder in an agate mortar. The powder samples were oven-dried at 100° C for 24 hours and then placed in a vacuum desiccator to cool. A 200-mg portion of each sample was weighed and placed in a small polyvial for short irradiation. At the same time another 200 mg of each sample were placed in high-purity quartz vials for long irradiations. Reference standards and quality control samples were similarly prepared.[11]

Neutron activation consisted of two irradiations and a total of three gamma counts (Glascock 1992; Neff 1992a). First, a short irradiation was carried out in which samples were sequentially irradiated, two at a time, for five seconds at a neutron flux of 8×10^{13} n/cm²/sec by being sent to the reactor core through a pneumatic tube.[12] A count of these samples for 720 seconds yielded gamma spectra with peaks for the elements with short-lived isotopes (Al, Ba, Ca, Dy, K, Mn, Na, Ti, and V). The samples in quartz vials were subjected to a 24-hour irradiation at a neutron flux of 5×10^{13} n/cm²/sec.[13] After this irradiation the isotopes in the samples were allowed to decay for seven days. The samples were then counted for 2,000 seconds on a high-resolution germanium detector coupled to an automatic sample changer. This counting period yielded spectra for seven elements with isotopes with medium half-lives such as La, As, Lu, Nd, Sm, U, and Yb. After an additional three- or four-week decay a final count of 10,000 seconds was carried out on each sample and yielded spectra of 17 elements with isotopes with long half-lives: Ce, Co, Cr, Cs, Eu, Fe, Hf, Ni, Rb, Sb, Sc, Sr, Ta, Tb, Th, Zn, and Zr.

QUANTITATIVE ANALYSIS OF
THE CHEMICAL DATA

The analyses of 375 samples produced elemental concentrations for 33 elements. Because Ni was below detection in a large number of specimens, it was dropped from the analysis. The remaining analytical data were transformed to log base-10 values for two reasons. First, this transformation compensates for the differences in magnitude between the more abundant elements, such as Al and Fe, and the much less abundant trace elements, such as the rare earths. Second, the multivariate statistical techniques used in this study assume a data set that is normally distributed, and log transformation yields a more nearly normal distribution for highly skewed data, such as trace element concentrations.

Ceramic sourcing typically involves definition of compositionally homogeneous groups of pottery samples of unknown origin. Based on the "provenance postulate" (Weigand et al. 1977), such groups are assumed to represent geographically restricted sources or "source zones." The location of source zones may be inferred by comparing the unknown groups to knowns (source raw materials) or by invoking the "criterion of abundance" (Bishop et al. 1982). In the present case true production locations of the ceramics are known, and such information provides the opportunity to evaluate how well the provenance postulate might apply in this test case. Is the provenance postulate a valid assumption? Do potters who use raw materials within a resource area make pottery that is distinct from that made in communities of potters who use other resource areas?

Demonstrating that the provenance postulate is a valid assumption for these data involves answering three related questions. First, are the behaviorally known groups statistically distinguishable? That is, given a sample from each community, could one assign unknowns to that community unambiguously? Because the data are multivariate elemental concentrations, grouping of the data must be assessed by using multivariate statistics based on the Mahalanobis distance (Beier and Mommsen 1994; Bieber et al. 1976; Bishop and Neff 1989; Harbottle 1976; Leese and Main 1994; Roaf and Galbraith 1994).

In the typical archaeological provenance study none of the ceramics analyzed can be assigned a source initially.[14] So the investigation usually starts with some kind of pattern-recognition analysis through which hypothetical subgroups are recognized.

The second question evaluating the "provenance postulate" concerns its application to northern Yucatán and the "recognizability" of the source-related groups. If one did not know the source of ethnographic pottery, could one identify pottery produced in particular communities through direct examination of the NAA data or through pattern-recognition techniques such as principal-components analysis or cluster analysis?

Finally, if subgroups are recognizable in the data, can compositional groups be linked to specific communities as in Guatemala (Arnold et al. 1991)? Because the chemical composition of pottery expresses that of the clay and temper, as well as any other additives (water and naturally occurring nonplastics), the composition of the pottery may have to be compared to that of mixtures of the raw materials combined during paste preparation in order to identify production communities. Can groups of similar composition be linked to specific communities that exploited resources within a specific geographical area? Are there other explanations for the chemically defined groups?

COMPOSITIONAL VARIATION IN TICUL POTTERY

One of the first questions answered about the 1988 data was whether individual kilns, and therefore individual households, could be recognized from the elemental patterns. Pairwise comparisons of the collections from each of the 1988 households revealed that the households were not significantly different from one another (for $p < .05$; Table 5.2). Similarly, the almost total overlap of all households in a principal components plot (PCA plot) indicates that the groups could

TABLE 5.2.
Pairwise Comparison of the Trace Element Centroids from Pottery Collected
from Each Household in 1988

Household	A. Tzum	A. Uc	F. Keh	M. Tzum	Miguel Segura	Raul Martin
A. Tzum		1.000	1.000	1.000	1.000	.995
A. Uc	.093		1.000	1.000	1.000	.997
F. Keh	.153	.120		.991	1.000	.994
M. Tzum	.147	.122	.184		1.000	.994
Miguel Segura	.152	.122	.181	.181		.993
Raul Martin	.306	.272	.326	.323	.332	

Note: F-ratio statistic between groups is below the diagonal; F-value probabilities are above the diagonal.

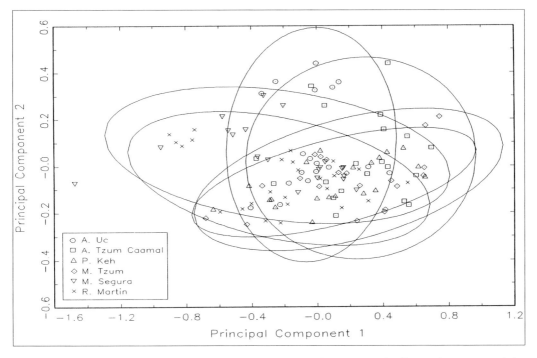

Figure 5.2. Principal components plot of the sherds sampled in 1988 with ellipses drawn around the 90-percent confidence limit for each potter.

not be differentiated without the behavioral provenance provided by ethnography (Figure 5.2).

The chemical similarity of the kiln wasters from different households was expected because in 1988 raw material procurement was not in the hands of household members but was the product of full-time specialists. First, clay was mined by three two-man teams who dug the clay from several mines at Hacienda Yo' K'at (Figure 5.1) and sold it to potters. There was no reason to believe that any one household ever obtained clay consistently from the same team of miners over time. Furthermore, the clay mined by each team of miners came from no more than 50 m from that of another team. Second, the same set of specialists that mine the clay also mine and prepare temper. Temper preparation is a complex process involving selection, mining, crushing, mixing, and screening of appropriate raw materials at the temper mines.[15] The end result is a behaviorally complex and highly variable combination of calcite, dolomite, attapulgite, and sometimes montmorillonite (see Arnold 1971:32–33). Even though there was no evidence that households consistently obtained their temper from the same specialists, all temper comes from the same mining location (Yo' Sah Kab; see Figure 5.1), and mining areas are no more than 300 m apart. Mining thus occurs within a small geographic area, and variability of mining location cross-cuts the entire population of Ticul potters.

Given the behavioral complexities of temper preparation and individual paste preparation, the chemically similar pottery produced by Ticul potters suggests that no inferences of raw material procurement or paste preparation can be made within a source-related group except that potters use raw materials in a particular resource area. In other words, chemically similar groups provide data on the relationship of pottery to a particular geographical area. In this case it does not provide data to answer questions about the way raw material procurement is organized, about the spatial distribution of resources, or about production intensity or scale.

We wanted to answer a second question about the data: Does the chemical signature of pottery made in Ticul change through time? Pairwise comparisons between the centroids of the 1964 sample (from A. Tzum) and the centroids of samples of each of the six potters collected in 1988 revealed no significant differences between the pottery of any of the households (Table 5.3). This result suggested that even though there appeared to be a slight shift between the 1964 ellipse and the 1988 ellipse in the principal components plot, the difference was not statistically significant (Figure 5.3).

Pairwise comparisons between the centroids of the 1964 sample and the entire 1988 sample for all potters, however, revealed statistical difference ($F = 3.219$; $p < .001$). Why was this? This difference may in-dicate individual variation. The 1964 sample came from just one potter (A. Tzum). Not only was his 1964 sample different from the combined 1988 samples, but his 1988 sample also differed from the remainder of the 1988 collection ($F = 1.596$; $p < .043$).

These tests reveal synchronic statistical differences between the centroids of A. Tzum and the rest of the 1988 sample and diachronic differences between the centroids of the A. Tzum 1964 and A. Tzum 1988 samples. The 1964 and 1988 samples, however, cannot be differentiated using a principal components plot. (These tests also served as the basis for combining the 1964 and 1988 samples from Ticul in differentiating Ticul pottery from that of Akil, Tepakan, and Mama in the discussion that follows.) When the chemical data were plotted along principal components 1 and 2, the plot revealed considerable overlap between the data sets from 1964, 1988, and 1994 but with a shift in the position of the 1994 90-percent confidence ellipse (Figure 5.3).

In summary, there are some statistical differences among Ticul potters in the combined 1964 and 1988 samples, but it is highly unlikely that these differences would be recognizable in an archaeological assemblage. By way of contrast, the 1994 sample contains pottery that clearly differs from the 1964 and 1988 compositions and would easily be identified in a pattern-recognition analysis. This compositional change in Ticul pottery between 1988 and 1994 appears to be the result of another behavioral factor that will be addressed in greater detail below.

DIFFERENTIATION OF THE
FOUR PRODUCTION CENTERS

Although pattern-recognition techniques of the elemental data cannot differentiate the pottery of different Ticul potters who used resources within a geographic resource area, the provenance postulate would suggest that communities known to exploit other resource areas should be recognizable in the compositional profile of the elemental data. Can the pottery from the communities of Ticul, Tepakan, Mama, and Akil thus be dif-

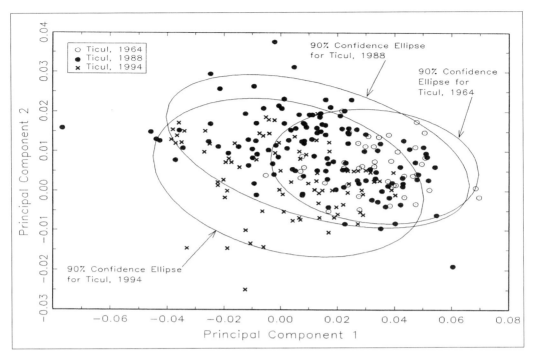

Figure 5.3. Principal components plot of the data points and ellipses of the 1964, 1988, and 1994 samples.

ferentiated? Sufficiently large samples are available from Ticul, Tepakan, and Mama to permit direct multivariate comparisons of ceramics produced in each community. Statistical outliers were removed from the Ticul and Mama groups before the groups were compared. In addition, a substantial proportion of the 1994 Ticul sample was found to be quite divergent from the 1964 and 1988 pattern and so was removed from the Ticul reference group.[16] After refinement the three reference groups are easily distinguished statistically. There is not a single misassignment out of all 292 specimens in the three groups. Because each specimen is treated as an unknown (i.e., is removed from the group prior to calculating its own Mahalanobis distance from the group centroid), the probability cutoff values demonstrate that the assignment of unknowns to the production centers of Ticul, Mama, and Tepakan is unambiguous. The chemical distinctiveness of pottery from the three production centers is clear from histograms of Mahalanobis distances from each group centroid (Figure 5.4).

TABLE 5.3.
Pairwise Comparison of Trace Element Centroids from Pottery Collected from the Ticul Kiln in 1964 with Pottery Collected from Ticul Household Kilns in 1988

Household	A. Tzum (1964)	
	F-value	Probability
A. Tzum (1988)	.834	.694
A. Uc (1988)	.785	.749
F. Keh (1988)	.815	.717
M. Tzum (1988)	.874	.648
Miguel Segura (1988)	.864	.660
Raul Martin (1988)	1.007	.49

The pottery from Akil is quite unlike the Ticul, Tepakan, or Mama reference groups. Unfortunately, the sample of pottery from Akil is too small to calculate Mahalanobis distances from the Akil centroid using the elemental concentrations. One way to circumvent this problem is to calculate Mahalanobis distances based only on a few of the largest principal components of the whole

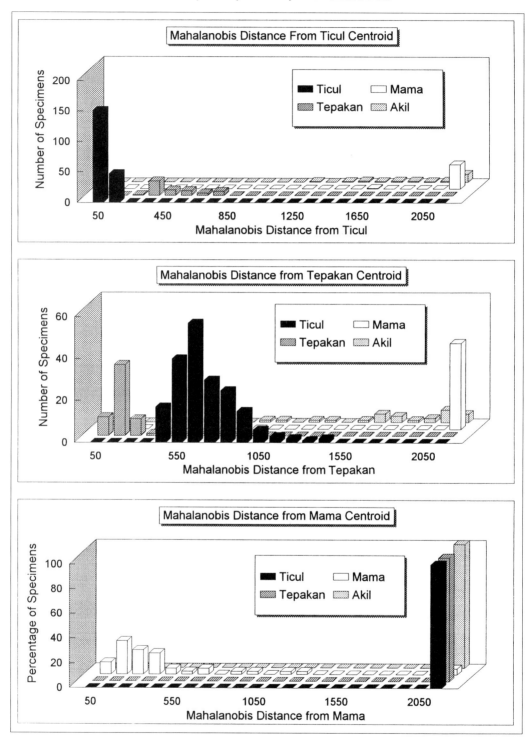

Figure 5.4. Histograms of Mahalanobis distances from the centroids of the three largest reference groups pertaining to modern Yucatán ceramic production centers.

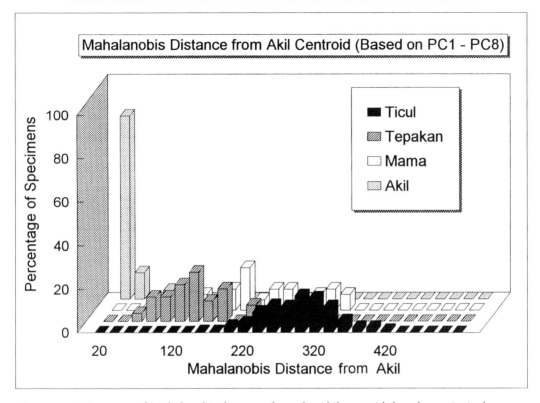

Figure 5.5. Histogram of Mahalanobis distances from the Akil centroid, based on principal components 1–8 of the Yucatán ethnographic data set (see Table 5.2).

data set. The Mahalanobis distances from the Akil centroid were thus calculated based on the first eight components of the data set, which subsume over 90 percent of the total variance. All Akil specimens are assigned unambiguously, and no members of other groups are erroneously assigned to the Akil group. A histogram of the components-based Mahalanobis distances from the Akil centroid shows that members of other groups are distant from the Akil group (Figure 5.5).

To some extent the known subgroup structure in the data can be recovered by principal-components analysis. A plot of the data on principal components 1 and 2 reveals that Mama and Akil can be differentiated from one another (Figure 5.6). The Ticul samples from 1964, 1988, and 1994, and those from Tepakan in 1994, however, cannot be separated based on these components (Figure 5.6). When principal compo-

nents 1 and 4 were plotted, however, the Tepakan samples were clearly separated from the Ticul 1964 and 1988 samples (Figure 5.7). The 1994 sample from Ticul overlaps with the 1964 samples from Ticul, the 1988 sample from Ticul, and the 1994 sample from Tepakan. When the total sample is plotted together with 90-percent confidence ellipses for the Tepakan group and the 1964 and 1988 groups from Ticul, it is clear that the 1994 Ticul sample includes many divergent specimens that are best linked with Tepakan, at least on principal components 1 and 4 (Figure 5.8). About half of the sherds from each of the four potters in 1994 occur in the Ticul reference group, and the remainder occur in the Tepakan group.

The chemical similarity of some of the 1994 Ticul sample with the 1994 Tepakan specimens can be explained by one major factor: the shift of the source of clay used in Ticul between 1988 and 1994. Beginning in

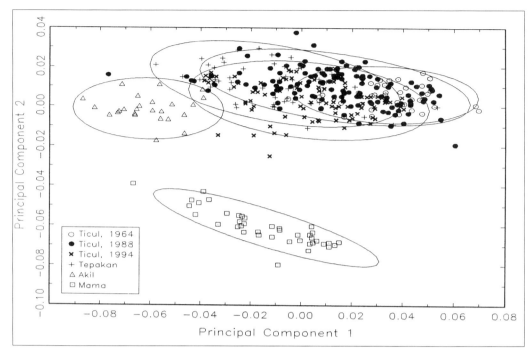

Figure 5.6. Principal components plot of the entire Yucatán ethnographic data set. Ellipses represent 90-percent level for membership in the reference groups.

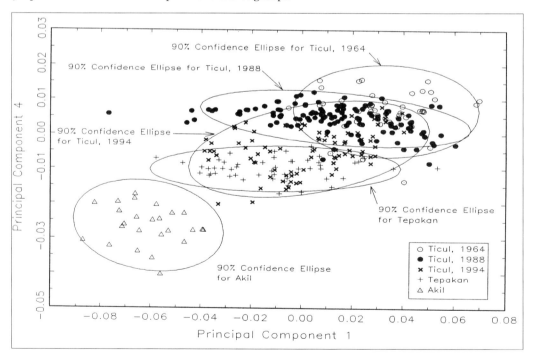

Figure 5.7. The Ticul, Tepakan, and Akil reference groups plotted on components 1 and 4 of the Yucatán ethnographic data set. Ellipses represent 90-percent level for membership in each group.

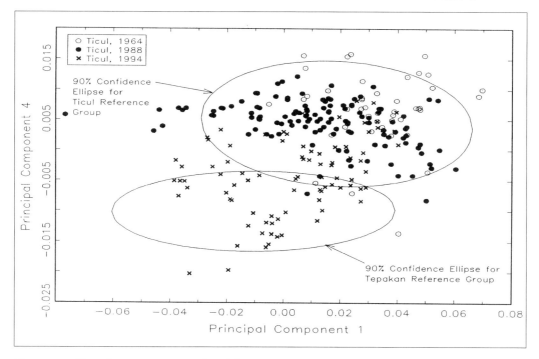

Figure 5.8. Plot of components 1 and 4 of the Yucatán ethnographic data set showing the Ticul reference group (combining the 1964 and 1988 samples) and Tepakan reference group (1994) 90-percent confidence ellipses. Data points for the 1964, 1988, and 1994 Ticul samples are differentiated by symbols.

Ticul between 1988 and 1994. Beginning in the late 1980s, the clay mined at the Ticul source (Hacienda Yo' K'at) had become increasingly scarce. Although there was clay elsewhere on the hacienda, the owner did not let the miners expand clay exploitation beyond an area of approximately 10,000 m². The amount of clay available in the terrain allotted for mining continued to decline, and specialists began abandoning their clay procurement at the hacienda. By early 1992 clay exploitation at Hacienda Yo' K'at had ended. In the meantime one workshop owner who had been banned from Yo' K'at in the late 1980s had purchased his own clay source some 80 km away in the State of Campeche. In 1991 another workshop owner had acquired exclusive rights to extract clay from an abandoned *sah kab* quarry in the same area.[17] During this same period a Tepakan entrepreneur had begun to transport Tepakan clay (from Dzitbalché) to Ticul by truck, selling the same clay to potters in both

communities. By 1994 all clay used in Ticul came from 80 km away in the State of Campeche.

The shift in the chemical pattern of 1994 Ticul pottery from that collected in 1964 and 1988 thus coincides with a shift from the Ticul clay source (at Hacienda Yo' K'at) to the clay source in the State of Campeche. Not surprisingly, a number of analyses in the 1994 Ticul sample fall within the range of variation of the Tepakan group on axes shown previously to separate Ticul and Tepakan (Figure 5.8). Because some of the 1994 samples are grouped with the 1988 Ticul sample, some wasters were made with the clay from Yo' K'at before it was abandoned. Separating the 1994 Ticul sample into Tepakan-related (Ticul-1) and Ticul-related (Ticul-2) specimens yields a clean partition of the sample on components 1 and 4 (Figure 5.9).

The resemblance of 1994 Ticul sherds to Tepakan sherds on one projection of the data

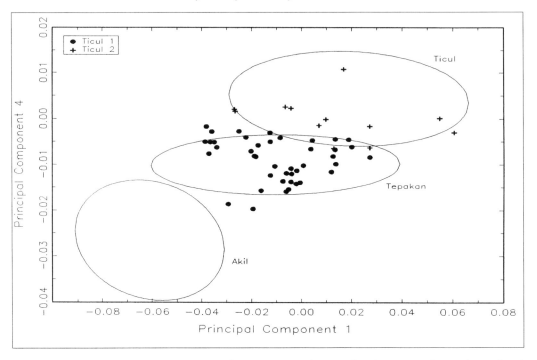

Figure 5.9. Plot of components 1 and 4 of the Yucatán ethnographic data set with Tepakan-related (Ticul-1) and Ticul-related (Ticul-2) specimens in the 1994 Ticul sample differentiated by using symbols. Ellipses represent 90-percent probability cutoff levels for membership in three reference groups.

(Figures 5.8 and 5.9) does not necessarily demonstrate that they are compositionally indistinguishable. In fact, because paste preparation intervenes between the raw clay and the analyzed sherd, it might be expected that the 1994 Ticul sherds should differ from the Tepakan sherds. The addition of temper to a clay is always a potentially confounding variable; the ratio of temper to clay is the potter's behavioral adaptation to reduce the plasticity of the clay so that he or she can (1) make pots without their sagging, (2) maintain the vessels' drying and firing properties, and, thus, (3) avoid damaging them. The ratio of temper to clay in Ticul pottery, for example, changed in 1988 because a new clay had been discovered at Yo' K'at that contained a substantial amount of nonplastics, and potters had to use less temper than previously.[18] This change, however, was not statistically evident in the differences between the 1988 sherds and the 1964 sherds.

Among the apparent Tepakan-derived specimens in the 1994 Ticul sample (desig-

nated Ticul-1), there are several whose p-values exceed 1 percent for membership in the Tepakan reference group (Table 5.4). There are, however, a larger number of the Ticul, Tepakan-derived specimens that would not be assigned either to the Ticul or Tepakan reference groups based on Hotelling's T^2 statistics calculated from Mahalanobis distances (Table 5.5). Histograms of Mahalanobis distances from the Tepakan and Ticul centroids (Figures 5.10 and 5.11) confirm the patterns suggested by the statistical groupings (Tables 5.4 and 5.5): Ticul-1 has a closer affiliation with Tepakan, but Mahalanobis distances from the Tepakan centroid tend to be greater than the members of the Tepakan reference group. A plot of chromium and thorium concentrations in the Ticul-1 specimens (Figure 5.12) reveals part of the chemical basis for excluding most of these specimens from the Tepakan reference group on multivariate grounds.

Although none of the 1994 Ticul-related specimens (Ticul-2) would be grouped with

TABLE 5.4.
Mahalanobis Distance–Based Probabilities
for Specimens in the Tepakan-Related Group
(Ticul-1) Compared to the Ticul and
Tepakan Reference Groups

ID#	Probabilities of Group Membership			
	Logged Elemental Data		PC1–PC8	
	Ticul	Tepakan	Ticul	Tepakan
DEA003	.000	.034	.000	10.758
DEA004	.000	.005	.000	.726
DEA005	.000	1.322	.002	38.533
DEA012	.000	.003	.000	2.488
DEA014	.000	5.490	.261	37.612
DEA015	.000	.013	.000	4.942
DEA016	.000	.007	.000	.983
DEA020	.000	.000	.000	17.466
DEA021	.000	.000	.000	.000
DEA023	.000	.000	.000	.109
DEA024	.000	.107	.009	5.999
DEA027	.000	.087	.104	13.616
DEA031	.000	.021	.104	33.822
DEA032	.000	.003	.468	6.856
DEA035	.000	.002	.120	4.951
DEA036	.000	3.493	10.497	20.389
DEA037	.000	.001	.142	35.918
DEA038	.000	8.171	.040	59.508
DEA039	.000	.577	.155	60.979
DEA040	.000	91.935	.010	61.391
DEA041	.000	.361	.101	96.457
DEA042	.000	.733	.262	9.249
DEA043	.000	2.317	.012	6.426
DEA044	.000	.001	.738	21.964
DEA045	.000	14.744	.001	58.026
DEA047	.000	.620	.009	93.683
DEA048	.000	.134	.399	12.182
DEA051	.000	5.923	.002	55.160
DEA052	.000	.131	.000	1.227
DEA053	.000	.866	.017	47.756
DEA057	.000	8.747	.010	96.611
DEA058	.000	.001	.067	23.732
DEA059	.000	4.010	.021	70.075
DEA062	.000	7.533	.002	22.459
DEA063	.000	22.751	.002	65.672
DEA103	.000	.505	.000	.865
DEA105	.000	.224	.000	3.586
DEA107	.000	.284	.000	6.702
DEA108	.000	.136	.000	.456
DEA109	.000	.089	.006	.665
DEA110	.000	.067	.000	5.135
DEA111	.000	.677	.000	12.742

TABLE 5.5.
Mahalanobis Distance–Based Probabilities
for Specimens in the Ticul-Related Group
(Ticul-2) Compared to the Ticul and
Tepakan Reference Groups

ID#	Probabilities of Group Membership			
	Logged Elemental Data		PC1–PC8	
	Ticul	Tepakan	Ticul	Tepakan
DEA006	.001	.001	2.256	4.803
DEA007	.000	.000	9.714	.010
DEA008	.000	.232	15.159	.914
DEA009	.000	.016	28.603	.157
DEA033	.004	.003	10.062	1.456
DEA050	.010	.002	14.707	.093
DEA054	.006	.000	17.794	.019
DEA113	.001	.001	.001	.013
YMAT31	.000	.000	.542	.003
YMAT40	.002	.000	.011	.000
YMAT54	.000	.000	.000	.000
YMFK30	.000	.000	43.076	.404

Ticul based on logged elemental concentrations, Mahalanobis distances calculated from principal components 1–8 confirm their relationship to Ticul (Table 5.5). The histograms of Mahalanobis distances illustrate this point further: Ticul-2 has a closer affiliation with Ticul, but most Ticul-2 specimens are obvious outliers in comparison with the Ticul reference-group members (Figures 5.10 and 5.11). The marginality of Ticul-2 compared to the Ticul reference group may result from divergent resource procurement and paste preparation practices employed during the time when the Yo' K'at mine was closing down. During this time temper sources expanded to a new location and paste recipes changed to adapt paste preparation to a new clay from Yo' K'at that had an increased amount of naturally occurring nonplastics.

In summary, although misassignment of a number of Ticul-1 specimens to Tepakan appears to misrepresent production patterns, it accurately reflects clay procurement because Ticul potters have recently begun to use clay from a source near Tepakan. This shift in

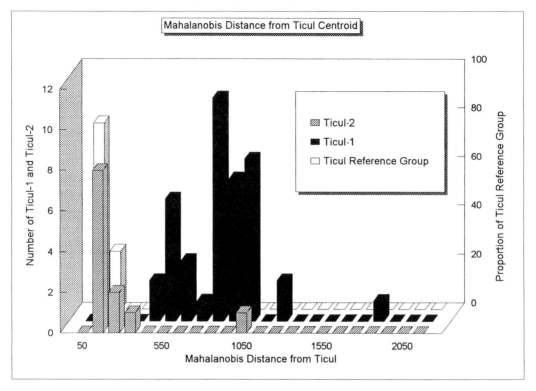

Figure 5.10. Histograms of Mahalanobis distances from the centroids of the Ticul reference groups for Tepakan-related (Ticul-1) and Ticul-related (Ticul-2) specimens in the 1994 Ticul sample. Frequencies of Mahalanobis distances for the reference groups are shown for comparison.

pottery compositions that match the Tepakan compositions: only 12 of the 41 specimens in the Tepakan-derived Ticul-1 group exceed a 1-percent probability cutoff for membership in the Tepakan reference group (Table 5.4).

Even though the differences in clay sources in northern Yucatán appear to be clearly manifested in the compositional data from the fired pottery, differences in added temper between the communities are still important. The effect of temper can be inferred from a principal components biplot based on the pottery from the communities (Figure 5.13); this shows that calcium and strontium pull data points in the opposite direction from virtually all other elements along component 1. Calcium is a significant component in calcite (Calcium carbonate) and dolomite (calcium-magnesium carbonate), and these minerals are the primary constituents of the tempering materials used in all of the com-

munities sampled here. Furthermore, strontium can substitute for calcium within the crystal structure of calcite. In her analysis of the ceramic raw materials in Yucatán collected by Raymond Thompson (1958) in 1951, Anna O. Shepard found that the tempering materials in all eight pottery-making communities studied by Thompson (including Ticul, Mama, and Tepakan) were calcareous (Shepard and Pollock 1971:8). In Ticul temper consists of calcite, dolomite, attapulgite, and sometimes montmorillonite (Arnold 1971:32–33). Furthermore, spectrochemical analyses of clays and pastes from Yucatán have also indicated that calcium is a significant component in Ticul paste[19] (Shepard and Pollock 1971:27) and in tempering materials from Tepakan[20] (Shepard and Pollock 1971:9) and Mama[21] (Shepard and Pollock 1971:9). Akil was not studied by Thompson, nor were samples collected there by Thompson or Shepard. Arnold and Bo-

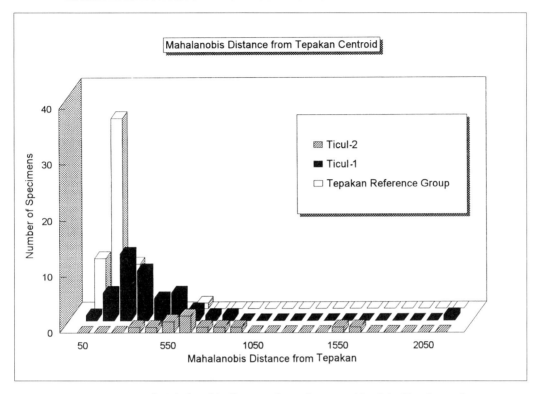

Figure 5.11. Histograms of Mahalanobis distances from the centroids of the Tepakan reference group for Tepakan-related (Ticul-1) and Ticul-related (Ticul-2) specimens in the 1994 Ticul sample. Frequencies of Mahalanobis distances for the reference groups are shown for comparison.

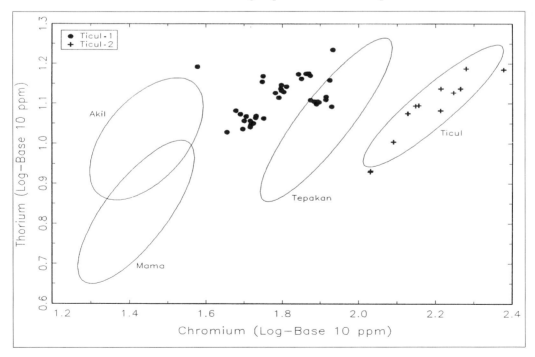

Figure 5.12. Plot of chromium and thorium concentrations in Tepakan-related (Ticul-1) and Ticul-related (Ticul-2) outliers from Ticul. Ellipses represent 90-percent probability cutoff levels for membership in three reference groups on these two dimensions.

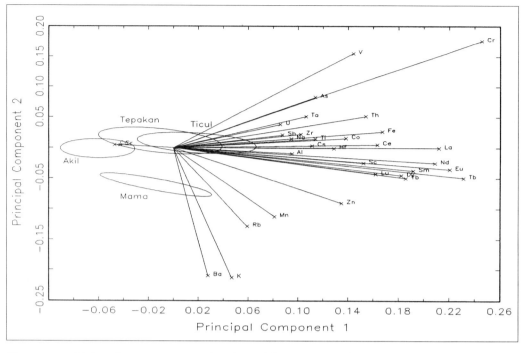

Figure 5.13. Biplot of components 1 and 4, derived from a principal components plot of the Yucatán ethnographic data set. Ellipses represent 90-percent level for membership in the reference groups. Vectors have been drawn from the origin to the coordinates for each element.

by Thompson or Shepard. Arnold and Bohor, however, visited Akil, Mama, Ticul, and Tepakan in 1968. Bohor analyzed raw materials from these communities using X-ray diffraction (Bohor, personal communication) and found that all of the tempering materials from these communities were calcareous.

There are certainly other sources of calcium and strontium in the pottery, but their contribution to the paste is probably minor relative to the potter's addition of temper. First, the water used in mixing the paste is well water and probably contains calcium because drainage in Yucatán is all subsurface and rainfall picks up calcium ions as it percolates through the limestone deposits that are throughout Yucatán. Second, Yucatán clays contain some naturally occurring calcite. The Ticul clay from Yo' K'at, for example, contains calcium in the form of calcite (Schultz et al. 1971:140; Shepard and Pollock 1971:27). Because calcite and dolomite are the principal nonclay minerals in all of the tempering materials from these communities, however,

temper rather than water is probably largely responsible for the presence of calcium and strontium in the samples.

Because strontium has similar chemical properties to calcium, tempering would be expected to enrich the strontium, as well as the calcium, in the clay and dilute the concentrations of other elements. This enrichment-dilution phenomenon can be removed by calculating best-relative-fit concentrations (see Harbottle 1976) for all data points relative to their group means, with calcium and strontium excluded from the calculation. When the resulting best-relative-fit data are plotted on components 1 and 2, and variation within groups due to this enrichment-dilution phenomenon is removed, the remaining between-group variation affords an exceptionally clear separation of the pottery from each of the four communities (Figure 5.14).[22] In this case the resulting patterns are a "clay" pattern resulting largely from the clay component and, secondarily, from the clay minerals in the tempering component

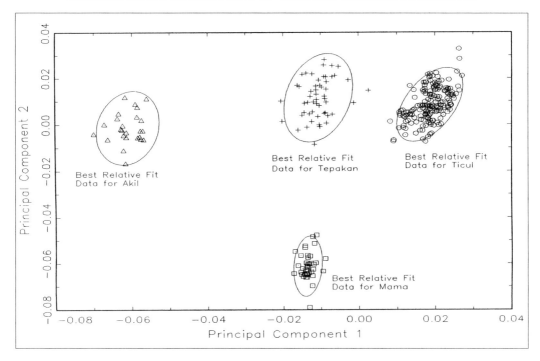

Figure 5.14. Best-relative-fit data for the four largest modern Yucatán reference groups plotted on components 1 and 2 of the Yucatán ethnographic data set. Ellipses represent 90-percent level for membership in each group.

veal a unique elemental pattern for each community. What is remarkable is that the use of the same clay in Ticul and Tepakan is no longer evident.

CONCLUSION

These analyses of contemporary Yucatán pottery collected over a 30-year period have several important implications for the study of archaeological pottery. First, even in a relatively homogeneous geological environment such as the northern Yucatán peninsula, neutron activation analysis of pottery from different communities can differentiate centers of production. The communities of Ticul, Tepakan, Akil, and Mama, for example, each make pottery that is chemically distinct. These communities are separated by distances ranging between 20 and 100 km and utilize distinct raw material sources. Even though Ticul and Tepakan used the same clay source in 1994, the composition of the pottery from these communities can still be separated using statistical

techniques. Clearly, NAA "works" in differentiating production communities that use discrete resource areas, but NAA can also separate production communities when they use at least one resource (clay in this instance) that is the same but use different tempering materials that contain clay minerals from their own local resource area. Because the four ceramic production centers sampled for this study are statistically separable, source-related subgroups might be recognizable in the analyses of archaeological pottery from northern Yucatán. Such analyses might begin by searching for subgroups in the data with principal-components analysis or cluster analysis. If the ethnoarchaeological data reported here were archaeological data, then the subgroups that coincide with the true groups could be identified by inspection of the first two principal components of the data (Figure 5.6). There is no question that Mama would be identified as a distinct group, and the nucleus of the Akil group would probably be identified as a distinct would probably be identified as a distinct group as well. Inspection of other combinations of principal components helps differentiate subgroups within the data points of the Tepakan and Akil specimens. On components 1 and 4 (Figure 5.7), for example, Akil is clearly distinct from the other two groups, and Tepakan is identifiable as a group intermediate between Ticul and Akil.

Second, these data should also be useful to archaeologists who seek to tie ancient pottery to production areas in northern Yucatán. The Yo' K'at clay source in Ticul is ancient (Arnold and Bohor 1977), dating to the period A.D. 800–1000 (the Terminal Classic period), and with the analyses of pottery produced in this study it should be possible to discover which kinds[23] of ancient pottery were produced in the Ticul region and in other communities sampled here.

Third, neutron activation analysis was not successful in distinguishing individual households in a single production community. This is probably always the case when all households obtain their clay and temper from the same geographic source location and follow similar paste preparation procedures. Because NAA appears to provide analyses of clay patterns from discrete resource areas, it is unlikely that NAA can identify individual households or the organization of raw material procurement. There are simply too many intervening variables—natural variability, raw material modification such as grinding and screening, changing paste preparation recipes, and a host of other procurement variables—that can obscure the relationship between chemical elements and human behavior (see Arnold 1981).

Fourth, the clay component of the pottery is the principal variable in distinguishing the chemical pattern of one community from another. This does not necessarily mean that NAA identifies clay "sources"; rather it identifies production locations where potters are obtaining the clay component of their pottery from a relatively small resource area around their community. This component may be one or more clays mixed by the potter

and may include (as it does in this study) temper with a clay fraction.

Fifth, this study casts new light on some of the perceived threats to the geographical resolution of chemistry-based provenance studies. Although paste preparation obviously affects bulk chemical composition, this study provides no empirical basis whatsoever for the fear that chemical distinctions among production centers might be obscured solely by paste preparation. The similarity of Ticul pottery made from Tepakan clay to the Tepakan pottery demonstrates that the compositional signal of the clay persists through variable temper preparation, variable temper composition (see Arnold 1971:32–33), and variable paste preparation between the two communities. When the major effects of temper are removed because of the dilution effect of calcium and strontium, the compositional groups are even more distinct.[24] The tempers added by the potters in Ticul, Mama, Tepakan, and probably Akil, however, also include some clay minerals (Arnold 1971: 32–33; Shepard and Pollock 1971:9), and even though the clay signal seems to be most responsible for the chemical distinctiveness of each community's pottery, the clay minerals in the temper appear to enhance the distinctive composition of the pottery from each community.

Finally, chemical patterning of pottery may change over time. As the Ticul case demonstrates, clay procurement locations may be expected to shift over time because of exhaustion of clay deposits and microlevel sociopolitical factors. The Ticul case demonstrates that the compositional effect of such shifts can be profound. If the Ticul pottery were an archaeological assemblage, a compositional study probably would have identified the 1994 specimens made from Tepakan clay as nonlocal, even though the clay, rather than the pots, was imported. Without truck transport and the asphalt highways of the modern Mexican infrastructure, however, ancient potters are unlikely to have traveled 80 km (the distance from Ticul to its 1994 clay source) to obtain clay. Consequently, such dramatic distortions in the elemental patterns are improbable in the archaeological record (see Arnold 1981, 1985: 51–81). Still, less extreme procurement shifts, which entail less dramatic compositional changes, must have occurred frequently. Over time the cumulative effect of such procurement shifts would "smear" the compositional data in the principal components plots from any single production center like it has in Ticul. This smearing effect appears to explain why compositional data from archaeological projects tend to be so much less discrete than the compositional data from ethnoarchaeological projects such as this one and the one in Guatemala (Arnold et al. 1991).

All of these conclusions reveal that the interpretive assumptions linking physical science data and human behavior can be successfully tested by using ethnoarchaeology. By carefully selecting contemporary pottery using behavioral criteria, and then analyzing this pottery using NAA, the archaeologist can identify those interpretations that are appropriate for understanding the past and those that are not. In this case, as has been suggested many times before, the chemical analyses of pottery reveal the corporate behavior of a community of potters who are exploiting raw materials within a discrete resource area of very limited size. When actual geographic areas can be identified by analyzing ceramic raw materials, the NAA of ancient pottery can provide a powerful tool for identifying intercommunity interactions across space and time.

Acknowledgments. This paper is a revised version of a paper presented at the symposium "Material Meanings: Critical Approaches to Interpreting Material Culture" at the Annual Meeting of the Society for American Archaeology, New Orleans, La., April 11, 1996. An earlier paper reporting only the results of the 1964 and 1988 data was presented in the symposium "Ceramic Ecology '94: Current Research in Ceramics" at the American Anthropological Association meetings in Atlanta, Ga., December 3, 1994. The fieldwork for this study was supported by funds to the senior author from the Wheaton College Alumni Association, the Wheaton College Human Needs and Global Resources Program, and the Wheaton College Faculty Development Fund. The financial support and encouragement of Ward Kriegbaum (vice president for Academic Affairs), Marilee Melvin (director of Alumni Relations), the Wheaton College Alumni Association Faculty Grants Committee, and Robert Stickney (director of the Wheaton College Human Needs and Global Resources Program) is greatly appreciated. The presentation of this paper at the Society for American Archaeology meetings was supported by the Wheaton College Faculty Development Fund and the Wheaton College Aldeen Fund. The authors also wish to thank Tom Riley of the Department of Anthropology of the University of Illinois for permission to sample the sherds from Ticul collected by Duane Metzger in 1964. The laboratory research was funded by grants from the National Science Foundation (BNS 8801707, DBS-9102016) to the Missouri University Reactor Facility and was supplemented by grants from the National Endowment for the Humanities (RK-20191–95) and from the Wenner Gren Foundation for Anthropological Research (Grant No. 6163) to the senior author to cover the consumable laboratory supplies. The authors are indebted to Cynthia Hays, James Cogswell, and Emma Poulter for able assistance with sample preparation and various other analytical tasks. Figure 1 was prepared by Rose Graham, and Pat Pupovac and Ellen Davis assisted in preparing the final manuscript. Finally, the time required to prepare this paper was supported by a grant from the National Endowment for the Humanities (RK-20191–95) to the senior author.

Notes

1. In this paper "chemical" or "elemental" data refer to a matrix of quantified major, minor, and trace element constituents.

2. Potters on waterways and with access to

watercraft do not fit this generalization (see Arnold 1985:35–57).

3. The potters were Alfredo Tzum, Raul Martin, Miguel Segura, Francisco Keh, Ademar Uc, and Miguel Tzum.

4. Among other aspects, Arnold studied the ethnotypology of Ticul wasters in 1965, and this information facilitated selection of a sample of wasters that included different types of firing accidents.

5. The kilns of Miguel Segura and Raul Martin were not sampled in 1994.

6. He had used the kiln in his father's house on Calle 17 and then constructed a kiln in a house lot on the corner of Calles 19 and 38.

7. Firing ceramics is a skill that takes considerable knowledge of the firing process, the burning characteristics of wood, and the causes of firing failures. Kiln construction also requires knowledge and a significant outlay of capital. Furthermore, kilns must be maintained by potters or they will fall apart over time because of rainfall and repeated firing. All of these factors influence why some potters do not have kilns and instead sell their unfired pottery to others. One regular client of this firing specialist was a workshop owner from Mérida who purchased raw materials in Ticul and transported them to Mérida for fabrication in his workshop. Then the finished vessels were returned to Ticul for firing. A second firing client was a local workshop owner who rented the kiln to fire his own pottery.

8. One of the potters sampled in 1994 (Miguel Tzum) said he purchased his clay from the owner of one of these workshops.

9. Although there were many wasters in front of her kiln, there were also many wasters covering an area 10 to 15 m to the northwest of it with such density that the ground was paved with them.

10. In 1968 there were at least four women potters in Akil, but all of these had since died.

11. Reference standards consisted of coal fly ash (SRM-1633a) and basalt rock (SRM-688). Quality control samples (i.e., standards treated as unknowns [SRM-278]) consisted of obsidian.

12. This procedure has been described by Glascock (1992).

13. This long irradiation is analogous to the single irradiation utilized at most other laboratories.

14. Wasters in direct association with a workshop or kiln are an obvious exception.

15. "Temper mines" is a free translation of the Maya phrase *Yo' Sah Kab,* which is located 3.3–3.6 km toward Chapab from the Plaza of Guadalupe in Ticul.

16. The significance of these compositionally anomalous Ticul specimens is discussed further below.

17. *Sah kab* is a marly, relatively friable material used for mortars, plasters, and surfacing materials and is extracted from subterranean mines. This material usually occurs below a layer of cap rock in Yucatán, and in some places a layer of clay lies below it (see Arnold 1971 for an elaboration).

18. "Temper" in Ticul includes both nonplastics (calcite and dolomite) and plastics (attapulgite and sometimes montmorillonite; Arnold 1971).

19. The calcareous nature of Ticul tempering material is also indicated by the fact that calcium oxide in the Ticul paste rose from 1.25 percent in the raw clay to 30.8 percent of the prepared paste (Shepard and Pollock 1971:27).

20. Tepakan pottery is also tempered with a local *sah kab,* which contains calcite (Shepard and Pollock 1971:9). In addition, Quiñones and Allende (1974:100) found that the *sah kab* samples they studied from Yucatán were low magnesium calcite and thus calcareous.

21. In 1994 potters mixed two parts *xlu'um hi'* with a little *chichi' hi',* two parts red clay *(chak k'at)* with one part white clay *(sak k'at).* According to Shepard's analyses, *xlu'um hi', chichi' hi',* and *sah kab* from Mama contained calcite.

22. The enhanced differentiation of groups achieved by factoring out dilution has led Beier and Mommsen (1994) to build several Mahalanobis distance–based grouping procedures around the calculation of dilution factors.

23. The avoidance of type-variety nomenclature here is deliberate. In the recent past Ticul has produced a red ware, an unslipped ware, and a ware slipped with the same body clay. It is thus possible that ancient production centers produced more than one "type" and "ware" of pottery.

24. This is only true for the Ticul sherds that were collected prior to 1994. It is not necessarily true for the pottery that was made with the Tepakan clay.

6

Formal and Technological Variability and the Social Relations of Production

Crisoles from San José de Moro, Peru

CATHY LYNNE COSTIN

What we find [in burials] is determined by the actors in ancient rituals, who put objects into graves because it seemed like a good idea at the time. —Morris 1992:108

Objects recovered from human burials comprise some of the most consciously constructed assemblages studied by archaeologists. Although subject to myriad human and natural postdepositional disturbances, their creation is likely not as unintentional as many of the loss- and discard-induced contexts with which we often work (Brown 1995; Morris 1992; O'Shea 1984, 1996). Burial assemblages are more likely to be "complete" representations of specific, bounded, intentional actions in the past and are therefore likely to signify a coherent set of thoughts or actions that come into play as a part of death rituals. Whether they directly mark the social status of individuals (Donnan and Castillo 1994; Pollock 1983), reflect social organization (Binford 1971; Goldstein 1976; Saxe 1970), or consciously deny or invert social distinctions (Hodder 1980; Pearson 1982), burials are part of a deliberate statement of ideology, some of which is an ideology of the social order. The challenge we face in mortuary studies is to develop theories and methodologies that can assist us in recovering some sense of what the "good idea" to which Morris refers might have been to the ancient peoples we seek to comprehend. In this chapter I propose a novel approach for inferring the social relations embodied in funerary events, namely, identifying the organization of production of objects deposited in graves as an indicator of social relations. Different production regimes—characterized by different technologies and different modes of organization—entail different types of social relations of production, which are associated with different elements of the social order. Production, as social labor, can reflect and even symbolize certain kinds of social and political relations. I argue that the social entities responsible for sponsoring/coordinating death ritual often made conscious choices among different kinds of production/distribution modes used to acquire the objects placed in graves. In choosing one production regime over another the individuals, kin groups, or institutions sponsoring interment may choose to express certain types of relationships (and not others) in the context of burial rituals. Thus, by identifying the organization of production of objects found in graves, we can infer the types of social networks and social relations that have been chosen for emphasis in these socially transitional contexts.

Death requires a restructuring of the social order because the loss of an individual rends the social network and alters the social identities of remaining living constituents within that social world: spouses become widow(er)s, subordinates become primary, children may be emancipated, political allies must shift their allegiance, supporters become leaders, and so forth. The larger the social network of the deceased individual, the more far-reaching, and potentially more disruptive, social restructuring may be. Ritual is a powerful mechanism in human societies for facilitating social reordering (Kertzer 1988). The rituals surrounding death are rites of passage for the living as much as for the dead. They are used to communicate the solutions to the social problems of status and identity reformulation faced by survivors as rights, duties, and resources are reallocated (Barrett 1990; Brown 1995). Funerary events are potentially contexts in which significant amounts of negotiation, disputation, alignment, justification, and sanctioning may occur. The new relationships and confirmed status-claims in the altered community are made manifest through death rituals and through the material culture that plays a part in those rituals. Both performative and material aspects of death rituals will reflect social structure and social dynamics. Many of these relations will be consciously or unconsciously coded in tomb construction, grave goods, and their production regimes.

Burials are the most archaeologically visible and recognizable parts of death rituals, and for several decades archaeologists have used mortuary analysis to reconstruct ancient social structure (see, among others, Beck 1995; Brown 1971; Chapman et al. 1981; Dillehay 1995; Goldstein 1976; O'Shea 1984, 1996; Saxe 1970; Tainter 1978). Whether "processual" or "postprocessual," "behavioral" or "structural," the archaeology of mortuary contexts has consistently focused on qualitative and quantitative similarities and differences among burials to identify aspects of social structure such as social categories and ranking and status systems. Studies of grave goods in particular have looked at the occurrence of certain objects and the makeup of assemblages to distinguish among social groups and reconstruct social organization.

In mortuary analyses little has been said of variability among the artifacts and their attributes within a single burial or how patterns in such internal variability may help us reconstruct and explain prehistoric social structure and social dynamics. Here I refer specifically to variability in form, materials, technique of manufacture, and style within a single burial assemblage; although perhaps innovative when applied to mortuary studies, such analyses are firmly entrenched in general archaeological method. Indeed, studies of morphological, material, technological, and stylistic intra-assemblage variability are critical to studies of nonmortuary contexts, where they are used to study functional variability (e.g., Braun 1980), the organization of production (e.g., Benco 1988; Blackman et al. 1993; Costin 1986, 1991; Costin and Hagstrum 1995), social and political competition (e.g., Feinman 1985), and social organization and differentiation (e.g., Hill 1979; Plog 1980; Pollock 1983). (See also the chapters by Stark, D. Arnold et al., and Chilton in this volume.) As in nonmortuary contexts, variability among funerary objects at this scale may or may not have been intended by or discernible to the participants in the funeral rituals. Nevertheless, variability at this scale of analysis has significance and utility for the archaeologist trying to reconstruct ancient social organization.

Here I adopt methodological and theoretical approaches from studies of production and exchange and apply them to mortuary assemblages to help reconstruct social networks and social structure. The identities of those who produced the objects placed in graves and the mechanisms through which these goods were acquired for inclusion in the burial assemblage will reflect aspects of social and economic structure as surely as production and distribution elucidate social structure among the living. Just as the dead did not bury themselves, they likely did not manufacture for themselves the goods included in their own burials. Thus, the production of mortuary goods, as production for consumption by others, is social labor. It is labor through which social and political relations can be expressed (Costin 1998b). Whether the goods recovered in mortuary contexts were produced specifically for the burial, accumulated for a long period of time before the death of the individual(s) interred, or collected/contributed at the time of the burial ritual, the organization and social relations of production and distribution will reflect social structure more generally. Furthermore, because burial objects in some societies are so strongly associated with the negotiation and maintenance of the social fabric, the social relations of their production will be those that most strongly anchor social relations—the social relations that support the social whole, not just the individual or small-scale, domestic subunits. I argue that in procuring goods for inclusion in graves, the social entities sponsoring the interment rituals consciously choose among different production regimes in part because of the particular social relations of production they represent. That is, I believe the symbolic value of the social relations (e.g., reciprocity, command, and so on) embodied in the production regime is at least as relevant to the ritual sponsors as are the functional/rational characteristics of production (e.g., efficiency).

It is now well established that production regimes are differentiated by a combination of organizational and technological characteristics (Costin 1991; Peacock 1982; van der Leeuw 1977). First is the number of producing units, which is often used as a proxy measure for the amount of specialization in the production system (Costin 1986). Second are the various relations of production between producers and consumers (Ames 1995; Brumfiel and Earle 1987; Sinopoli 1988). Third, production regimes can be distinguished technologically by their use of mechanized "mass" production technologies at one extreme compared with individual handcrafting at the other (John E. Clark, personal communication 1994; Zubrow 1992). Finally, distinct production regimes entail differing amounts of skill and labor investment, which reflect the nature of the labor pool and, indirectly, the relationship between producer and consumer (Costin and Hagstrum 1995). Methods for measuring the degree of specialization, characterizing producer-consumer relations, identifying manufacturing techniques, and assessing skill and labor investment are well developed for nonmortuary contexts. I adopt these methods directly in this work.

I commence the analysis with the fundamental assumption that certain aspects of intra-assemblage variability reflect (1) the number of production units that made a particular class of objects in the assemblage and (2) the ways in which production was organized (Arnold 1991; Costin 1991; Costin and Hagstrum 1995). In general, the relative amount of standardization or diversity in a well-defined assemblage is proportional to the number of producers that created the assemblage, that is, the degree of specialization (see Rice 1981, 1991; Stark 1995; Wright 1983). Other production characteristics, such as labor investment and skill, also reflect the organization of production (Clark n.d.). I believe that by identifying the social relations of production and distribution associated with materials intentionally included in burial assemblages, we can estimate the size of economic networks and infer the nature of economic relationships/interactions among those memorializing the dead. From these conclusions it is possible to make further inferences about the character of social structure and political organization in ways analogous to those used for studying production and exchange within the domestic and political economies of the (purely) living (e.g., Brumfiel and Earle 1987; J. Clark 1991; Clark and Parry 1990; Feinman 1980; Gero 1983; Wailes 1996).

NORTH COAST BURIALS

I illustrate this approach with data from the North Coast of Peru. The Prehispanic societies of the North Coast of Peru are a particularly opportune focus of such study for a number of reasons. First, archaeological and ethnohistorical data suggest that the dead remained important nodes in the social structure (see papers in Dillehay 1995). Burial locations, whether under house floors, in central plaza areas, or in artificial mounds, were a part of the social landscape. Second, the often elaborate tombs and significant quantities of grave goods recovered in North Coast burials suggest that interment was a focal part of the death ritual. The burial rites themselves were significant enough to constitute a major iconographic theme in Moche art (Donnan and McClelland 1979). Third, traditional approaches to interburial variation—looking at tomb construction and grave goods—suggest that for the North Coast we can get a fairly straightforward "read" on some aspects of social structure, especially rank and gender (e.g., Luis Jaime Castillo, personal communication 1995; Conrad 1982; Donnan 1995), without the worry of encountering ritual leveling, disguising, and inversion identified in other parts of the world (e.g., Pearson 1982; see O'Shea 1996 and papers in Beck 1995, which argue that this "problem" is not insurmountable).

In the course of my recent work with grave goods from the site of San José de Moro, one particular class of objects—miniature ceramic vessels called *crisoles*—interested me as vehicles for investigating the social significance of intra-assemblage variation in grave goods. *Crisoles* have heretofore been consistently overlooked amidst the spectacular ceramic finewares and metal objects recovered from many North Coast burials. But it is precisely because they lack the intrinsic value of precious metals and iconographic complexity of decorated ceramics that I suggest they may reflect certain aspects of social structure—those rooted in the local community—that are overlooked when conclusions are drawn only from concentrations of wealth and exotic goods.

CRISOLES

The term *crisole* refers to the small, crude, handmade "finger pots" recovered in a limited number of contexts on the North Coast of Peru. They are reported most frequently in burial contexts (Heyerdahl et al. 1995:158, 176), but they have also been recovered in fill (Heyerdahl et al. 1995:99), dump (Hayashida 1995), and cache/offering (Donnan and Cock 1985:74–81:Figures 38–40) contexts. They date from at least Middle Moche through Inka times (A.D. 400–1532), although the majority of reports in the literature pertain to the Moche period (A.D.

100–700) and immediately succeeding the Transitional phase (A.D. 700–900).

In prehistoric contexts *crisoles* are often recovered in large quantities. For example, approximately 400 were recovered from a ritual context at Pacatnamu (Donnan and Cock 1985). Some fill contexts at Tucumé yielded thousands of these small vessels (Heyerdahl et al. 1995:99). At San José de Moro they generally numbered in the hundreds or thousands in tomb contexts (see discussion below).

The specific function of *crisoles* is rarely addressed explicitly in the literature; they are at best referred to as some form of "offering." In the only published work that I am familiar with that mentions the actual use of *crisoles,* Alfredo Narváez (Heyerdahl et al. 1995:176–177) suggested that they were used as cups in *chicha* (maize beer) drinking. According to his local informants, until the first half of the twentieth century, empty *crisole*-like vessels were heated until red hot and dipped into a large container of *chicha*. The hot *crisole* warmed the *chicha*, which was then drunk. This warmed *chicha* was said to have medicinal properties. The archaeological recovery of often huge numbers of *crisoles* in or near public spaces—often discarded together—suggests that they were used in large public gatherings, perhaps feasts or other community events.

In this chapter I present data from a preliminary study of *crisoles* from the site of San José de Moro in the Jequetepeque Valley and suggest how they might be studied as reflections of ancient social structure.

SAN JOSÉ DE MORO

The Complejo de Moro consists of a large (365 ha) archaeological site with at least two culturally and functionally distinct sections that together represent more than 1100 years of continuous occupation (roughly A.D. 440 through the Colonial period). The two sectors are the 350-ha Chimu period Algarrobal administrative complex and the 15-ha cemetery and habitation complex at San José de Moro. The *crisoles* discussed in this chapter were recovered from the cemetery at San José de Moro.

San José de Moro was clearly an elite cemetery. Looted for decades, it is almost undoubtedly the original provenience of some of the finest pieces of Moche ceramic art illegally removed from Peru. Legitimate excavations in the 1950s (Disselhoff 1958a, 1958b), 1970s (Chodoff 1979), and 1990s (L. J. Castillo, personal communication 1995; Castillo and Donnan 1994; Donnan and Castillo 1992, 1994) have yielded materials from the Middle and Late Moche, Lambayeque, Cajamarca, and Chimu cultures. The most recent excavations were begun in 1991 under the direction of Christopher Donnan and Luis Jaime Castillo and continue today under the direction of Luis Jaime Castillo, Andrew Nelson, and Carol Mackey. I joined the project in 1995 as a consultant on the ceramic analysis. The current excavations at the site must be characterized as salvage work. Most of the mounds are so badly looted that there is little chance of fully reconstructing their form or function although ongoing stratigraphic excavations will help determine their sequence of construction and use. The small open area that has remained undisturbed by looters was spared destruction primarily because the woman living nearby could not tolerate the looters' dust blowing into her house and chased away all potential diggers. Today the site is under additional threat because of the expansion of the small village of San José de Moro; not only is the modern village expanding onto the site, but soil with cultural materials is regularly mined from the site for use in making adobes.

In the most recent field campaigns excavation units were placed judiciously by the project principal investigators in areas believed to be undisturbed by looters and modern construction.

Since 1991 several dozen burials have been located and carefully excavated. Of these, ten contained *crisoles*. There is a bimodal distribution in the number of *crisoles* recovered from the burials (Table 6.1). Four

Table 6.1.
Numbers of Whole *Crisoles* Recovered in
San José de Moro Graves, 1991–1995

Burial number	Number *Crisoles*
111	4
319	10
115E	42
104C	62
314	774
102	1057
26	1180*
30	1680*
41	1700*
103	1982

*approximate

burials had fewer than 75 *crisoles;* the other six had more than 750, with a mean of 1395 for the six graves with abundant numbers of *crisoles.*

Crisoles were commonly superimposed on most other grave goods and/or in side niches in the chamber tombs (see Castillo and Donnan 1994:Figure 3.21). This placement indicates that at San José de Moro *crisoles* were placed in the tombs toward the end of the interment process. In the most densely filled tombs *crisoles* fill the spaces between clusters of larger, more elaborate grave goods. The orientation and clustering of *crisoles* suggest some or all may have originally been placed inside shallow, perishable (gourd) plates or bowls and then set into the tombs in groups. In one burial (319) ten *crisoles* were placed in a large, rounded sherd roughly the size and shape of a shallow gourd bowl.

TOMB 314

In this section I present data on *crisoles* from a single tomb (314) at San José de Muro in order to demonstrate my methodology and speculate about the function/meaning of *crisoles* in Prehispanic North Coast life and death. Based on ceramic cross-dating, the tomb dates to the Terminal Moche era or the

Transitional phase, as it is called by Luis Jaime Castillo. Tomb 314 is a deep, boot-shaped tomb characteristic of Moche and Transitional lower-middle elite (see Donnan 1995:Figure 2). The tomb contained the remains of two adult females and a child 3 to 5 years of age. The adult females were almost certainly buried at the same time and were "stacked" one on top of the other. They were either wrapped individually in separate cane tubes or placed together in a single cane "coffin" with a cane partition between them. In addition to the *crisoles* discussed below, the females were interred with approximately 15 whole ceramic vessels and 2 clay house models *(maquettas)*.

PRELIMINARY ANALYSIS OF *CRISOLES* FROM TOMB 314

The excavators recovered approximately 774 whole *crisoles* and perhaps a dozen broken ones from Tomb 314. Among the intact *crisoles* 731 were undecorated, and 43 bore some form of modeled or incised decoration, almost exclusively anthropomorphic. None was slipped or painted.

PLAIN *CRISOLES*

I selected an approximately 25-percent random sample of the 731 whole, plain *crisoles* ($n = 174$) from Tomb 314 for detailed analysis. This analysis included measurement of four formal metric variables (maximum height, maximum diameter, orifice width, and wall thickness), recording of incidental technological information (including surface marks, evidence of forming and finishing techniques, firing characteristics), and macroscopic paste characterization. All *crisoles* in the sample were drawn. An additional ten vessels were selected nonprobabilistically for analysis because they appeared to be unique in terms of size or form. The results of the analysis are summarized below:

Technology. The plain *crisoles* are technologically quite similar to one another. Virtually all the plain *crisoles* were manufactured from the same kind of clay and exhibited evidence of the same basic forming techniques. The clay is medium gray, rough textured with

very small inclusions (probably all natural inclusions in the clay rather than added temper). Vessels were essentially "pinch-pots," made with one or two fingers in the vessel and the thumb placed on the exterior and used to form the neck constriction. Evidence of hasty construction includes rough exteriors, asymmetrical (misshapen) form, fissures, unsmoothed joins, and "unfinished" (pinched, irregular, unsmoothed) rims. Surface "finishing" ranges from none (rough surface) to minimal smoothing. Finger marks are still clearly visible on nearly 20 percent (32/174) of the vessels in the random sample, including a few otherwise noted as "well-made" (defined as symmetrical, with a well-defined shoulder break and an even, squared-off rim).

Most *crisoles* were poorly fired—either at extremely low temperature, very quickly, or both—if they were fired at all. My field notes suggest facetiously that they were "warmed, not fired." Most have a crumbly texture, and several of them broke easily with the minimal handling necessary to measure them. Most have a wide gray core, which indicates they were just beginning to oxidize on the surface when they were removed from their "firing" environment. Many are fire clouded on the bottom, which suggests to me that they were set into a low fire.

Morphology. Virtually all the *crisoles* in the probabilistic sample are "jar"-shaped: they have a height greater than their maximum diameter, with a restricted orifice (Figure 6.1). Nevertheless, within this general-shape category there is a high degree of morphological variability. Neck forms range from being characteristically slightly inverted, to straight, to everted. Some examples have a clear break at the shoulder, whereas others slope from orifice to body without a clear break. As with neck angle, there seems to be a continuous distribution of shoulder forms. Lip form also varies widely, including squared, pointed, rounded, and beveled. Bases are most often rounded or slightly rounded. Neck, shoulder, lip, and base forms do not co-vary in any meaningful way. Overall, despite the variability, there do

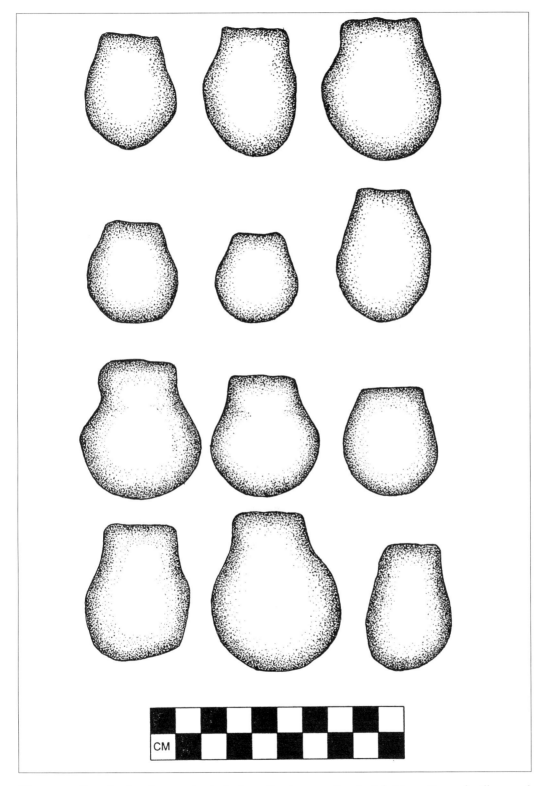

Figure 6.1. Sample of undecorated *crisoles* from Tomb 314 at San José de Moro. Examples illustrated here were selected randomly from among those included in the full analysis.

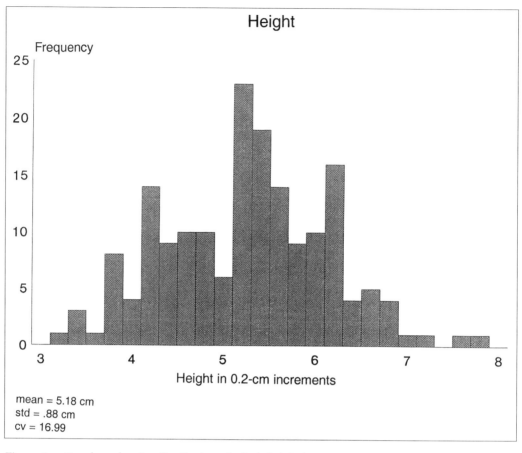

Figure 6.2. Bar chart showing distribution of crisole height in centimeters.

Table 6.2.
Summary of Metric Attributes of *Crisoles* from
San José de Moro Tomb 314 in Centimeters

	Mini-mum	Maxi-mum	Mean	Standard Deviation	CV
Height	3.20	7.80	5.18	.88	16.99
Diameter	3.10	6.35	4.40	.58	13.22
Orifice	1.25	2.40	1.70	.21	12.45

not appear to be discrete jar forms within the group, although in a few cases two or more *crisoles* appear to be remarkably similar, based on both objective and subjective criteria.

Although all the *crisoles* are extremely small, there is a substantial amount of variation in metric dimensions and proportions given their diminutive size (Table 6.2).

Among the randomly selected group, height ranged from 3.20 cm to 7.80 cm with a mean of 5.18 cm, a standard deviation of .88 cm, and a coefficient of variation (CV) of 16.99 percent. Maximum body diameter ranged from 3.10 cm to 6.35 cm with a mean of 4.40 cm, a standard deviation of .58 cm and a CV of 13.22 percent. Among the nonprobabilistically selected group ($n = 10$) were vessels as small as 2.45 cm in diameter and 2.85 cm in height and as large as 7.7 cm in diameter and 8.35 cm in height. All individual metric attributes have multimodal distributions (Figures 6.2–6.4), but—with the exception of the clearly aberrant forms—there are no clusters based on metric attributes, indicating the assemblage cannot be objectively divided into size or shape (form) categories. The height-to-diameter ratio is unimodal (Figure 6.5), and a plot of height by diameter reveals no

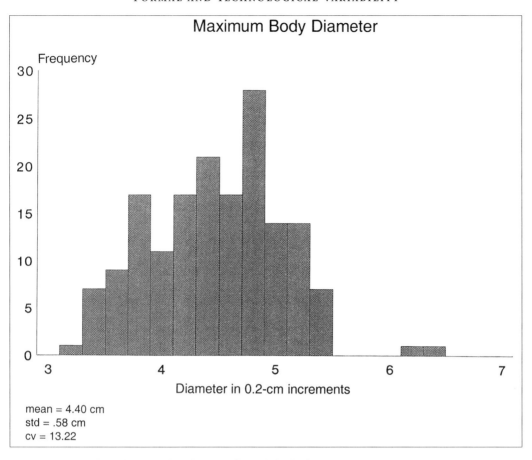

Maximum Body Diameter

Frequency

mean = 4.40 cm
std = .58 cm
cv = 13.22

Figure 6.3. Bar chart showing distribution of crisole body diameter in centimeters.

clear clusters (Figure 6.6). Morphological variation does not co-vary with size differences.

Many of the plain *crisoles* are asymmetrical in one or more of their metric attributes; just under 10 percent were coded as "extremely asymmetrical/warped." I had assumed that this was a reflection of their hasty manufacture or the lack of skill of their producers. However, Alfredo Narváez suggests that some *crisoles* from Tucumé were not only unfired but actually placed in tombs while still wet, which led to their deformation (Heyerdahl et al. 1995:176), presumably from slumping, contact with other goods, or pressure from the fill.

Three pieces were included in the nonprobabilistic sample because they had significantly different forms from the usual jars. These were a spherical vessel without a neck, a "flask"-shaped vessel, and what appears to be half of a crudely formed miniature double-chambered vessel.

Interpretation. In general, the plain *crisoles* are characterized by extremely low labor investment, low amounts of skill required to form them, and a lack of standardization. All of these traits are characteristic of production systems in which the relatively unskilled or untrained can participate (Costin and Hagstrum 1995). I interpret the technological homogeneity of the assemblage as a reflection of the vessels' extreme local manufacture and crude simplicity rather than as an indication that they were manufactured by a relatively small number of individuals. The poor quality and high degree of metric variation among the plain *crisoles* suggest hasty, almost ad hoc, production by a large number of untrained individuals (see

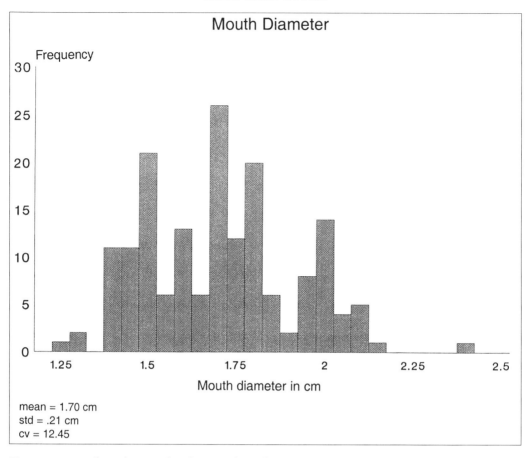

Figure 6.4. Bar chart showing distribution of *crisole* mouth diameter in centimeters.

Hayashida 1995:140 for a similar conclusion that Inka period *crisoles* were manufactured very rapidly and/or by inexperienced potters). Indeed, my working hypothesis is that the *crisoles* were made in a short period of time by a relatively large number of inexperienced individuals immediately before or during the death rituals.

FACE *CRISOLES*

Most (41/43) of the decorated *crisoles* bear anthropomorphic facial features—eyes, noses, mouths, and/or ears—so I refer to the decorated group as "face *crisoles*." As a class, face *crisoles* are similar to the plain *crisoles* in that they are basically jar-shaped, but on the whole they are somewhat larger than the plain *crisoles*.

There are several dimensions of variability among the face *crisoles*. First, there seem to be differences in the entities/personages represented. As discussed below, some grouping was possible on the basis of the presence or absence of certain facial features. Some of these vessels appear to be possible portraits of some sort or another because they emphasize individual facial characteristics (for example the figure that lacks one eye, illustrated in Figure 6.7g).

Second, the face *crisoles* were clearly made by many different individuals. This is evidenced by a constellation of highly variable attributes, including the use of different tools and techniques, different "styles" of representation, and a high degree of formal variability.

Technology. As with the plain *crisoles*, the face *crisoles* were manufactured with a set of

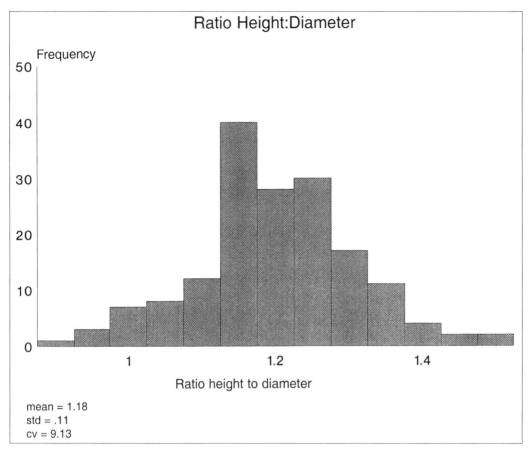

Figure 6.5. Bar chart showing crisole height-to-diameter ratios.Figure 6.5. Bar chart showing *crisole* height-to-diameter ratios.

relatively simple, easy-to-grasp techniques. The vessel bodies of the face *crisoles* were generally formed using the same finger-pinching method described for the plain *crisoles*. There is, however, variability in the techniques and tools used to fashion the facial features. Eyes were made by cane stamping (Figures 6.7b, 6.7f) or with a sharp tool moved in a circular fashion (Figures 6.7a, 6.7g). On some, anatomical details (ears, noses, and "chins") represented in relief are solid pieces of clay added to the vessel wall in the appliqué technique; whereas in other examples ears and noses are hollow, formed by simultaneously pushing out on the wall of the already formed vessel from the interior while using two fingers on the exterior to push in against the finger on the interior. Mouths were most often formed with a sharp

tool, but the exact form and gesture vary. Some mouths are thick, others thin. Some were made with one gesture, others with two. Some were made with the point of a tool using a dragging motion, others by pressing the long side of the tool into the wet clay.

Morphology and "Style." Although most decorated *crisoles* are miniature anthropomorphic "face-neck" jars, there is quite a bit of variability in form and representation. I used these formal and iconographic variables, along with technological criteria, to divide the face *crisoles* into several groups.

Group 1 is the "basic" (most common) form (Figure 7a). The face is on the neck of the vessel; the individual has modeled ears and a nose made with an appliqué technique. The figure lacks a chin. Eyes are oval to circular; many appear to have been made by

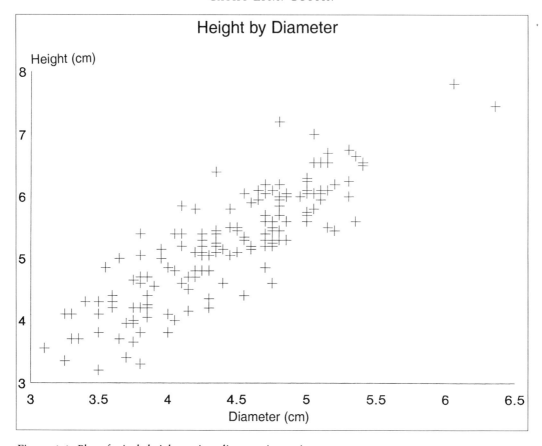

Figure 6.6. Plot of crisole height against diameter in centimeters.

dragging a sharp tool in a near-circular motion (the start and stop points are clearly visible), but a few were stamped with a round, hollow tool (possibly a cane or bird bone). The mouth is a thin, straight line, also made with a dragging motion using a sharp, pointed tool.

Group 2 vessels are stylistically similar to those in Group 1 but were made with a different technique. The ears and nose were formed by pushing out from the interior of the vessel. Eye sockets were indented as a result of the pinching/pushing motion used to shape the nose. Eyes are more circular and likely were stamped with a cane or other type of hollow tube.

Group 3 vessels are more heterogeneous in their technological attributes than some other groups (Figure 6.7b). I grouped them together largely because they have a clearly demarcated protrusion below the mouth. I

identify this protrusion as a chin. Given the general paucity of facial hair among Andean males and the lack of representations of facial hair in representational art across time and space in Prehispanic Peru, this protrusion is likely not a beard. Noses and ears were consistently formed using the appliqué technique. Eyes were likely made by impressing some form of hollow tool (bird bone or cane), but variation in size and shape clearly indicates they were not all made with the same tool. My impression is that most, if not all, of the vessels in this group were made by different individuals, because different tools were used to make the eyes and mouths.

Group 4 vessels are also somewhat heterogeneous (Figure 6.7c). They are much like *Group 3*, with appliquéed noses, ears, and "chin" protrusions. What sets them apart from *Group 3* is the greatly exaggerated nose, which includes impressed nostrils that

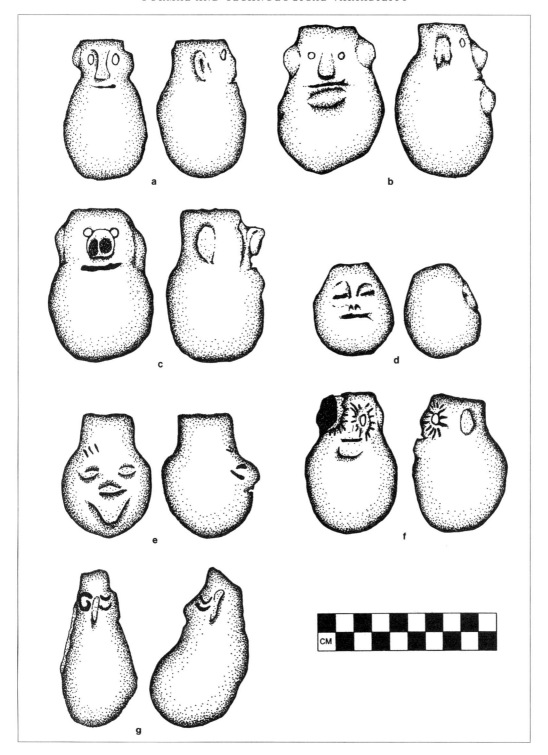

Figure 6.7. Sample of face *crisoles*: *(a)* Group 1; *(b)* Group 3 (note prominent chin); *(c)* Group 4 (note prominent nose and nostrils); *(d)* Group 5 (note tear shape and different manner of representation); *(e)* Group 7 (note face on jar body); *(f)* Group 8 (note lines radiating from eyes); *(g)* ungrouped (note different shape and possible missing [blind] eye).

are usually round (although one example has triangular nostrils made with the end of a pointed tool). This figure may represent an anthropomorphized bat, a common figure in Andean North Coast iconography. As with *Group 3*, my subjective assessment is that stylistic and technological variability indicate face *crisoles* in this group were made by several different individuals.

Group 5 consists of three relatively small, tear drop–shaped vessels (Figure 6.7d). There is little relief in the modeling of the nose and eye sockets (which were formed at the same time with a single pinching gesture); eyes and mouths are represented by thin lines made with a sharp stick. There are no ears. In contrast to the other groups, the overall technological, formal, and stylistic similarity of these three vessels and their formal and stylistic distinctiveness from the other face *crisoles* suggest that they were all made by the same person.

Group 6 consists of two undecorated vessels with a unique, complex in-curved neck that gives them an hourglass form. They are not the same size, and both are misshapen (asymmetrical). Given their irregularity, it is difficult to assess the likelihood that they were made by the same person.

Group 7 vessels are placed together because they all have the face represented on the body of the vessel rather than on the vessel neck (Figure 6.7e). Other than this trait, they are formally and technologically quite different from one another, and I deem it highly unlikely that they were made by the same person.

Group 8 consists of two vessels linked "iconographically" but almost certainly made by different people (Figure 6.7f). The distinguishing characteristic of these is that the individuals are represented with "rays" radiating from their eyes. Otherwise, they differ markedly in terms of face location and tools used to form the face.

Eleven of the 45 face *crisoles* were not placed in these eight preliminary groups. Some differ slightly in terms of technology or representation, whereas others differ significantly from all the groups.

Interpretation. There are several possible explanations for the diversity observed in the face *crisoles*. Most fundamentally, the high degree of technological variability suggests that a large number of "artisans" is represented in this subassemblage. Like the plain *crisoles*, the face *crisoles* were apparently made rapidly within a short period of time. If a single individual had been responsible for their manufacture, I would expect her or him to facilitate rapid production by using the same set of tools and gestures to make all the objects. This is clearly not the case. Some variability may be explained because these are possibly crude attempts at (self-)portraiture or because different deities, mythical characters, or other beings were represented. My impression is that the face *crisoles* are so variable stylistically and technologically that they might come from different "workshops" or even pottery-making technological traditions. Yet the homogeneity of the materials suggests they were all made in the same location or at least made of clay obtained from the same source. As with the plain *crisoles,* the characteristics of the face *crisole* subassemblage indicate that a relatively large number of inexperienced producers participated in the events surrounding the manufacture of these vessels, although material homogeneity and fragility of the pieces suggests they likely worked in close proximity to one another.

SUMMARY AND DISCUSSION

The *crisoles* are an outstanding data set with which to study issues of labor organization and social structure. Variability/standardization should be particularly meaningful for this class of objects because we are not confronted with many of the complications inherent in most studies of assemblage variability, such as the length of time over which the assemblage accumulated, uncertainties about functional differences, and incompleteness of the assemblage (see Costin and Hagstrum 1995:622–623). First, it is extremely likely that the *crisoles* recovered from any one burial were all made within a short period of time rather than acquired over the life of an individual (as might be expected for some of the finewares). Thus, variability reflects the number of producers working within a narrow window of time. Second, it is likely that the *crisoles* were made soon before they were used and were made near to where they were used because storage and/or transport of these vessels would have been troublesome in light of their fragility. Because they were recovered in the graves, I argue they were likely made specifically near and for the burial ritual. Third, the burial context means they are a "complete" assemblage. Because they are the "direct and purposeful culmination" (O'Shea 1984:39) of some part of the burial ritual—likely *chicha* drinking or a broader pattern of feasting followed by their careful and intentional placement in the grave—I work under the assumption that they form a set of objects that was complete and meaningful to the participants in the events surrounding the interment.

Crisoles from burial contexts at San José de Moro are characterized by material and technological homogeneity and formal variability. In many contexts material homogeneity is a strong argument for production within a single workshop or by a limited number of producers (Arnold et al. 1991; Costin 1986; Hegmon et al. 1995). However, the other production attributes of the *crisoles* argue forcefully against the idea that these vessels from Tomb 314 were manufactured by only a few individuals. The material homogeneity does suggest, however, that the *crisoles* were all manufactured in a geographically restricted area or that all producers used the same clay source. The undecorated *crisoles* are so simple that their technological similarity cannot be used to argue for a small number of production units. The level of skill manifested in these vessels is so low that virtually all members of the community could have possessed the basic knowledge necessary to produce one of these pinch pots. Indeed, even a small child would likely be capable of participating in this activity. The high degree of unsystematic, formal variability in shape and size provides

compelling evidence that a large number of untrained or inexperienced individuals participated in the manufacture of the plain *crisoles*. The technological, formal, and stylistic/iconographic variability among the anthropomorphic face *crisoles* suggests strongly that a large number of distinct producers created them as well. The material homogeneity of these vessels suggests some sort of coordination of this large number of producers.

In sum, the technological, material, formal, and stylistic attributes of the *crisoles* suggest that they were individually handmade by a relatively large number of untrained individuals—that is, not by ceramic specialists—at or near the burial site soon before their final placement in the grave. Based on comparisons with other contexts of recovery at other sites, I suggest the *crisoles* may have been used as part of a *chicha*-drinking event that was a part of—perhaps culminating—the funerary rites.

The *crisole* data suggest a number of interesting questions that require further reflection. What does it mean when objects are made by hand when technologies exist to make them more "mechanically"? What does it mean to have members of a large labor pool each produce a few objects, when the technology and organizational structure are available for specialized, "mass" production? What does it mean when these low-output, individually "crafted" objects are extremely crude—made with little investment of time or energy by unskilled, untrained labor—rather than elaborate and skillfully wrought, as are the labor-intensive goods we usually contrast with "mass-produced" wares? And, finally, why are so many of these exceedingly rough vessels found in burials whose other attributes mark them as "elite"?

Although the *crisole* data are in and of themselves intriguing and suggestive of the size of the social network participating in the burial rites and the mode of socioeconomic integration of the community, these data can be further illuminated by comparing them with the production characteristics of two other classes of ceramic materials recovered in North Coast burials: (1) the finewares that are also included in most middle- and upper-class burials and (2) the extremely rough, almost "unfinished," mold-made pieces that are included in some burials. Although I do not yet have the level of detail from San José de Moro burials specifically to compare with the *crisoles,* a general characterization of these objects will place the significance of the *crisoles* in broader context. The key dimensions of contrast are diversity/variability compared with homogeneity/standardization, and finewares compared with coarsewares.

I consider first the possible social significance of the diversity/homogeneity dichotomy and the choices that are made to emphasize one property or the other. The variability among *crisoles* cannot be explained adequately by abstract technological constraints. From Moche times onward North Coast populations had the ceramic mold technology necessary to make large numbers of identical vessels. We have many examples of sets of objects that most certainly came from the same mold, including a few from San José de Moro burials. If the objective of funeral sponsors and participants was to merely "fill" the grave with large numbers of objects, the technology was available to mechanically "mass" produce objects. Thus, I see it as significant that the choice was made to include hundreds or thousands of individual, handmade objects in particular San José de Moro tombs. The diversity—or individuality—must have had strong social significance to those participating in the San José de Moro death rituals.

The preference for representing diversity in certain contexts is repeated in other classes of burial goods as well. For example, in late Moche graves the variety of ceramic forms generally increased with the absolute number of vessels (Donnan 1995). As Donnan and Mackey (1978:209) summarized for late Moche burial inventories: "For the most part, the variety of ceramic objects is directly proportional to the number of ceramic objects. This suggests that a variety of vessel forms in the grave was preferable to multiple examples of a limited number of forms."

What does this intra-assemblage (within tomb) diversity mean? It may be a reflection of social personae; among the Transitional Moche the formal and functional diversity of the objects placed in tombs likely reflected the diversity of social roles a person played in life (Luis Jaime Castillo, personal communication 1995). By extension, then, this may also reflect the number and/or diversity of social ties, if we assume that as the number of social activities in which a person participates increases, the number of persons she or he interacts with, or is responsible for, will also increase. It is my fundamental contention that the relative amount of diversity among the grave offerings—whether it is stylistic or technological diversity—is a measure of the number of nodes in one's social/political network.

To elucidate further the possible social meaning of *crisoles,* I compare them with another kind of relatively crude, but *mold-made* rather than handmade, vessel that also appears occasionally but in large numbers in high-status North Coast burials. In contrast with the *crisoles* discussed here, these vessels—recovered from the same burials—were clearly made from the same mold, in the same workshop, and perhaps by the same person. Mold-made vessels imply relatively few producers. By extension, in this context where large numbers of identical vessels are consumed in the same place, they also suggest the ability of consumers to commission or control the artisans who made the vessels in a relationship that is different from the relationship between a consumer and a multitude of individual "nonprofessional" producers.

The *crisoles* and the mold-made vessels were manufactured under different production regimes. The *crisoles* represent the coordinated efforts of a large number of mobilized nonspecialists. In contrast, the mold-made vessels represent sponsored production from a single, discrete, specialized production unit. What are the social and political implications of (1) different production systems/regimes as they are engaged to produce objects for mortuary rituals and (2) the concomitant restructuring of the social order? The *crisoles* represent something being brought to the funerary ritual by a large number of individuals. They are personal and immediate, reflecting the direct involvement and participation of many people. In contrast, the mass-produced, mold-made objects are something even one individual can provide; as commissioned items from a workshop, they are likely something the social group underwriting the burial brought to the ritual, and they reflect a different form of premeditation and control over the event and all it symbolizes.

The difference here is analogous to the difference between a "potluck" supper and a catered dinner. The former may embody an ethic of cooperation and mutual dependence for the success of the event, even if one person brings a seventy-nine-cent bunch of carrots and another a ten-dollar bottle of wine. Here large numbers of people are allowed to participate and express social unity without a great investment being required. But the potluck may also reflect open competition among participants. In either interpretation of the potluck, we observe direct participation in the conduct of the event by a large number of individuals. In contrast, the sponsored or catered event codifies a fundamentally asymmetrical relationship, where one entity has the power/wealth to create and sponsor an event, and the guests are passive consumers of the festivities, dependent on the largess of their hosts, which goes uncontested in this particular context. The issue is not so much the presence (or absence) of social asymmetry as it is the symbolic representation of active participation and contribution to the system despite differential investment.

The amount of variability among *crisoles* suggests that the social entity responsible for the interment could or should call on many different individuals/entities to create and participate in the death ritual. That widely constituted social network is then commemorated in the interment through the inclusion of the individually handmade *crisoles*. I speculate that the San José de Moro *crisoles* rep-resent offerings to the dead/participants in the burial rituals by different persons. Perhaps the reason the *crisoles* are so highly variable is that each participant had to form his or her own *crisole*, perhaps for a drinking ritual prior to interment or perhaps only for inclusion in the actual burial.

The *crisoles*, then, may recall an interdependence between community and elite. By Moche times on the North Coast we are dealing with a highly stratified society where elites had the ability to differentially command labor and material resources. Yet in certain instances, among them the class of burial rituals that involve *crisoles*, one of the final "statements" that was made before the tomb was closed was a gesture that symbolically included the community in a direct way. In contrast with the handmade *crisoles*, the use of mold-made vessels to "fill" a tomb suggests a different sort of social relations. Here the implication is that the community—or at least a direct tie to it—is no longer needed in the same sorts of ways. In the two production systems labor (and fealty) ties are different, akin to the differences between corvée and retainership as modes of labor recruitment. In the former case an ideology of reciprocity is maintained, even when wealth and power differences are highly imbalanced. In the latter case there is no ideology to bond socially the commander and the commanded. Furthermore, although it is conceivable that participants could procure cheap, mass-manufactured items from workshops to personally place in the tomb, we are still left with a different social or emotional sentiment. Given the Andean tradition of identifying craft items and their makers through makers' marks (Donnan 1971; Hastings and Moseley 1975), the connection between crafting and social identity in the Andes (Costin 1998a), and the individualistic nature of at least the face *crisoles*, I imagine the participants were including a piece of themselves in the grave by personally making the objects.

I have suggested that the degree of formal, material, and technological diversity among ceramic objects in North Coast burials represents the extent of economic ties and social networks among social entities sponsoring burial rituals and the communities/polities in which they live. *Crisoles* and finewares represent different aspects of those networks and, as such, different power bases. Finewares were commissioned and/or acquired as items of social currency (compare Reents-Budet 1994, 1998). Finewares were likely manufactured by and accumulated from many sources over a long period of time. There is much evidence from many Moche burials that many classes of grave offerings, including some of the attendant human remains, were older and/or had been used before placement in the burial. Because I do not yet know the exact mode of acquisition for the finewares, I can propose several plausible scenarios of social and political significance. Most fundamentally, the finewares represent an expenditure of wealth and labor, in addition to reflecting the social roles of the interred individual. If commissioned directly by the deceased or by the social group sponsoring the interment, the finewares represent the ability to command skilled, specialized labor. Because finewares are differentially distributed in burials, they represent differential ability to command wealth and labor, reflecting the hierarchical nature of North Coast society and access to power through control of wealth (see D'Altroy and Earle 1985 on wealth finance systems). In contrast, if finewares were accumulated as gifts during politically charged social events over a long period of time, or were acquired as donations immediately before or during the death rituals, they represent ties among elites of relatively equal social standing. Here power is represented as embedded in ties to other elites (analogous to Blanton et. al's [1996] network strategy).

The *crisoles* also represent the extent of social and economic networks, with a critical difference: the *crisoles* do not, at least on the face, represent a significant direct expenditure of wealth or labor. As such, they reflect command of a very different kind of labor pool, one that is neither highly skilled nor specialized. They also represent a very differ-

ent form of power: power that derives from leaders' ability to mobilize community labor and support on a consensual basis (similar to the corporate strategies outlined by Blanton et al. [1996]). The basis of this power is given material expression in the inclusion of individually handmade *crisole* offerings during the period of crisis when community structure needed to be redefined and rewoven.

In conclusion, the organization of the production of North Coast burial goods reflects elements of social and political organization: alliances among elites as expressed through circulation and accumulation of valuable items of social currency; sponsorship of mass-production as indication of class separation; and mobilization from a large number of producers as indication of socioeconomic integration between classes. During the socially and politically tumultuous end of the Moche era, all of these production regimes were manipulated to furnish objects for graves, albeit in different proportions that may have varied by rank, gender, or geographic location. Expansion of this study to include a much larger sample of burials will provide needed insight into fluctuating modes of social ties and networks in this still enigmatic culture.

Acknowledgments. This study would not have been possible without the extreme generosity of Luis Jaime Castillo, who opened his site, data, laboratory, and house to me, and I would like to express my gratitude that this collaboration was possible. Andrew and Chris Nelson were responsible for much of the actual excavation, particularly that of San José de Moro burial 314, and I thank them also for their generosity in letting me work with the *crisoles*. I benefited greatly from discussions with both Luis Jaime and Carol Mackey as I began my speculation on the ugly and overlooked *crisoles*. Chris Donnan and Frances Hayashida provided data and useful insights about these objects. Elizabeth Chilton, John E. Clark, and John Papadoupolis read earlier versions of this chapter and provided crucial and often thought-provoking comments on the work.

7

On Typologies, Selection, and Ethnoarchaeology in Ceramic Production Studies

Philip J. Arnold iii

It is an axiom of archaeology that material culture reflects human behavior (e.g., Binford 1962). Furthermore, most archaeologists would agree that artifact production, consumption, and disposal are important dimensions of that behavior. There is considerably less consensus, however, concerning the ways that archaeologists evoke and interpret human behavior from the material record.

This chapter focuses on artifact manufacture as an important field of material culture studies. Specifically, I discuss ceramic production and consider how archaeologists might better investigate the relationships between pottery manufacture and the material record. This presentation emphasizes ethnoarchaeology as an appropriate tool to facilitate this goal. By ethnoarchaeology I refer not simply to studies of contemporary material culture but also to the specific application of such studies to archaeological situations. Furthermore, my discussion of ethnoarchaeology concentrates less on validating source-side models with the archaeological record and more on using causal relationships as a means to investigate variation in ancient production organization. I contend that the cultural composites generated by this approach are considerably more useful than the same ethnographic examples that are invariably trotted out to inform the archaeological record.

I divide the following discussion into several sections. First, I present a brief critique of two current approaches used to address pottery production studies. The first approach employs a typology of ceramic manufacture that presents pottery making as conforming to specific production stages. The second perspective views manufacturing activities as differentially transmitted behaviors according to a neo-Darwinian model of natural selection. I conclude that both approaches are wanting in that they are fundamentally descriptive endeavors that mask significant variation in production activities.

Following this critique I discuss the use of ethnoarchaeology to study pottery manufacture. I suggest that production organization is best addressed as a dynamic phenomenon in which technology is not a matter of production "stages" or the result of "selection" but rather a conscious behavioral strategy that reflects the producer's past experiences and future short- and long-term goals. Using data from ethnographic and archaeological contexts in southern Veracruz, Mexico, I demonstrate how ethnoarchaeology can be used to create a composite picture of the past. Such composites are crucial in that although they are linked to the present via uniformitarian principles, they nonetheless enable archaeologists to identify variation that may not exist within the ethnographic or ethnohistorical records.

A CRITIQUE OF TWO METHODS

Like other areas of archaeological research, studies of pottery production and consumption have begun to focus increasingly on behavioral dynamics, variation, and explanation. No longer confined to their previous role as chronological markers, ceramics have become more relevant to issues of economic interaction, social organization, subsistence activities, and ideology (Miller 1985; Rice 1987; Sinopoli 1991). Pottery manufacture, as a subset of ceramic studies, has received considerable attention as a means to elucidate the economic, social, and ideological behavior of producers and consumers (e.g., Arnold 1985; Bey and Pool 1992; Rice 1996a).

Two approaches characterize current attempts to understand ceramic production activities. The first procedure classifies production organization into discrete stages or "modes" and situates these types along a continuum of behavior (Peacock 1982; van der Leeuw 1976). Important dimensions used to formulate these categories include the amount of energy input, the size of the production unit, the context of the production unit, and the amount of generated output. Production types also rely heavily on ethnographic, ethnohistorical, and ethnoarchaeological data ("ethno-info") to validate the existence of production stages (Rice 1987).

A second approach to ceramic production is characterized by framing manufacturing activities as responding to pressures that operate within a neo-Darwinian selectionist milieu. These pressures derive from the context of ceramic manufacture (production technology) and pottery use (performance characteristics) and are overlain by the effect of differential consumer demand (e.g., Neff 1992b; O'Brien et al. 1994). A selectionist perspective is thought to (1) avoid the essentialism inherent in typological classifications and (2) move explanation away from the "extreme assumption" (Neff 1993:32) of adaptationism that purportedly characterizes research into pottery production and consumption

(Neff 1992b:170; see also Jones et al. 1995: 18; O'Brien et al. 1994).

Typological and selectionist programs can provide useful insights into production activities, albeit at different scales of analysis and in reference to distinct questions. If the goal of investigation is to categorize production organization and/or compare production between contexts, then reference to a typology is essential (e.g., Dunnell 1971; Santley et al. 1989). On the other hand, if the intent is to catalog the engineering issues that *may* have affected ceramic production or consumption within a particular historical context, then a selectionist view may be preferable (Neff 1992b, 1993; O'Brien and Holland 1992: 50–52; O'Brien et al. 1994).

Despite these potential contributions, both approaches suffer from serious shortcomings. Below I outline the major aspects of the typological and selectionist frameworks and identify several problems with each. I conclude that the two programs are unsatisfactory in helping to access the variation in ancient ceramic production that is not already documented through ethno-info. Furthermore, I argue that both are essentially descriptive exercises and are constrained in their application by a lack of logical independence between the phenomena under investigation and the data used to confirm propositions about those phenomena. Ultimately, neither approach will draw us closer to explaining the variation and development of pottery making in ancient societies.

TYPOLOGICAL APPROACHES TO CERAMIC PRODUCTION

Reference to a sequential model of production is by far the most common way of characterizing pottery making and its organization. Within this model manufacturing behavior is compartmentalized into a series of discrete production stages or modes (Peacock 1982; van der Leeuw 1976). Criteria considered important include the quantity of products, the location and size of the production area, and the diversity of manufactured goods (Costin 1991; Rice 1987:186). Production organization is "understood" or "explained" by situating manufacturing activities along a series of increasingly intensive input and/or output behaviors.

Archaeologists have begun to voice dissatisfaction with this static, typological view of the past (Shennan 1989b; Teltser 1995a; van der Leeuw 1991; see also Chilton, Stark, Wobst, this volume). Questions that require more dynamic information can rarely be addressed adequately using these production categories. Ironically, van der Leeuw, who is sometimes implicated in the "misuse" of these models, makes it very clear that these production types cannot be used to address questions of behavioral dynamics: "Clearly, such juxtapositions cannot in any way be construed as representative of actual changes in the organisation of pottery-making. They remain an *a posteriori* construct of the researchers, and they say little about the real nature of changes which are or were taking place" (1984:720).

Costin (1991) provides one of the most thorough critiques of the typological approach to understanding ceramic production. Her criticisms highlight three problems: (1) a lack of comparability as different schemes emphasize different dimensions of variability; (2) a proliferation of terminology, resulting either in similar terms for different organization or different terms for the same basic phenomenon; and (3) conceptual schemes derived from a limited ethnographic and/or archaeological database.

In response to these concerns Costin (1991:Table 1.1) proposes a "multidimensional typology" that highlights such variables as production context, concentration, scale, and intensity and explores their co-occurrence along several different continua. Through the intersection of parameters and values Costin (1991:8–9) is able to bundle the variation into an eight-part typology for the organization of specialized ceramic production.

This new scheme supplies a considerably more precise tool for characterizing production activities. For example, Costin's (1991) model specifies a wider array of potential production contexts and consumer audiences. More important, her discussion constitutes a more socially sensitive treatment of pottery making that stands in contrast to the overly economic emphasis that characterizes the more common production sequences.

Nonetheless, Costin's (1991) approach has its own drawbacks. For example, rather than simplifying the current situation, her discussion significantly expands the dimensions of possible production variation. In other words, the eight-part typology exacerbates the proliferation of terminology; it does not mitigate the problem.

In a recent critique Clark (1995) argues cogently that Costin's (1991) reconstituted typology suffers from two serious limitations: (1) a failure to differentiate dichotomous and continuous variables and (2) a conflation of distinct levels of abstraction. For example, Clark (1995:283) proposes that "attached" and "independent" specialization do not fall along a single production continuum, as Costin's (1991) typology implies. Rather, an individual producer or production entity may act as both "attached" and "independent" producer at the same time. The fact that a producer may simultaneously conform to both types (i.e., both ends of the continuum) undermines the logic that represents "attached" and "independent" as end points along a single continuous variable.

Clark (1995) also notes that a variable such as "context," which is used to differentiate production types, actually conflates the distinct dimensions of "elite sponsorship," "affiliation of producers," "the sociopolitical component of the demand for their wares," and the utilitarian vs. nonutilitarian nature of the product (Costin 1991:Figure 1.4). "Context," therefore, represents several separate parameters that may reappear as diagnostic variables within different levels of the typological hierarchy (Clark 1995: 283–285). Again, the conflation of these values calls into question the assumptions behind the production typology. It is not surprising, therefore, that the overall classification is found to be troublesome: "That her categories of craft specialization appear descriptive and explanatory is merely an illusion generated from conflating four levels of abstraction into one conceptually-muddy category of craft specialization.... Costin's explanatory level really concerns the organization of production, a level not addressed in her paper, and her descriptive level concerns parameter values of intensity, scale, and so forth, which are used inconsistently" (Clark 1995:285).

More problematic for the present discussion, however, is the continued emphasis on types of production organization in Costin's (1991) model. A major drawback is that all typologies, even those constructed at a finer scale of resolution, necessarily minimize within-group variation, and it is precisely this variation that provides potential insight into the dynamic quality of production organization and activities (Arnold 1991a:3; Rice 1984; Wobst, this volume). Furthermore, we must always keep in mind the distinction between precision and accuracy—increased accuracy of observation does not necessarily follow from more precise tools or methods of data collection (Arnold 1991a:155; Skibo 1992:27).

Other problems undermine the utility of Costin's (1991) continued reliance on production types. Typologies often privilege a particular trait as representative of a constellation of attributes, many of which are then assumed to have been present in the prior condition (Feinman and Neitzel 1984:44). Finally, typological approaches may foster a perspective of change in the archaeological record that emphasizes comparatively abrupt shifts in behavioral organization at the expense of more gradual transitions (Jones et al. 1995:20; Rice 1984).

A typological approach to pottery production, regardless of how fine-grained its resolution may be, is limited by its static, descriptive nature. Issues of change are extremely difficult to address; when change is identified, it usually takes on a somewhat punctuated appearance. Typologies are intended to summarize traits, and single characteristics are often expected to bear the weight of an attribution to a complex system state. Finally, the summary nature of classification minimizes within-group variation, and variation is crucial in modeling the operation of ancient behavioral systems.

SELECTIONIST APPROACHES TO CERAMIC PRODUCTION

Partially in response to these concerns with typologies, some archaeologists have turned to neo-Darwinian selection to account for change in ceramic production and consumption (Neff 1992b, 1993; Neiman 1995; O'Brien and Holland 1992; O'Brien et al. 1994). This approach eschews the "transformational view" of typologies, in which "differences are substituted for change" (Teltser 1995a:54), in favor of the selectionist agenda that views change as a function of quantitative differences within "analytically discrete variants" (Teltser 1995a:53). This latter approach is essentially what evolutionary biologists refer to as "population thinking" (e.g., Mayr 1982).

Viewed from a selectionist perspective, temporal variation (i.e., evolution) in ceramic production organization is a two-part process that results from the creation of variation in manufacture followed independently by the differential transmission of that information. According to the selectionist view, human behavior may contribute to the creation of variation; it does not, however, contribute to the differential transmission of that variation (Jones et al. 1995; Neff 1992b, 1993; Teltser 1995b).

The independence between the creation of variation and the transmission of that variation is a central tenet of neo-Darwinian selection and differentiates it from Lamarckian evolution (Dunnell 1981; Mayr 1982). A Lamarckian view conflates the production and transmission of variation, thereby allowing an organism to "self-select" traits in response to perceptions about the environment. Unlike the passive role that an organism is afforded in neo-Darwinian selection, Lamarckian evolution permits an organism to be an active participant in "fixing" traits within the population over time.

According to the selectionist perspective, the Lamarckian view is flawed in that it requires an organism to correctly forecast future conditions (Dunnell 1981; Jones et al. 1995:19; O'Brien and Holland 1992:42). Neff (1992b:146) succinctly makes this point when he argues that to "direct evolution through innovation, humans would have to solve future problems and exploit future opportunities, and would have to anticipate the impact of particular solutions on conditions and events in the more long-term future." The apparent reasoning behind this statement is that all innovation is considered functional (e.g., Dunnell 1978), that no trait becomes fixed in the population for reasons other than its original function, and that either (1) humans do not behave in anticipation of future (either short- or long-term) conditions or (2) that decisions made in anticipation of future conditions never improve "reproductive success" (i.e., information transmission).

Unfortunately, the selectionist view on this particular issue is simply wrong. Contrary to selectionist claims, Lamarckian evolution does not dictate that organisms "solve future problems" or "exploit future opportunities." Lamarckian evolution contends that organic mutability derives from an organism's habitual behavior within the context of its immediate environment (Lamarck 1984 [1809]). The basic fact is that neither Lamarckian nor Darwinian evolution was designed to project change into the future; instead, both evolutionary perspectives focus on the circumstances that have brought about the appearance of an organism *at a given point in the present or the past* (Mayr 1982:354). Noteworthy is the fact that Mayr (1988:96), an evolutionary biologist cited often in the selectionist archaeological literature, characterizes selection as an *"a posteriori"* construct, invoking the same term that van der Leeuw (1984:720) uses to discuss production typologies. In other words, like ceramic production typologies, selectionism is a descriptive activity that accommodates the evidence.

Neither Darwinian nor Lamarckian evolution looks toward the future; both were constructed to account for events that have already taken place.

Even when confining treatment to ancient ceramic production and consumption, most selectionist applications do not independently establish environmental constraints and selective pressures; rather, *these conditions are inferred based on properties of the material culture* (cf. O'Brien et al. 1994:266–268). Selective pressures are reconstructed according to expectations regarding the "fitness" of artifacts. Ceramic "fitness" is thought to result from "superior performance at meeting the needs of producers and consumers of pottery under given environmental conditions" (Neff 1993:28). To use fitness in this way implies that the "needs of producers and consumers" and the "given environmental conditions" are already known, even though these conditions are precisely what the selectionist agenda purportedly attempts to establish (e.g., Leonard and Reed 1996:604; O'Brien et al. 1994:266; Teltser 1995a:60). Thus, expectations about the context within which pottery performs are proposed to account for the formal properties of pottery, and these same formal properties are presented as substantiating the interpretation of the "selective environment" (e.g., Neff 1993; O'Brien and Holland 1992). The logical pitfalls of such tautological reasoning should be easy to appreciate and were raised in the biological literature some 20 years ago (e.g., Gould and Lewontin 1979). Nonetheless, these serious and legitimate concerns are dismissed as "red herrings" by advocates of the selectionist agenda (O'Brien and Holland 1992:39).

Thus, the persistence of a given ceramic trait is presented to account for its own appearance, thereby committing the fallacy of "retrospective distortion" (Pinch and Bijker 1987:28). The interesting issue for archaeologists is not simply whether a trait serves a specific function but why that particular response was adopted instead of other possible behavioral responses. "There is more than one way to skin a cat" goes the well-known dictum, or as Cohen (1981:202) wryly observes, "In evolution, all bets are on."

In some cases archaeometric analysis is invoked to establish ceramic "fitness" (e.g., Neff 1992b, 1993; O'Brien and Holland 1992; O'Brien et al. 1994). Archaeometric studies play a crucial role in understanding the function and use context of ancient pottery. Nonetheless, many such studies adopt an approach akin to the "Law of the Metric" (Arnold 1994). This rule implies that all statistically significant differences in the performance properties of ceramics, such as tensile strength or thermal conductivity, were obvious to the producers and consumers of the pottery. Skibo (1992:27) makes a strong case against this simplistic notion when he states, "Not all differences, even statistically significant differences, are behaviorally significant. The archaeologist must determine behavioral significance based, usually, on ethnoarchaeological or ethnographic information." In other words, our ability to measure and evaluate properties in the present does not always translate directly into prehistoric recognition (also Braun 1983:107–108).

Advocates of selectionism respond to this critique by proposing that the awareness of metric variation is not important because it concerns only the creation of variation, not the fixing of variation in the population (O'Brien and Holland 1992:52; O'Brien et al. 1994:268). This response ignores the issue of how consumers consistently selected traits of which they were supposedly unaware. Furthermore, I am unconvinced that measuring properties of ceramics is no different from "measuring beak length in a group of finches" (O'Brien and Holland 1992:52). Certainly the physical act of measuring may be similar, but most anthropologists would agree that a finch exercises considerably fewer "choices" in "making" its own beak than a potter exercises in making her or his own pottery! Furthermore, the finch plays a backseat role to the natural environment in determining whether its beak characteristics are selected. In contrast, ethno-info clearly indicates that ceramic producers play an active role in establishing the "success" of their products within the *cultural* environment (Arnold 1985; Arnold 1991a; Arnold and Nieves 1992; Kramer 1985).

A final problem with the selectionist agenda is the almost singular emphasis on fitness (i.e., performance characteristics) in reconstructions of ceramic production and consumption. According to the biological literature, "fitness" is not the sole means of accounting for the persistence of traits. In many instances traits improve reproductive success but do not contribute to the "fitness" of the organism (Mayr 1988:104–105). For ceramic production fitness, as defined by "superior performance" (Neff 1993:28), may be less important to the consumer than the cost involved in acquiring the vessel. Because the producer of the ceramic has considerable latitude in dictating the cost to the consumer (i.e., negotiation), the individual responsible for "variation" (the producer) directly affects the "environment" within which consumer "selection" is carried out. Some pots may be more "successful" because they are less expensive or are easier to acquire, not because they transfer heat more rapidly, are less susceptible to thermal shock failure, or are more resistant to physical impact. In fact, if ceramic "success" and "fitness" is to be archaeologically established through relative sherd frequencies (e.g., Neff 1992b; O'Brien and Holland 1992), it may be worth remembering that the most frequently occurring sherds within an archaeological assemblage may represent vessels that have a shorter use life (DeBoer 1974; Mills 1989), not containers that last relatively longer because of superior performance!

Thus, the selectionist approach to ceramic production poses three key problems. First, it is limited by its insistence that the producer is a relatively passive participant in an environment devoid of cultural interaction. Second, neo-Darwinian selection as applied to archaeology is a fundamentally descriptive activity conducted within the framework of historical particularism. Finally, although advocates of neo-Darwinian selection apparently believe that the restricted emphasis on quantitative analysis makes their approach more "scientific" (Neiman 1995:29–32), in reality this emphasis simply makes selectionist archaeology narrowly quantitative.

In sum, neither the use of production typologies nor an emphasis on neo-Darwinian selection is liable to increase appreciably our understanding of pottery production, its organization, and its change through time. Production typologies necessarily mask considerable variation that is an informative part of the material record. Neo-Darwinian selectionism in archaeology is often tautological and negates the role of the producer of variation (i.e., the potter) as an agent who affects the cultural environment within which selection is carried out (e.g., Dobres and Hoffman 1994; Pfaffenberger 1992; Rice 1996a:185). Finally, both approaches view cultural transitions as if the past were moving toward the present, fostering a progressive, overly functional, and linear characterization of change. This is the "Standard View of Technology" (Pfaffenberger 1992); its implications of "progress" and "functionalism" have been questioned by a number of social scientists (e.g., Bijker et al. 1987; Dobres and Hoffman 1994; see also Dobres, this volume).

PRODUCTION ORGANIZATION AND ETHNOARCHAEOLOGY

Given these difficulties, how might archaeologists address the organization of ceramic production? As noted above, a large part of the answer has to do with the questions that are asked. The questions I find most interesting involve the nature of variation in ancient ceramic use-related activities. I submit that a program of ethnoarchaeology provides one of the more effective means to address this variation (Arnold 1991a, 1998).

Ethnoarchaeology is a two-stage process. It involves the search for causal relationships between behavior and material culture in the present and the use of these relationships to investigate variation in the material record of the past. Ethnoarchaeology is *not* simply mapping a contemporary houselot or track-ing the use life of an extant piece of pottery. If research conducted in contemporary settings does not directly address an archaeological problem, the study remains ethnographic, no matter how thought-provoking it may be to archaeologists (cf. Stark 1994:197).

These causal relationships, or "relational analogies" (Wylie 1985:95), are subject to the same inferential parameters as all source-side reasoning. The strongest analogies, therefore, are those that are able to mitigate cultural caprice; in other words, the best candidates for these uniformitarian assumptions are the supracultural mechanical, physical, and/or chemical properties of artifact production, utilization, and discard. These supracultural linkages are least likely to change through time and, thus, afford the most appropriate means to explore the unknown past in terms of the known present.

Archaeometry can be very important in this regard because it provides a frame of reference that utilizes uniformitarian assumptions to characterize past behavior as reflected in material culture. As noted above, however, I do not believe that the strength of archaeometry is in documenting subtle differences in performance characteristics and then using those differences to validate our preconceptions about the past. Rather, the principles of physics and chemistry that guide archaeometry are best employed as fixed inferential reference points used to identify and measure variation in material culture.

Environmental conditions provide another set of important relational analogies (e.g., Arnold 1985, 1993). Ironically, ecologically informed studies of pottery manufacture have recently come under attack as theoretically "naive" (Stark 1993b) or as representing the "extreme assumption" of adaptation (Neff 1992b:170, 1993:32). These criticisms are misguided at best. Like other supracultural parameters, the uniformitarian assumptions that link the environment and pottery production are central to investigating variation in the archaeological record.

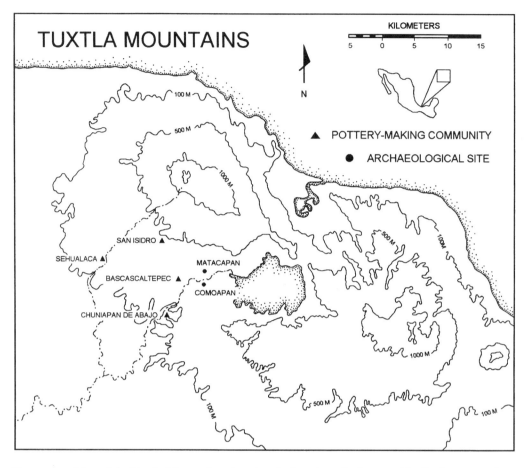

Figure 7.1. Map of the Tuxtla Mountains, showing the location of ethnographically documented pottery-making communities and the archaeological sites where evidence for ancient ceramic production has been recovered.

Monitoring variation in ancient activities is a central theme in ceramic production studies. But as Costin (1991:8) notes, the number of ethnographical and/or historical examples of pottery manufacture is extremely limited. Are we to assume that these few documented cases represent the entire range of ancient production activities? If not, how do we use these limited cases to access the potential range of variation? We do it by establishing the causal relationships in the present, applying those relationships to the archaeological record, and monitoring variation in terms of the knowns. This sequence is essentially the program of middle-range research and theory building outlined by Binford (e.g., 1977b, 1982; ed. 1981).

CERAMIC PRODUCTION ORGANIZATION IN THE TUXTLA MOUNTAINS

Over the course of the last decade, research carried out in the Tuxtla Mountains of southern Veracruz, Mexico, has been devoted to studies of contemporary and ancient ceramic production (Figure 7.1). This research includes two components. First, a program of ethnoarchaeological investigation was undertaken among a group of 50 household potters (Arnold 1988, 1990, 1991a, 1991b). This study was designed to explore variation in contemporary production activities and to generate "relational analogies" that would serve as indices against which the archaeological record could be assessed.

The second research component includes the application of these relationships to the archaeological record at Matacapan, a Classic-period (A.D. 300–900) site also located within the Tuxtla Mountains (Santley et al. 1987). This latter research investigates variation in the scale of production activities and has thus far identified three different, contemporaneous production organizations at the site (Arnold 1989; Arnold and Santley 1993; Arnold et al. 1993; Pool 1997; Pool and Santley 1992; Santley et al. 1989).

The background to these studies has been presented elsewhere (Arnold 1991a; Arnold and Santley 1993; Arnold et al. 1993) and will not be repeated here. Rather, I confine this discussion to one aspect of ongoing research, namely the relationship between variation in production technology and variation in production organization. First, I discuss the use of updraft kilns among contemporary household potters in the Tuxtlas. I argue that conventional expectations of production scale, output, and environmental conditions do not differentiate open firing from kiln firing within the study group. Rather, the need to organize ceramic production in terms of available activity space appears to be the primary force affecting firing decisions.

I then employ the relationship between the use of space and production organization to investigate an ancient Mexican production context. I argue that the spatial arrangement of production facilities strongly implicates manufacturing activities beyond the domestic organization. Coupled with independent production data, these findings contradict the perception that intensive, suprahousehold manufacture was not a part of the ancient Mesoamerican economy (Gary Feinman, personal communication 1996), a position based primarily on the lack of evidence from ethnohistoric and Contact-period documents.

This research also suggests that production technology is not necessarily related to production scale and/or intensity (Arnold 1991a, 1991b). This finding is important because the typological approach to pottery making frequently relies on differences in

production technology to segregate "stages" of manufacture (Peacock 1982; van der Leeuw 1976). Furthermore, the data indicate that production technology does not simply change as a result of selection for "superior performance." Thus, explanations of variation based on assumptions regarding improvements in firing atmospheres or greater fuel efficiency are not supported by the Tuxtlas ethnographic data.

CONTEMPORARY KILN USE IN THE TUXTLA MOUNTAINS

Contemporary potters in the Tuxtlas practice both kiln firing and open firing (Arnold 1991a). Research has demonstrated, however, that this choice is not based on many of the factors commonly discussed in the ceramic production literature (e.g., Arnold 1985; Costin 1991). For example, the variation in firing technology in the Tuxtlas is not a product of environmental differences because all potters are subject to the same basic climatological patterns. Nor are differences in firing strongly associated with distinct types of clay or temper. Production output (i.e., number of vessels manufactured) is not a factor because there is no significant difference in output between one community of potters that fires in the open and one community that fires in kilns. Finally, production context does not determine firing activities because all of the potters studied manufacture ceramics within their residence for a market that includes themselves and consumers from outside their communities.

The single overt difference between the two firing strategies is the kinds of fuel used (Arnold 1991a:59–60). Updraft kiln firing requires hardwoods dense enough to slowly heat the kiln and then sustain sufficient heat to fire the pottery. Open firing, in contrast, is completed in considerably less time and can be accomplished using palm fronds, dried sticks, and other rapid-burning combustibles. This pattern mirrors what Gosselain (1992b) notes for African potters—namely, that the time involved in heating pottery strongly conditions the choice of fuel. Given this association, it is difficult to

Table 7.1.
Fuel Use and Firing Efficiency in the Tuxtlas:
Open Firing vs. Kiln Firing

Firing type	Amount of Fuel Used	No. of Vessels	Percentage of Firing Loss	Total of Vessels/ Carga
Open	⅓ carga	25	31.5	51
Kiln	1 carga	40	21.0	32

establish whether a preference for hardwood "causes" kilns or whether the choice to use kilns elicits a preference for certain types of hardwood.

Kilns provide important benefits to potters, including greater control over the firing atmosphere. Nonetheless, kilns are not without costs; they require additional outlays of time and energy for construction and maintenance. In fact, one potter in the Tuxtlas fired her ceramics in a neighbor's kiln, stating that she did not produce enough pottery to make kiln construction and upkeep worthwhile (Arnold 1991a:54).

Perhaps more important from the perspective of "performance," kiln firing in the Tuxtlas is *less efficient* than open firing. As noted above, a considerable amount of the heat produced in kiln firing goes toward heating the facility itself, not toward heating the pottery (Gosselain 1992b). In fact, Rice (1987:162) notes that small updraft kilns, similar to those used in the Tuxtlas, "have a particularly unfavorable ratio of heat distribution with respect to pots versus structures." As a result, kiln use in the Tuxtlas is associated with a greater demand for firewood, not less (Arnold 1991a:59–60).

Of course, an increased requirement for fuel is not inefficient if there is a concomitant increase in the number of successful vessels produced per firing. It is certainly true that on average more pots are fired per episode in the Tuxtlas kilns than through open firing (Arnold 1991a:52, 55). Nonetheless, when we compare the ratio of successfully fired ceramics to the amount of fuel consumed, kiln use is still not characterized by superior performance (Table 7.1).

On average, kiln firing in the Tuxtlas uses a single *carga* ("load") of wood per episode. A *carga* weighs approximately 35 kilos (also see Sheehy 1988), and an average of 40 vessels constitutes a kiln load. The average firing loss for kilns in the Tuxtlas is 21 percent, yielding an output of approximately 32 successful vessels per *carga*.

Open firing, in contrast, requires about ⅓ of a *carga,* and an average potter fires 25 vessels per batch. This value produces an uncorrected ratio of 75 vessels per load of fuel. When the 31.5-percent firing loss is factored in, open firing generates approximately 51 successfully fired vessels per *carga*. In other words, open firing is almost 60 percent more efficient in terms of fuel than kiln firing. Given these differences, coupled with the fact that the fuel used in kilns is increasingly costly and difficult to obtain (Arnold 1991a: 59–60), kilns in the Tuxtlas hardly constitute greater "fitness" through a technology that provides "superior performance."

What forces are affecting the use of kilns in the Tuxtlas? Conventional treatments of pottery manufacture link changes in production technology to differences in the scale of manufacture, the production climate, the intensity of output, or the targeted consumer market (Arnold 1985; Costin 1991; Peacock 1982; van der Leeuw 1976). In contrast to these expectations, however, the Tuxtlas data indicate that kiln use is a response to restrictions in available activity space within houselots. In other words, kiln adoption is a spatial, not a technological, decision. The separation of "spatial" from "technological" is, of course, artificial because spatial factors can and frequently do influence technological decisions (e.g., Nelson 1991). Unfortunately, the relationship between spatial availability and manufacturing organization is rarely addressed in the ceramic production literature.

Open firing is a "spatially flexible" activity (Arnold 1991a:100); it can be relocated in response to changes in wind conditions, characteristics of the firing area, or even the occurrence of other activities within the residential compound. But in some regions of the

Tuxtlas the terrain minimizes the space available for houselot activities. When pressure on available space increases, specific, fixed locations for firing result. But as open firing becomes more spatially dedicated, the potter is unable to mitigate the effects of microenvironmental change through activity relocation. A different response is required to alleviate these unpredictable conditions. Kilns, by virtue of their greater control over the firing atmosphere, provide a means to lessen the impact of microenvironmental change when activity relocation is not an option.

The choice to use kilns in the Tuxtlas strongly correlates with the amount of space within the houselot that can be devoted to production activities. First, the size of houselots is significantly larger among potters who practice open firing than among those who use kilns (Arnold 1991a:110). Thus, there is greater opportunity to relocate firing activities within these larger houselots. Second, the distance from the actual residence to the firing area is significantly greater for open firing, again reflecting a larger area within which firing activities are conducted. Furthermore, the actual number of discrete activity loci is much higher for open firing, and in comparison to kiln use, open firing is carried out within a greater diversity of locations within the houselot (Arnold 1991a: 111–112). Finally, the organization of houselot maintenance is significantly different between the kiln-using potters and potters who fire in the open. This distinction in refuse management provides an additional, independent index of different spatial pressures within the respective houselots (Arnold 1990; 1991a:120–137).

Firing technology, therefore, responds to factors beyond the quantity of vessels generated or the need to use fuel efficiently. Among the contemporary Tuxtlas potters, kilns are adopted in those situations in which available space for firing activities is restricted. Fixing firing activities on the residential landscape minimizes potential task interference, but it also requires a technological response to reduce the impact of microenvironmental variation on firing conditions. The adoption of kilns, with their protected firing chamber and improved control over the firing atmosphere, represents just such a conscious response on the part of certain Tuxtlas potters.

ANCIENT KILN USE IN THE TUXTLA MOUNTAINS
As mentioned above, ethnographic observations should constitute only the first step in an ethnoarchaeological research program. The second step is to apply these findings to an archaeological context and explore variation in production organization. Research at Matacapan uses the information on spatial organization and pottery making to inform our interpretation of production activities (Figure 7.2). Specifically, we have argued that pottery making within the Comoapan complex, a particular area on the outskirts of Matacapan, was large-scale and nonresidential (Arnold 1991a; Arnold et al. 1993; Santley et al. 1989). This interpretation rests in part on the spatial arrangement of production facilities and evidence for intensive waste management.

Prior to our research at Matacapan and Comoapan the overwhelming majority of Precolumbian pottery production was considered small-scale, nonintensive, and characterized by open firing. In fact, by the early 1980s the available data indicated that kiln use was primarily an Old World phenomenon, introduced into Mesoamerica during the Colonial period (e.g., Arnold 1985:218). Nonetheless, soon after we first encountered the Comoapan production area we realized that it was different from just about anything else that had been reported from Mesoamerica. The production area covered 4 ha^2 and included the remains of at least 36 kilns clustered in approximately eight separate units, each associated with waster dumps. The very presence of kilns was noteworthy; their frequency was an additional surprise.

Artifacts from surface collections indicated a ceramic assemblage that was extremely skewed toward the production of three wares in a restricted range of forms (Arnold et al. 1993; Pool 1990). Furthermore, neither surface nor excavated data revealed substantial

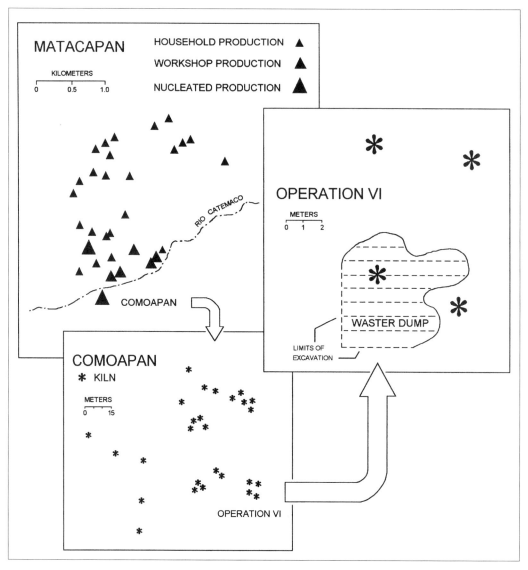

Figure 7.2. Map of ancient ceramic production locations at Matacapan and Comoapan, highlighting the spatial relationship between kilns and a waster dump within the excavated area of Operation VI.

domestic-related refuse, suggesting that production at Comoapan was segregated from residential activities (Arnold et al. 1993; Pool 1997; Santley et al. 1989). Along with the kilns, these characteristics implicated an intensive production area.

Nonetheless, several possible scenarios could account for the patterning. The area might be a palimpsest of individual, independent firing activities carried out over a rela-

tively long period of time (e.g., Costin 1991:29). The production area might also represent a clustering of residentially oriented pottery making. A third possibility is that Comoapan might result from more formally organized production carried out on a comparatively large scale.

Fortunately, the ethnographic data gathered among the Tuxtla potters provide a reference point to investigate potential production variation within the Comoapan complex. As noted above, residential kiln use in the Tuxtlas (and elsewhere) generates a specific structure in the location of firing facilities, maintenance activities, and the formation of midden deposits. Within the houselots of kiln-using potters, waster dumps are commonly situated directly adjacent to the firing facility. The consistent placement of debris in this location is a function of spatial limitations and concomitant segregation of both production and waste-management activities. Locating dumps next to kilns provides the additional option of using larger broken sherds as saggars to separate vessels within the kiln or as an added layer of insulation across the top of the kiln. The one-to-one ratio of kilns to waster dumps was a common residential pattern within the Tuxtlas and elsewhere (Arnold 1991a).

Within the Comoapan complex, however, the pattern consisted of several kilns associated with a single dumping area. In fact, whereas the ethnographic ratio of kilns to dumps was essentially 1:1, the Comoapan ratio was more than 3:1. It was clear that, despite a lack of comparable Mesoamerican archaeological or ethnohistoric analogs for large-scale pottery manufacture, the Comoapan pattern diverged considerably from what was known for residential production.

Research into activity organization, location, and maintenance suggests that the spatial distribution of activities is sensitive to the scale and intensity of those activities. When several facilities within an area are used simultaneously, and waste generation is relatively high (as it is in pottery making), a common response is to increase the maintenance of space by centralizing waste disposal (e.g., Schiffer 1987). This response minimizes the impact of debris on activity performance. The fact that similar patterning was exhibited in the Comoapan complex suggests that pottery manufacture in this area was characterized by intensified production conditions. In this case the presence of kilns is not an indicator of production intensity because ethno-info clearly associates kilns with residential production. Rather, the *spatial structure* of production facilities, refuse areas, and waste management suggests more intensive production efforts (Arnold 1991a; Arnold et al. 1993).

Joined with the *independent data* on the skewed ceramic assemblage, the physical location of the production complex, and the lack of domestic artifacts, the organizational attributes of Comoapan imply a level of intensity rarely identified for ancient Mesoamerica (Arnold et al. 1993; Pool 1997; Santley et al. 1989). This degree of production intensity is associated with increased consumer demand, greater production output, and overall production consolidation at Matacapan during the later portions of the Classic period (Arnold and Santley 1993; Arnold et al. 1993; Kneebone 1990).

The simple fact that there is no "precedent" for this organizational structure in the Mesoamerican ethnographic or ethnohistorical literature is irrelevant. Again, if we confine our ideas about the past to models derived wholesale and exclusively from ethno-info, then we must assume that all ancient variation is represented in extant contexts. I am uncomfortable making that assumption; in fact, I am far more interested in exploring the differences between the past and the present than in simply accommodating archaeological data to models based solely on contemporary behavioral analogs.

CONCLUSION

The ethnoarchaeological approach presented here responds to many of the limitations inherent within both the typological perspective and the neo-Darwinian selectionist agenda discussed above. Research undertaken in the Tuxtlas is not designed to validate a type of production organization; rather, these studies explore the range of ancient variation that ceramic production assumed in Mesoamerica. Thus, concerns that characterizations of Comoapan (e.g., Santley et al. 1989) do not conform to a reconstituted typology (Costin 1991:29) simply miss the point. Moreover, the Tuxtlas research demonstrates that different production organizations often co-occur and that characterizations of pottery making based primarily on continuous variables may be less fruitful than commonly assumed.

Nor does this research accept the selectionist posture that past experience and future goals are irrelevant to the differential transmission of cultural traits. Contemporary potters in the Tuxtlas, and the ancient potters of Comoapan, adopt(ed) production strategies that make sense given their environmental conditions. However, these traits were not "selected for" by some vague, noncultural environment. Rather, potters make intentional, informed decisions based on prior activities, perceptions of short-term and long-term circumstances, and expectations regarding the consumers they serve. Discussions, both elsewhere (e.g., Pfaffenberger 1992; Dobres and Hoffman 1994) and in this volume (e.g., Chilton, Stark, Wobst), consistently demonstrate that patterning in technological decisions results from a complex combination of social, economic, and political circumstances. Collapsing these behavioral dimensions into the catch-all phrase "selective environment" and then objectifying that "environment" via analysis of ceramic performance characteristics represents the worst kind of reductionism.

Contrary to the position advocated by selectionists, the belief that potters may contribute to the "success" of the variation they produce is neither naive nor misguided. In fact, Dunnell (1989:39) notes that "Lamarckian evolution is not inherently unscientific"; rather, he simply believes that biological evolution, as we currently understand it, is better accounted for by the mechanics of Darwinian selection. Dunnell is certainly correct with respect to biological evolution; however, *cultural* change, as we currently understand it, is best accounted for by acknowledging the collective effect of individuals as agents (i.e., producers *and* selectors) of that change. As Stephen Jay Gould (1997:22) recently observed: "Genetic variation is Mendelian, so Darwinism rules biological evolution. But cultural variation is largely Lamarckian, and natural selection cannot determine the recent history of our technological society"(see also Mayr 1988:79,122).

A second drawback to many current "explanations" of technological change results from the manner in which archaeologists reconstruct diachronic patterns. Looking backward from the known, archaeologists view change as moving toward a fixed point, as "becoming" or "adapting." The potters, however, are behaving within their present and are acting in terms of past, present, and possible future conditions. The challenge to archaeologists, therefore, must be to develop methods and theories that allow us to project ourselves into the past with confidence, assess the variation that exists, and look toward the future in terms of that variation (e.g., van der Leeuw 1991). In this paper I have argued that a program of ethnoarchaeology provides an important first step in building such methods.

Ethnoarchaeology is a tool, a tool that generates dependable standards against which archaeological phenomena can be assessed. The purpose of these standards is to anchor the past in terms of reliable constants and facilitate the identification of variation in the material record. I believe that the differences between the past and present are considerably more exciting and potentially informative than cross-cultural similarities. Despite acknowledgments that variation is important in models of ancient pottery making, archaeologists continue to emphasize ethnographically informed typologies of production organization. At the same time, neo-Darwinian selectionism denies the potter's ability to actively participate in "fixing" technological choices that they themselves might make. Neither approach is liable to improve appreciably our understanding of ancient ceramic production organization or to clarify changes in the technology of pottery manufacture through time.

To achieve this understanding, archaeologists must be willing to entertain the possibility of *composite pictures* of the past, pictures that combine the properties of very diverse production organizations. The argument that no "prior example" of a production organization has been documented is only relevant if we insist on confining our interpretations of the past to the behavioral systems of the present. Instead, I contend that archaeologists must be willing to bundle the behavioral continua in new and different ways. *The archaeological record, not the ethnographic record, provides the organizational diversity and variability that archaeologists seek to understand.* But first we must be able to isolate that variation, not homogenize it within a static typology or remand it to a passive attribute whose archaeological occurrence lies at the mercy of an environment stripped of cultural influence. A robust program of ethnoarchaeological research can provide an important avenue for isolating and, ultimately, explaining the behavioral variation represented in the archaeological record.

Acknowledgments. The archaeological and ethnoarchaeological research discussed in this paper has been supported by the National Science Foundation, Sigma Xi, the Mellon Foundation, and the University of New Mexico. I would like to thank Elizabeth Chilton for the invitation to participate in the symposium from which these ideas are drawn and contribute to the edited volume. Dean Arnold, Elizabeth Chilton, Shannon Fie, and two anonymous reviewers provided comments on earlier drafts that improved the version presented here. Shannon Fie also contributed significant time and energy in assisting with the computer generation of Figures 7.1 and 7.2.

8

Style in Archaeology or Archaeologists in Style

H. Martin Wobst

This chapter represents an archaeology of style. Almost 30 years ago I took a seminar at the University of Michigan entitled "Style in Archaeology and Ethnology." Run by archaeologist Robert Whallon and the late ethnographer Richard Beardsley, it exposed archaeological thought about style to the ethnographic present. How well would archaeological theory hold up in that scenario? Seminar papers were to scan archaeology for theory relating to style and to see how well that theory would work with ethnographic, rather than archaeological, data.

I selected Yugoslavia for my ethnographic scan. The Balkans had been on my mind since I was fifteen, when I had hiked with some friends around Albania, from Kotor in Montenegro to Skopje in Macedonia. I almost naturally settled on Yugoslavia as the area for my dissertation research, and I have since traveled there frequently. My scan for ethnography dealing with material culture hit pay dirt in Yugoslavia. In contrast to anglophone ethnography, many Yugoslav ethnographers have focused on material culture and have systematically collected and described it. This is particularly germane for archaeologists because the material categories in the ethnographic literature there include some often seen by archaeologists (such as metal tools or pottery) and others rarely encountered (such as carved wood, rugs, and clothing). Moreover, what is reported tends to be sensitive to the social affil-iations of the maker or user, an axis that archaeologists at that time considered particularly interesting and useful.

My scan for pertinent *archaeological* theory left me relatively empty-handed: what was considered "stylistic" by archaeologists then was simply form that could not be explained "any other way" (see, for example, Conkey and Hastorf's historical discussion [1990:3]). "Any other way" usually meant not having any "functional" explanation (Dunnell 1978:199; Sackett 1973:321; Whallon 1968:224); and "functional explanation," for archaeologists at the time, usually meant "form related to the processing of matter and energy" (Binford 1965; see Flannery's [1972:400] cogent critique) as, for example, in the different shapes of working edges required to interact with meat, soil, or stone.

That most archaeologists then could not see stylistic form as having function left me dissatisfied: Why put time into something that did not have "function"? Why go the extra mile to commit "style" to material culture if that did not serve any function?

Ultimately, I resolved the contradiction between vacuous archaeological theory and rich ethnographic data in the paper "Stylistic Behavior and Information Exchange" (Wobst 1969), which was published eight years after its completion (Wobst 1977). Without repeating its arguments, my paper pointed to some important functions of style. I reasoned that style should be about form conveying information (whereas the usual archaeological "functions" had been about form interacting with matter and energy), a point I illustrated with dress in Yugoslavia's ethnographic present. In my reading of the Yugoslav ethnographic matrix at the time, individuals varied their dress (well beyond what was needed in defense against the elements) to make statements about their social affiliation.

I have remained interested in style ever since. In this chapter I scan archaeological style again, by sketching changes in my views. I point to lingering shortcomings in archaeological stylistics but nevertheless reiterate my optimism about archaeology and the domain of style. In fact, I consider style one of the most promising and dynamic avenues for archaeological research into society.

STYLE AFTER THIRTY YEARS OF STYLISTIC RESEARCH

Scanning the horizon for new developments relating to style in archaeology, I find that many things have not changed dramatically since 1969. Archaeological knowledge about style is still quite limited (see, for example, Carr and Neitzel [1995b:452–454] for a list of important open questions). Even though their number has grown significantly since the seventies, only a few prehistoric case studies contain style as a central variable (see, for example, Braun 1977; Chilton 1996; Conkey 1978; Engelbrecht 1978; Hardin 1983; Hodder 1982b:218–228, 1984; Hodder and Orton 1976; Leroi-Gourhan 1982; Newell et al. 1990; Plog 1980; Shanks and Tilley 1987b:155–171; Voss 1980; Washburn and Crowe 1989; Whallon 1965). Many case studies simply consume theory rather than develop, or probe for, new insights. Theoretical experiments using archaeological data are still quite rare.

Protracted debates about style have taken place over the past 30 years. Processual archaeologists have fought amongst themselves about style—in the lengthy iconographic and isochrestic battles (see, for example, Sackett [1977, 1982, 1985, 1986] vs.

Wiessner [1983, 1984, 1985]); in the skirmishes about variable grouping (Cowgill 1982) vs. object grouping (Doran and Hodson 1975; Hodson 1982); and in the turf wars among evolutionists (Braun 1995; Dunnell 1978; Hill 1985), behavioral archaeologists (Schiffer 1976), and Binford and first-generation Binfordians (Binford 1989; Binford 1983; Binford and Binford 1968)—as to who had more to say about the term. Processualists and postprocessualists have battled over whether stylistic form got to be where it is through action (Hodder 1982b) or behavior (Carr 1986; Carr and Neitzel, eds. 1995; Schiffer 1996). And massive tomes of ethnoarchaeology (Arnold 1985; David et al. 1988; DeBoer 1990; DeBoer and Lathrap 1979; Faris 1972; Graves 1981; Hayden 1987; Hodder 1982b; Kramer 1979, 1982; Longacre 1981, 1991; Longacre and Ayres 1968; Longacre and Skibo 1994; Miller 1985; Moore 1986; Smith 1994; Wiessner 1983, 1984; among many others), historical archaeology (Leone 1984; Leone et al. 1989; McGuire 1988; Paynter 1988; Pearson 1982), and history (Schiffer 1991) now grace our bookshelves, reminding us that the world relative to style is more complex than archaeologically anticipated and that archaeological common sense about style is often wrong.

By now, exhaustive schemes have patented virtually every aspect of the production of material cultural form, including many stylistic variables (Carr and Neitzel, eds. 1995; Schiffer and Skibo 1997). And quite a few researchers have pushed their own scheme as the only guaranteed access to theory about style. There is even talk that style as dealt with in much of the extant literature has become passé, has died, and should be quietly buried (Boast 1997; Schiffer and Skibo 1997).

I consider it premature to talk about the death of style in archaeology: to me, talk about the end of style is as hegemonic as talk about the end of history—it represents an effort to silence readings alternative to the accepted story and thus an effort to suppress learning. To me, style is one of the most interesting and dynamic aspects of the material culture corpus to learn about. As long as stylistic theory and method have barely scratched the surface, we have no good reason to abandon the concept.

STYLE REFLECTING VS. STYLE INTERFERING

Twenty years ago many of my readers mistook style as *reflecting* social affiliation (or other messages). In that reading style is the dead-end output of something that is there before material (and exists in the absence of material culture). Style is something that, once established, automatically rains down into its material traces. Treating style as the *material correlate* of social affiliation would represent a similar misreading. Behind that term also hides the assumption of a one-to-one mapping of something that pre-exists and has essence without its material traces, the material traces being so completely correlated with it that one could use "canned inference" to get from them automatically to that essence, be it social affiliation or other messages.

In many archaeological cases to which my 1977 article was applied, the data were interpreted as "reflecting" the group affiliation of their archaeological subjects, and some of their variables were said to constitute "material correlates" of social group affiliation or other information. This misreading was shared by some prominent critics in the discipline (see, for example, Hodder 1982b:56; Shanks and Tilley 1987b:142).

Such a reading attaches the wrong exclamation marks to my 1977 paper. At the time, I definitely did not think that style (as a message of social affiliation in the Yugoslav examples) would automatically ooze out of some essential qualities of its bearers. I thought that style was added materially by individuals into their social contexts, that some important social attributes were not knowable without material signaling, and that many social attributes and even social units could not even exist without that same material signaling. I understood that the bearers of dress *were materially confronting a need* when they talked materially about so-cial group affiliation so that others could/would take notice (Wobst 1977:322–324, 327; see Shanks and Tilley 1987a:94), thereby helping to constitute the variable "group affiliation," which would be quite different without that material signaling.

Over the last two decades I have become much more explicit about this. To me, the database of archaeologists consists of the material products of, and precedents for, human action (Wobst 1978: 303, 307). Lately, I have begun to refer to human artifacts more concisely as "material interferences" or "material interventions," that is, as intentions to change something from what it was to what it should be or to prevent change that would take place in the absence of those artifacts (Wobst 1997a). The term *interference* emphasizes that artifacts are entered into contexts that humans want to change (or that would change in undesirable directions if they did not enter artifacts in such contexts). Humans artifactually interfere where they cannot, or choose not to, accomplish (or prevent) change by other means. "Other means" are nonartifactual ones: speech and other sounds, gestures and other motions, odors, and touch.

Within this realm of "material interferences," style refers to aspects of form that "talk" or "write" and that are "listened to" or "read." In contrast to artifactual form that interferes with matter or energy, "stylistic form" on artifacts interferes materially *with humans*. Animals interfere materially in matter and energy, and primates are particularly adept at it (McGrew 1992; Wrangham 1994). But even primates do not often materially interfere with each other. *Style* defined in this way is virtually exclusive to humans. As the language and tool chest with which we materially interfere with each other, style is that part of our artifactual repertoire that makes us human.

STYLE, INDIVIDUALS, AND SOCIAL GROUPS

Over the last three decades my definition of *style* has become steadily more encompassing, in ways that do not necessarily make it easier to work with. In 1969 I stressed the role of "style" in talking about social units—helping individuals and groups of individuals to broadcast, or bring about, their social affiliation or their groups: "By summarizing an individual's economic and social situation, stylistic messages play a more active role in the integration of social groups" (Wobst 1977:327); and: "If, through the messages on his [sic] clothing, home, and other artifacts an individual says: 'I am an individual who belongs to social group X,' he [sic] is also saying that he [sic] is conforming with the other behavioral norms and with the ideology behind these norms" (Wobst 1977: 327–328).

Now I hear much more when I listen to style, although not necessarily all at once or with equal loudness. For example, style talks as much about individuals as it does about social units. It is very difficult to maintain social groups through time and across space without reifying (and thus helping to constitute) individuals' social affiliations. But aspects of form that materially proclaim a social group also allow us to assess individual commitment to that group. Style is *always* there by the grace of individuals; individuals cannot easily prevent others from evaluating their talk about *group membership* also as talk about themselves as *individuals* (whether or not they want that to happen). Even uniforms talk about individuals while negating or classifying them. Thus, style always talks loudly about individuals. How loudly, in which contexts, with which objects and attributes, and by whom are important inter- and intracultural variables. Archaeologists should be well positioned to address this variability but have not done so, with a few noteworthy exceptions (see, for example, Handsman and Leone 1989; Shanks and Tilley 1987a:Chapter 3; Voss and Young 1995).

If social groups are difficult to imagine and maintain without materially affirming their presence, what about "individuals"? It is almost impossible to play the role of "individual-consistently-different-from-others" for any length of time, or in any but the smallest population, without support from one's material shell (dress, body modifications, surrounding material accoutrements). *Material interferences* help people imagine and believe in an individual's individuality. Without them individuals would need to continually act out their individualism. That would be quite expensive in terms of matter and energy and might carry with it considerable potential for conflict and stress. Instead, aspects of the individual's material shell (can) do the talking.

This argument is not about the primacy of the individual over society; they are inseparably reflexive. The following example may help to illustrate this. For argument's sake let us imagine all individuals wanted to constitute themselves as individuals different from everyone else. We would be sorely mistaken if we were to expect completely different "individual styles" as the outcome. Even "flaming individualists" need to talk materially so that others can hear "flaming individualist" rather than any number of other possible messages. Thus, even the message of "individuality" needs to be conveyed in socially conventional terms. It will *socially* vary and change, much like messages of social affiliation.

Material discourses about "individualism" constitute and reify the social group regardless of the priorities of individuals. Once humans begin to materially interfere with each other, style is inseparably about society *and* about individuals. Without this mutual material reification neither individuals nor social groups would be able to persist through time or extend across space.

STYLE, HEGEMONY, AND LIBERATION
Without style social cloning and social classification are next to impossible. Style allows people to surficially approximate others and thus to hide their own individuality. It gives humans virtually unlimited space for reifying themselves in difference to others (see, for example, Leone 1984) or to lie about, or otherwise materially deflect from, their self-experienced self (see, for example, McGuire 1988; Pearson 1982, Root 1984; Roveland 1989; Tilley 1984). Style is what reifies

hegemony. But style also reifies resistance, as well as material challenges to hegemony *and* resistance. Once material culture talks, style is a tool for subjugation and a tool for liberation and empowerment, often in the same material dimension, at the same time, and in the same place. For example, school uniforms are introduced for American secondary education of 1998 as a tool to remove students' messages of wealth, poverty, ethnicity, or access to the drug culture. By lowering their pants (males) or raising their skirts (females) a bit, uniforms become vehicles for messages of resistance or for inventing a local discourse concerned neither with rebelling nor conforming (Hamilton 1998:A19).

Style talks about the design of the stage on which humans act (e.g., Baram 1989; Fletcher 1984), it talks about stage directions for humans (Coleman and Elsner 1994; Thomas 1990), it chronicles action in progress (Mizoguchi 1993), it talks about humans acting (Deetz and Dethlefsen 1967), and it helps to constitute human actors (Handsman and Leone 1989) and entire theater companies (Fritz and Mitchell 1987). Style extends human communication about all of these topics well beyond the limits set by biology (Steele and Shennan 1996). But although style potentially increases the reach of human communication in space and time, it also keeps that communication channeled, ensuring that it remains objectifiable, and thus, observable, controllable, and censurable (see, for example, Shackel 1993).

Over the course of their evolution humans have remarkably expanded discourse via material form. From one vantage point this may be viewed as potential liberation from parochial constraints. From another vantage point all human social scales have become subject to material interference, from the largest to the smallest, including entirely private ones. For example, satellite TV and the World Wide Web allow humans to constitute social groupings that span the globe. But "material interferences" are also behind a loss of independence and autochthony in local contexts and behind the ever smaller range of contexts where individuals may re-

main outside of this material discourse, whether by not talking or by not listening. Style liberates and enslaves simultaneously.

THE VISIBILITY OF STYLE

I used to see style primarily in the most visible attributes of form and in the end products of design and manufacture. For example, in 1969 I said that "those artifacts are more appropriate for stylistic messages (regardless of other articulations) which are more visible" (Wobst 1977:330) and that "the less an artifact is visible to members of a given group, the less appropriate it is to carry messages of any kind" (Wobst 1977:328). Now my expectation for suitable stylistic habitats has become significantly broader. I see no reason why something invisible in use should not potentially interfere with humans. This category includes variables related to raw material extraction and movement, artifact production, and artifact disuse (discussed below).

It was Sackett (1990) who forcefully pushed for some of this kind of variation to enter into the discussion of style. He considered low-visibility aspects, with cohesive distributions, to be the unconscious result of ethnicity (and thus helpful to the archaeologist's reconstruction of social groups). Where I differ with Sackett is in the potential for this kind of variation to consciously enter the social field and to be read as social interference by others.

RAW MATERIAL EXTRACTION AND MOVEMENT

Let us begin with the extraction and movement of raw materials. These activities shape the variables of finished tools well before their "working edges" are put to work on matter, energy, or information. Many of these variables are difficult to see in their use contexts (see, for example, Stark, this volume). In *those* contexts it is difficult for anyone but the user/maker to assess if there are preferred or broad ranges of raw materials, if the sources are nearby or faraway, how much variance there is in color, and if raw materials differ by task, tool type, or social context. Nevertheless, the ultimate distribution in these variables results from individuals entering form into their social field in ways they thought appropriate or satisfying. The actions that relate to raw material extraction and movement often take place over more space or time and in broader social fields than the energy and matter uses of the artifacts. Thus, variation added in this phase also potentially talks about social contexts in process and about humans interfering with humans materially. It is my hunch that much of the exotic material that finds its use in parochial tasks derives its primary utility not from marginal efficiency and effectiveness but from its marginal utility for messaging in, and reshaping, local communication matrixes.

Tool Production

Many aspects of production are invisible to the observer of artifacts in use, and many production steps or choices will end up modifying the "inside" of artifacts. Yet although they will not jump into the eye of observers at the time of use, they have *potential* to interfere significantly in the social field. This kind of style is often separated from the "visible" style and is referred to as technological style, technology, technological organization, or technological choice (Chilton, this volume; Dobres and Hoffman 1994; Lechtman 1977:6; Lemonnier 1993; Nelson 1991; Reedy and Reedy 1994; Stark, this volume). For example, the number of production steps is virtually invisible when an artifact is finished and placed into use. Yet this dimension is as variable as the shape of the finished artifacts (and associated with it in some specifiable way). Thus, Abbevillian and Solutrean bifaces are clearly different in their finished shapes. Their difference is easy enough to eyeball, but it is the number of production steps (as one important variable) that helps analysts (and agents) to operationalize shape difference and to relate variations in finished form to different social considerations, goals, or constraints.

At the same time, of course, what is "invisible" to the archaeologist may be quite noticeable and important to the users and other makers (Stark, this volume). Sometimes it might even be that relative "invisibility" that makes the attribute important to the maker or user, as, for example, in badges—such as alumni or lodge pins, wedding bands, circumcision—that signal to ego and to other members the individual's membership in a closed group.

Production that remains invisible in use takes place in the social field and thus potentially talks, potentially is listened to, and potentially intervenes with humans (see, for example, Dobres 1995a; Sinclair 1995). Why should production interfere any less in individual action than the ultimate context where the artifact is supposed to be used? After all, manufacturing selects the ultimate attributes of use; it takes places in, and helps to constitute, the social field at the time of manufacture. The attributes selected, added, modified, or deleted at that stage in an artifact's life *potentially* talk as loudly as the ones that are most visible in the context of use.

Artifact Disuse

Form exposed to disuse, loss, discard, and decomposition (and the habits, rules, and ranges for these behaviors) may transmit as much information, or transmit information as loudly, as the surfaces visible in use. People become differentially disassociated from artifacts by tool function, working edge, task, social context, and surrounding activities. Variation in disused form may talk louder about society or interfere more aggressively with people than the surfaces of tools while they are in use (see, for example, Hodder 1982b:Chapter 8; Moore 1982, 1986).

Of course, how people interact with discarded artifacts is highly variable among and within cultures. But there is no good reason why communication should cease once artifact use ceases. For example, whole areas are defined by what we discard there as "garbage dumps," with a number of implications for what we would do there ourselves or what we assume others to be doing there. What is garbaged helps to define in binary opposition that which is viewed as "useful," "functional," or "proper." What has been discarded is often read as dangerous, taboo, or improper—to be handled only with considerable forethought and the greatest of care if it is not to be avoided altogether. Artifacts may thus often be read more carefully and consciously after discard than before discard.

Usually, "disuse" takes significantly longer in the "life" of an artifact than does "use." The disuse phase usually is in the field of vision of subjects. It must be a *potential* font of information for, or about, them, and a *potential* tool for changing social contexts and individuals. Compositional attributes of the artifact interior, invisible in use, often become visible when the item decays, as in the paste and temper of pots, the mud of bricks, or the clay linings of pot interiors.

MELLOWED FUNCTIONALISM

My 1977 paper is often viewed as having been smack in the middle of the processualist wave (see for example, Dietler and Herbich 1989; Hodder 1991b:27, 64; Miller 1985: 55). In writing it I had more of a sense that I was changing the emphasis in the direction of social questions and social variation (see also Murray 1987:287). On the other hand, like many processual archaeologists, I have distanced myself more explicitly from narrowly functionalist, optimizing, and biologizing approaches since then. I do not want to belittle these approaches here, nor do I consider them to be irrelevant or second class. They are vital for understanding a number of scales with which humans may, and often do, evaluate aspects of each other's material shells.

But where material culture communicates, functionalist considerations need not have been paramount in the social field of the archaeological subjects. Tool makers, users, and discarders learn what they consider relevant in their own history and social context. It is our archaeological challenge that we have to feel our way to the material constituents of that history and context. Without that history and context there is little to guide us on how to scale and evaluate action or on which among the many possibilities to

choose as currency for that interpretation. In the present, in various social contexts and historical trajectories, goals of actors range from satisficing to maximizing, from altruism to egotism, and from abject hedonism to the belief in having to suffer for ultimate redemption. In varying histories and contexts humans may feel compelled to use any of these states as a rationale for materially interfering with others (or with themselves).

Humans enter artifact making and using contexts with considerable knowledge (of history). They also know what they would like to do there and what they would like to avoid doing; they have experience in having satisfied, or having failed to satisfy, such wants before. They have seen others succeed or fail under similar circumstances. They possess the ability to improvise, experiment, and innovate. They also have some practice in anticipating who will be there, who will potentially be exposed to their artifacts, how these people will likely respond, and what should be done via artifacts to make them change their anticipated response. Note that I do not assume that humans crave or need change. They interfere materially also where they feel it necessary to "keep things on track as always." In other words, the belief that things would change in undesirable directions unless artifacts were entered to prevent it is at least as forceful a motivation as the desire to change the context or the course of history. In both cases these "interferences" are driven by the assessment that without one's material intervention the local context would be different in undesirable ways and that one's artifacts (and aspects thereof) would be of help in moving things in desirable directions.

All of these considerations are inseparably contextual and social. The subjects' experience, memory, knowledge, vision, and actions are all contextually conditioned, socially embedded, and discursive. If we want to interpret why subjects interfere materially in society, we need to take the temperature of the context they enter and direct our interpretation at the way in which that context is likely to have been modified—and ended up being modified—by that material interference.

It is clear to me that intentionality of action does not place humans outside of "function," but the functionality of human actions is contextual rather than universal and socially rather than mechanically conditioned. It is here that I have found Giddens's term *enstructuration* so useful, a term that entered the archaeological literature in the early 1980s (Giddens 1979). At position *artifacts-plus-one* the social context and the social history of relevance to the subject have been changed (as have the context and history of other subjects in the social field). Each material intervention modifies the histograms for the distribution of form; it changes the material precedents and thus the templates for future artifacts, whether that interference was designed to keep things the same or to make them different. Things will actually be different in either case.

In the same context there usually are material act(ion)s of domination and of resistance, and they are both reasonable from the vantage point of the respective subjects; or the subjects might avoid taking part in either domination or resistance. Which interference looks reasonable and worthwhile is bound to be different for the higher and lower ranks in a ranked society, for members of high and low classes or castes, and for Chassidim or Hutterites. Giddens's enstructuration paradigm allows for contemporaneous social actors to arrive at different optimal solutions (even in the same social context), something that is very difficult to accommodate in many of the overly functionalist paradigms.

Such a paradigm allows for social contradictions, discontinuities, even pathologies by our standards, and for unresolvable tensions in the social field. It takes them for granted as part of the normal human condition. Without them there would be little reason to keep artifactually interfering in the social matrix. It allows us to keep complexity in the picture. It also allows for everyone "becoming" without ever really getting there; and it allows for differentiation, variation, and assimilation as day-to-day and usual features of the social scene. To me, these are the challenges and the pleasures of social life. Style is central to them all.

THE ALL-PERVASIVENESS OF STYLE

Did I just lead myself *ad absurdum*? If style is that aspect of our material world that talks and interferes in the social field, is there a place where style is not, where some aspect of the artifactual record does not convey information among those who come in contact with it? Is there the possibility of some aspects talking and other aspects not talking? Have we constructed an oxymoron, a variable with only one state—talk?

I held in 1977 and I hold now that once there is style, style is all pervasive (Wobst 1977:326). Once some artifacts talk, all do, independent of the intent of the producer or user. Regardless of what the reader chooses to read, the entire material inventory is reading matter if some aspects need to be read or are read. Imagine a lengthy book in which only three pages contained text. All pages would need to be scanned to find the typed pages, regardless of the writer's intent. Lack of writing would not identify the empty pages as being outside the realm of communication but as pages with "zero" as their variable-state-for-communication. If dress communicates things sometimes, then even nakedness talks, regardless of the wearer's intent. It is read as a refusal to talk via dress or as maximal contrast to dress (rather than as an essential state of nature or a "prewriting" state of material culture). This is nicely illustrated in the interpretation of ancient Greek statuary: its state of undress makes more sense as a state of fashion—a fashion that talks even louder than dress itself (Bonfante 1989). Where some aspects of the material inventory consciously talk, others are, or need to be, evaluated for potential messages, regardless of the intent of the participants. In that sense style has been all pervasive ever since it entered human discourse.

THE CONSCIOUSNESS OF STYLE

Humans are not necessarily conscious of this all-pervasiveness; they are not equally conscious about what is being said in different realms of material culture; and they are not equally secure about the meaning of what they are reading in different material cultural categories. Depending upon context and history, some realms will talk louder (and will be read more often and/or more intensely) than others, and some will talk softer. To be read, some realms may require more material intervention than others, and some will not be "read" at all, if reading implies consciousness.

There is the possibility of some serious talking taking place while nobody is listening and of some serious listening taking place while nobody is consciously talking. Loud talk is not necessarily the most complex or redundant material interference: at the time of the Baroque style in Europe, the more "baroque" Rococo attracted attention; but at the time of the Rococo, it was the spare and stark Neoclassical style that was noticed and adopted. In the United States suburban front doors are read with greater interest than back doors, and suburban lawns talk with greater intent and are read with greater interest than suburban sidewalks. "Art" is read with greater attention to detail than are "doodles," and knives talk more often than nails. The inside of pot walls is of considerably less interest than their decorated outside; fire trucks are observed with greater attention than other trucks; and sneakers have considerably more to say than rubber boots (Gladwell 1997). What is heard and what is not, and what talks and what does not, is forever in discursive motion, in change, and in tension.

STYLE IN FUNCTION

If style is ever present, the separation of material form into domains that separately interfere with matter, energy, and humans is, of course, purely heuristic—it is not based on any "natural" allocation of form to essential logical categories. The "working edge," that is, the part designed for interacting with matter or energy, may potentially interfere as much in the lives of humans as aspects added to tools in addition to the working edge, with no other purpose than to materially intervene with humans.

Let us assume for argument's sake that tool matter-and-energy functions were the only considerations. Even then, "functionally" appropriate or not, each new tool modifies the social field. It reshapes the template for what is thought or known to be practical. It modifies the reference points against which actors can evaluate themselves and others. It exposes everyone's practical reason and reasonable practice. How well does my working edge approximate that of Alphonse's? How effectively does my working edge say "I am a competent tool maker"? How convincingly does my working edge differ from that nincompoop's over there?

In that way working edge mechanics are inseparably interwoven with social dynamics, even in perfectly "functional" aspects of artifacts. The relative functionality of the working edge interferes with, modifies, constrains, rebels against, or reinforces the model that future artifact makers will employ—in making the given kind of tool, in thinking about toolmaking, and in thinking about the social field. To what degree do working-edges approximate the functional ideals? Is working edge form continuous across the possibilities, or does it grade without interruption from one use function to the next one? Are some kinds of edges confined to given kinds of matter? Are some edges taboo for some matter, whereas others are multimaterial? Such questions expose the social dimensions of working-edge variance—dimensions that are not exhausted in energy-matter explanations. Working edges help to constitute, constrain, or alter the social field, whether or not the makers or users are conscious of it.

ISLANDS OF STYLISTIC SIMILITUDE (OR THE FLAT EARTH SOCIETY)

How can something all pervasive and ever present be interesting to study? In standard archaeological practice it is not. Stylistic research often is a scan that pulls from the archaeological record sets of form that are internally identical but maximally different from their respective logical neighbors (see, for example, Hodson 1982:23; Shennan 1988:195–196; Whallon 1982:128; Whallon and Brown 1982:xvii). In that way standard archaeological practice generates an oxymoron, a variable with a single state.

This is well caricatured in Whallon's (1972) analysis of archaeological practice in Owasco typology: at each step in a typological (read stylistic) scan, that attribute is selected which keeps within-group variance at a minimum and between-group variance at a maximum. The "ideal type," for which we can substitute the "ideal style" in the argument here, is entirely without internal variation and differs, attribute by attribute, from all other such constructs. Variation *within* types is compartmentalized into smaller islands (varieties, etc.) a step down the classificatory ladder, again to minimize variation within the new group and to maximize contrasts between that group and others.

The focus is not on learning how humans materially interfere in each other's social spheres but to identify all actions in which humans interfere with each other *in exactly the same way*, as if humans wanted to convey exactly the same information to each other. That, indeed, would be oxymoronic. For what kind of information is transmitted if everyone tells everyone else exactly the same thing? Imagine a group of people who sent each other identical emails day after day. Recipients would soon delete these messages from their screens without reading them; senders would stop sending email, or they would change the message to stimulate renewed reading. What actually is pulled out from the archaeological continuum via stylistic homogenizing is not interference in other lives or humans communicating with each other but islands of form within which there is no communication.

Of course, there may be circumstances in which people may actually want to tell each other exactly the same story in the same way or in which they may be forced to do so. But that type of storytelling is only one of many. It should be the exception rather than the rule and take place to satisfy severe constraints and in contrived settings, and it should be restricted to a few categories of artifacts.

On the other hand, one can always and very easily generate data that will have this structure. A strategy of "sorting until shared form is discovered" is bound to succeed even if the archaeological record consisted of nothing but random numbers. In that case archaeologists would select the few *identical* random numbers from the record and use them to infer the reasons behind the entire highly varied but random communication system—surely, a vacuous project in any paradigm.

MEA CULPA

In part the strategy caricatured in the previous section can be blamed on a narrow reading of my 1977 paper. In the parlance of that time, if style was directed toward conveying information and social affiliation was one of the topics that needed to be addressed, how else but with identical messages could members of the group convey that they belonged to a given group? When people applied my paper to their slice of the archaeological record, they went looking for sameness in form that was unrelated to matter or energy functions. That sameness would identify the members affiliated with a given social group. Congruence within groups went hand in hand with the expectation of total disassociation between groups. As a result, one ended up with spatio-temporal entities with virtually no variation in form. A research dead end was the result. People had only two states: group member (be the same as others) or not (be different). Either people were each others' clones, or they refused to be grouped.

Where talk is not allowed to vary within groups, and where values that logically link form to other groups are suppressed, group *formation* and group *process* are hard to make visible. As a matter of fact it is hard to relate that variance structure to anything because there *is* no variance. The result is not a chronicle about lived lives but about a utopia (or hell!). In treating populations as if they approximated that utopia archaeologists hold up model societies free of internal variation, whose members are incapable of social states other than sameness. In that way archaeologists serve particular social or political agendas that help to *bring about reductions of social variance in the present.*

This kind of archaeological output must itself be read as material interference in social process (in the past *and* in the present). It has past subjects declare their material unwillingness to vary and their lack of tolerance for social variability, tensions, and contradictions. If the present looks at the past for alternatives to contemporary social relations, it will not find them (the process actually reduces the potential for social alternatives in the present). If this is the only strategy by which to serve up the past, archaeology must have a distinctly conservative effect on modern templates for action. It has archaeologists forever providing utopias dear to administrators—peopled with subjects united in their subscription to symbols of, and templates for, action and neatly bounded in space, time, and personnel. Such studies make it easier for people to imagine their own social docility and for administrators to conceive of, and help bring about, docile underlings.

PARADIGMATIC OXYMORONS

Even if people had no other desire than for others to recognize, read, and internalize their message of group affiliation, the conclusion that this would generate an internally homogenous surface of identical aspects of form is unrealistic, as I have pointed out a number of times (Wobst 1977:329–330, 1978). Even under these assumptions the message of sameness should be more variable in space and time than the model of a perfectly cohesive spatio-temporal entity with internally identical messages. If messages of group affiliation are interferences, designed to change that which preceded them, one would expect them to be particularly glaring where group affiliation is particularly contested and where people need to seriously counteract group fission. Thus, the message *should* vary in intensity across a group.

People validate that their messages are the same against their experience of other people's material culture. Given learning and error theory, even if everyone wanted to do nothing but produce messages identical to those of the other group members, one should get clinal change in form across space at a given time and gradual change of form through time in a given place (Wobst 1977: 328–329; 1994; *contra* Voss and Young 1995:92).

Of course, the spatial reach of some communication media, such as the printed word, television, or email, may smooth the contours or decrease the gradients on that clinal map or affect the rate of change through time. The same should be produced by improvements in transportation, by mass production, and by the provision of standardized prototypes (as in metric standards or flag laws, among others).

There is another reason why contiguous, contemporaneous material sameness will not result from everyone's intention to let "sameness" materially hang out. That is because it is not "material sameness" but *"material-sameness-that-wants-to-be-read-and-recognized-as-such"* that is of importance here. Through time, that "sameness" needs to be modified so that it continues to be read or recognized as such. For example, that with which sameness has been contrasted might have changed (the enemy's symbols might have become different, or the standards of what people view as "practical" might have changed), forcing a change in the symboling of sameness. Or the given signal might fail to attract the same attention as before. Or the intended readers might be getting bored, so the amplitude of what is to be read has to be changed. Or there might be competition along the axis of sameness, which would force continuous fine-tuning of an individual's scores on the group's histogram for sameness. In short, even talk about sameness forces change and variation and within-group variance in most conceivable social scenarios.

The search for social groups is only one of many reasons why archaeologists often structure their data into internally homogenous types. Virtually *any* archaeological sorting begins in this way, regardless of the researcher's problem direction or research perspective (Hill and Evans 1972). That should make us a bit uneasy because before we have formulated any idea the data have been structured already—structured with no particular sensitivity to the future questions that one may want to resolve with them. Such data do not fit well with the paradigmatic goals of any of the major contemporary paradigms in archaeology—particularly not with those that strive to explain the social articulations of artifacts.

THE PROCESSUAL DILEMMA

Suppose you were a card-carrying processual archaeologist trying to evaluate expectations about human behavior in variables $X, Y,$ or Z as variable W changes. If successful sorting had preceded you, it would have predigested the variation in your material world into islands of homogeneity, and not much of that variation would be left for your analysis. Such a data structure would be most inelegant for your purposes. As variable W's value changed, objects assigned to an "island" (a specific set of formal messages) could not vary much because they had been grouped to suppress that variation. All of the objects in each group should produce essentially the same set of recurrent values. And because you had grouped the objects for maximal contrast between groups, it may even be hard to demonstrate that the same relationship was responsible for the massively contrasting forms in the other groups.

Biological, behavioral ecological, evolutionary ecological, and sociobiological hypotheses all depend on variance in the variables to be explained. Because our islands of similitude do not leave any within-group variance, we must conclude that they do not lend themselves to these kinds of approaches. For talking about relationships we need variance, not groups that minimize variance. A sensitive processual analysis should start with a data structure that *maximizes* the variance of the *explanandum*.

Processual archaeologists often complain about their lack of success in social theorizing (see, for example, Flannery 1972; Redman et al. 1978), or they are accused of such impotence by their paradigmatic opponents (see, for example, Hodder 1982a; Leone et al. 1987; Miller 1982:84). This failure may simply be due to the suppression of variance that precedes most archaeological analysis because a) in the absence of variance there can be only very weak resolution among competing ideas and b) the paradigm aims to explain, predict, or retrodict variation with general theory—where there is no variation, there is no (need for) theory!

THE POSTPROCESSUAL DILEMMA

A similar argument can be applied to many postprocessual exegeses of archaeological contexts. Much postprocessual analysis also starts with data structures that minimize within-group variance and maximize between-group variance. In that way material aspects most sensitive for chronicling action and subjects' sensitivity (and contributions) to social structure are eradicated before interpretation has had a chance. The variance thus eradicated circumscribes the ways in which people acted and, thus, what they believed was their room for action.

Some of the best-known, early, postprocessual case studies add variation by means of binary oppositions. But this strategy hard-wires the brains of subjects quite perniciously. In that way subjects unavoidably have binary oppositions of cultural determinism raining down from their brains into artifact form. Style is relegated to being an output of nonvarying structuralist principles, and what variation is observed in the record does not impinge on those binary generating variables. Although the archaeological record is varying, it remains epiphenomenal, an exemplar of human nature, which itself remains essential as a matrix of binary oppositions.

It is the range and variation among socially constituted (and socially constituting) actions within a group and the interstices between groups, in their historical contexts, that chronicle agency and structure. The unthinking application of the extant method kills these data before analysis has started. The call is thus for keeping variance on the inside of the in-group analysis and for bridging variance between the islands of similitude so that action can be contextualized and interpreted.

Could it be that most processual archaeologists are not convinced by the interpretations of historic and prehistoric contexts in the postprocessual vein because the structuralist data (and theory) behind many contextual readings detract from the plausibility of agency?

Domination-resistance and Marxist approaches fall somewhere in between processualist and postprocessualist practice when it comes to style. Often dominators or the dominated are treated as internally nonvarying, bounded entities in the same way that many processualists define social groups. Once that is accomplished, research then changes to other variables. Or hegemony is defined in the processual way, and resistance is structured as its stylistic binary opposition. Again, style often ends up as something that is resolved, there, and uncontested except in opposition, cohesive so that all of its material referents point in the same direction, and nonvarying through time and space within the time-space boundaries it helped to define.

In sum, the inherited ways of classifying and grouping, before more problem-directed research and interpretation begin, are often not conducive to the paradigms in vogue. They may prevent the resolution of central paradigmatic questions because they structure information insensitively. Often they weed out exactly that information that the paradigm is interested in (see also Chilton 1996 and this volume; Wobst 1997b).

STYLE IN PROCESS

Although style is always there, it never quite gets there. Style never arrives full-blast and then stays there; it is always in contest, in motion, unresolved, discursive, in process. "Talk about" always indicates an imbalance, and human information exchange never

reaches a state in which that imbalance is ultimately resolved. Even binary oppositions, or the contest between domination and resistance, are too motionless to do justice to the dynamics of communication of which they are a part. Applied uncritically and insensitively, they instead destroy the relevant information about variation. They take away from style in motion, in process, in contest, unresolved, in tension, internally varying. Let me illustrate this in a number of different ways.

Let us suppose an archaeologist has sorted out Style X as bounded in Area A and Period 5. We have known since our introductory archaeology class that this plateau of sameness appears as a two-dimensional battleship if it is plotted through time in a given place and as a time-transgressive process if it is plotted in space-time (Deetz and Dethlefsen 1967). At a very simplistic level of process the perpetrators of Style X include early adopters, follow-the-leader adopters, and late adopters. They are completely different in social position and in their rationale for adopting. As this example indicates, material form that is the same does not predict that the processes associated with it were similar. In fact, the very sameness of style predicts behavioral difference depending on the space-time coordinates of the identical form. *The same form differentiates different sectors of the community differentially and places the same sectors of different communities into different time slices.* For example, in data over which we have good time control, as in cemetery studies, the early adopters of the cemetery decoration of death-heads in Boston are separated from their counterparts in Halifax Center, southern Vermont, by many generations, over a distance of only 100 miles. And the late adopters in Boston are contemporaneous with the early adopters in Northampton 80 miles away (compare with Deetz and Dethlefsen 1967 and Hägerstrand 1967). Throwing them all into the same pile does injustice to them all. It removes form from its messaging context, it removes people from their social milieu, and the research universe thus circumscribed is a hodgepodge of unrelated, decontextualized, noncontemporaneous outcomes of actions.

Take the case in which the makers or users actually want to broadcast the same message. If they keep passing it off in the same way, it becomes harder to hear because people get used to hearing it. To remain audible it needs to be varied, to become noticeably louder, softer, more complex, or starker; the material medium might need to be changed; or it might need to be embedded in different contexts or different personnel. Thus, where there is material change, there is not necessarily change in what is being communicated! Change is necessary simply to communicate the same message.

We are all part of one or the other stylistic rat race—the constant tension, variation, and motion that is style in our society. Style keeps people on their toes and allows no rest. One never fully gets there with style. In one process style at the top is copied below on the scale of demonstrating access to matter, information, and appropriate social contexts. As long as style at the top is changed faster than it can be copied from below (Cohen 1974), everybody will go on copying up for a never-ending sense of social accomplishment. Although the material trace of this system is massive and continuous material change, the social pyramid thus reified stays the same, as do the processes of that reification.

The reverse of this can also be observed in our society—a process by which people "borrow up" to gain social capital. Baggy pants, blue jeans, dance, music, and graffiti are copied from the street, helping to individualize the people at the top of the social ladder in their social context there. The street tends to stay much the same (Gladwell 1997).

Thus, quite often in material interferences, the more things change, the more they stay the same.

PRACTICAL REASON AND STYLE

This observation provides a smooth transition to another assumption afflicting much stylistic analysis in archaeology: that stylistic processes at work in one's own society will also be found in the societies in our archaeological field of vision. For example, archaeologists tend to look for stylistic process primarily in the most processed extreme of the material cultural inventory: rims rather than bodies among the sherds and highly processed tools in lieu of unmodified flakes. In that way a single currency (degree of processing) is naturalized archaeologically. Even in U.S. society, although no doubt important, this scale—degree of processing—is only one of many for communicating materially. It happens to be the most energy-intensive one. Thus, it tends to privilege communication among the upper layers of society, at least if our society is taken as example.

The "practical reason" (Sahlins 1976) of our society in stylistic analysis is imposed uncritically on the archaeological record of other societies. Stone and pottery are taken to be full of stylistic meaning. What prior knowledge do we have to assume that the materiality of fauna, roads, field borders, distance distributions, zoning maps, plow scars, firewood, fire-cracked rocks, kitchen gardens, and urinals were not more important media for talking than were dinner- and tableware? Communication by means of material modifications is arbitrary and dynamic. It becomes less so only in context, given knowledge of the history and change in trajectory of that context, and with a fine-toothed sensitive assessment of the distribution of variation.

Do all societies communicate with equal intensity with their communication currencies? Across the same number of media? With as much variance among the media? Globally our society must be close to the possible maximum in terms of talking via the material record. Yet even in our society there are important (discursive) differences between subgroups in the degree to which material culture is consciously committed to artifacts and is consciously read.

Ultimately each society's members are differentially tied into the stylistic games of their time; they use talk to differentiate themselves, and they differentially react to attempts to channel or control their material talk. They are also differentially tied into the material communication web in the same place through time, even if all they are trying to do is to communicate the same things about themselves. It is clear that this dynamism is underexplored archaeologically. The material dimensions that constitute this discourse and are sensitive to it are not anticipated in extant practice.

To bring this material communication into the picture, we need to anticipate it theoretically, observe it in its variation, and relate it to society. It is this dynamism that makes style so much fun to see in action. It is also this dynamism that makes style such an irrelevant bore if this variation is kept out of the picture! In the task of getting this most human of human activities to center stage, in its infinite variability and variation, the range of present anthropological paradigms leaves plenty of room for action on style, for people ranging from the most context-bound post-processualist to the most grandiose, grand-theory builder.

In closing, rather than celebrating the death of style, I would like to suggest to my readers that a more appropriate title for this chapter would have been "Style into Archaeology" or "Archaeologists into Style"!

Acknowledgments. This chapter is dedicated to my students at the University of Massachusetts, who have helped me enormously in revising my style of style, and to Greg, Natalia, and Jude, who are much more style conscious than I will ever be. The anonymous readers provided useful devil's advocacy. Although I have not adopted all of their suggestions, they have certainly made me think quite a bit. *Ich möchte diesen Aufsatz auch meinen Freunden widmen-Gockel, Helmut, Mickefett, und Wozzeck, mit denen ich 1959 Jugoslawien erlebte. Ohne Euch wäre ich heute völlig anders!*

9

An End Note

Reframing Materiality for Archaeology

MARGARET W. CONKEY

Everyone agrees: material culture is, and long has been, the heart of archaeology. So why, at the close of the century and the turn of the millennium, should there be something "new"? How can there be something more to be said? Is it that, once again, the reengagement of archaeology with more and more varied theoretically informed approaches to material culture has been stimulated by recent developments in sociocultural anthropology and related "cultural studies" that have (for a variety of intriguing reasons) brought back a focus on/interest in/attention to materiality and to the constitutive nature of material culture in the creation, transformation, and practice of culture? Is this, yet again, another of the so-called parasitic "paradigm lags" (after Leone 1972) of anthropological archaeology?

A simple paradigm-lag model cannot explain the current situation. In fact, if anything, one must acknowledge the important and integrative role that archaeological perspectives have played on an international scale in facilitating the veritable revival of materiality and the study of material culture in sociocultural anthropology and related fields. But to chart out these relationships and influences, interesting as they may be, is outside the scope of this end-chapter. What can be said, however, is that it is not the case that anthropological archaeology is rediscovering materiality and culture, as could be argued for sociocultural anthropology and

ethnography (see, e.g., Frank 1998; Guss 1989; Miller 1987; Pfaffenberger 1992; Stocking 1985; Thomas 1991; and Weiner and Schneider 1989). Both subdisciplines—archaeology and sociocultural anthropology—are, of course, being influenced by wider theoretical trends and shifts in the circumstances of research that necessarily reorient and redefine our objects of knowledge and the implicated objects of study.[1]

Rather, archaeology has always been defined as, defined by, and often degraded for its grounding—sometimes to the point of empiricist tyrannies—in the material: "the record" of things, artifacts, features, forms, and patterns. What is and has been new—and what thus allows for, if not calls out for, a volume like this one—is the simultaneous convergence of at least two trends: on the one hand, a growing (albeit sometimes grudgingly) admission and acceptance (though hardly a universal one) of theoretical diversity and multiplicity within and for archaeology; and, on the other hand, a somewhat mature (at last!) attitude about the potential utility of and inspiration from conceptual resources in a wide array of disciplines—an opening out that is more thoughtful and selective than the usual straightforward borrowing, long thought to characterize how archaeologists build theory and method. Although archaeologists have long admitted in their concept of "style" and in the study of material culture of past societies that there may be more than one way to "plow a field" (or "skin a cat," or whatever metaphor you prefer), we are at last able to admit more openly and more productively that there is more than one way to do archaeology. This volume, in its array of papers, is testimony to this admission and, even more so, to a willingness—and an ability—to take old concepts and approaches and think them through again, rework them, put them to work in new ways, and, above all, to provide new insights that, nonetheless, merely open out into further inquiry rather than closing off with premature "conclusions."

In taking up the task of preparing an "end-chapter" for this volume, I rediscovered that the usual requests from editors are not so easy to fulfill. They inevitably want something that "integrates" the volume, "summarizes" the chapters' findings, and yet "draws out the implications" of the volume. Edited volumes are always an unruly challenge to the idea of coherence, consistency, integration, and that somehow scholarship, and especially publications, should be about "closure" or "tying it all up with a neat red bow." I cannot claim that this will or even should happen, especially with a volume like this; it is not the editor's nor contributors' intent to provide a singular agreed-upon program or programmatic statement about how to study material culture in archaeology. This, I think, is a good thing. The subtitle I would write for this book is not "How to study material culture in archaeology" but "Ways to think about materiality for archaeology."

The volume explores *some* of the ways that archaeologists engage with material culture, with an underlying push towards a veritable expansion—through reconceptualizations (often rather radical ones)—of what has heretofore gone on under the rubric of "stylistic analyses" and other approaches. This set of papers, however, is not merely stylistic or typological or ethnoarchaeological analysis with new labels. This is more than serious scrutiny of prevailing concepts. There are theoretical and methodological concerns raised here that, in general, are ripe for debate and discussion across the disci-

pline—concerns that are taken up through the lens of how archaeologists can and do engage with material culture. As one reviewer of the volume pointed out, the volume includes papers that revisit historically significant problems, such as the chapter by Wobst and his self-reflexive consideration of his 1977 style paper (Wobst 1977), as well as the chapter by Dean Arnold et al., who revisit a longitudinal ceramic sourcing study in the Yucatán. Numerous papers make important assessments and critiques of key archaeological concepts and methods, such as typology (P. Arnold, Chilton, Dobres). Both current and long-standing topical foci of archaeological analysis are to be found here: mortuary analysis (Costin), agency (P. Arnold; Dobres), gender (Dobres), ethnicity (Stark), ethnoarchaeology (P. Arnold; Stark; Arnold, et al.), and style (Wobst).

Yes, as with most edited volumes, there are difficulties in integration. Not all theoretical perspectives are strongly or visibly represented, although some (e.g., selectionist approaches) are elegantly critiqued (in P. Arnold). Several theoretical infusions resonate through a number of papers, most notably, the set of ideas and concepts galvanized by "technology and culture" and "technological style/style-in-technology" approaches (in Chilton, Dobres, and Stark, for example). In fact, production itself is not only given more attention (than is final form or product) but is invigorated and refined. Overall, the volume reflects and itself constitutes the wider interest and emphasis on "making culture," whether from practice theory, agency, enstructuration, technological style, and/or the analysis of artifact manufacture. Many chapters deliberately and interestingly reframe aspects of production to show not only how we can apply these ideas and approaches to different contexts (e.g., Costin's chapter) but how we can expand the very notion of production itself (e.g., P. Arnold's chapter).

In framing the symposium at the Society for American Archaeology meetings (1996), where many of these papers were first presented, organizer and editor Elizabeth

Chilton asked, "After a decade of post-processual approaches, after almost 30 years of feminist theory, and after a renewed interest in materials science approaches, how far have we come in our interpretations of material culture?" It would be nit-picking, but perhaps true, to suggest that postprocessual approaches have been visible for nearly two decades, or that feminist theory, despite its heralded 30 years in anthropology, is still almost negligible in the archaeological literature (even in that which is concerned with gender). As for the papers at the SAA session, and even within this volume—which is only a subset of the SAA papers (which included ones by Hosler [1996], Pfaffenberger [1996], and Skibo and Schiffer [1996])—one would have to say that they indicate a strong and positive contribution of materials science approaches, relatively little influence of postprocessual theory (except that people agreed to participate in and be identified with a public SAA session [and now a book] that was about "meaning"), and, unless the mention of gender constitutes feminist theory—which to me it certainly does not—nothing noticeably influenced by or about feminist theory, except for the Dobres chapter. The volume, however, is much more about two things, no matter what the theoretical or analytical inspiration was for the papers: it is about "critical" approaches, and it is about variation in material culture.

WHAT'S "CRITICAL" ABOUT
THESE APPROACHES?

A dictionary definition of *critical* lists (1) "given to fault-finding or severe judgments; carping" and (2) "exhibiting careful, precise judgments and evaluations" (Funk and Wagnalls 1973:319). The very word *critical* has, in the past few decades in scholarly circles, taken on an air of being theoretical and therefore (*contra* Culler 1994) elevated, abstract, and sophisticated (if not to some pretentious), as in "critical theory." Even without this recent overburden, being "critical"— as in making a critique—is the kind of notion that makes many senior scholars cringe, although most of us expect and even hope for

ongoing, critical reworkings of disciplinary concepts and concerns, including those we ourselves promulgated, adopted, and/or promoted: one generation's solution(s) becomes the next generation's problem(s). Although most people expect that a critical approach will tend toward the first of the dictionary definitions, this volume is notably full of critical approaches of the second sort: careful, precise evaluations. The papers in this volume are singularly healthy in their critical approaches; across the board they recast the objects of their critique, they render them more usable, and they show how a wider net can be cast with reframed concepts that have been put to scrutiny.

Wobst's chapter (chapter 8) is not so much critical as it presents a long-awaited self-critique of an approach to style that Wobst published in 1977, an approach that has been so widespread and influential over the past two decades that one can refer to an interpretation as being "Wobstian" (see Stark, this volume). Many of us have occasionally suggested that we find it unlikely that after so many years Wobst would hold the same premises or make the case for "style" in quite the same way. But in the absence of his own statement, this has been just a guess. Here Wobst has to confront the fact that the approach he laid out in 1977 was perhaps far more influential than he had ever intended; certainly, he says here, it was taken far beyond its original scope and in ways that he had not imagined or foreseen. This chapter by Wobst is worth the wait: Wobst is again original and provocative, and although he is, admirably, not going to give in on certain key aspects of the original argument about what "style" is about, he nonetheless expands, refines, and reframes these ideas. With a critical assessment of the "use life" of "Wobst 1977" he breathes new life into a notion of "style" that is, once again, eminently usable. This chapter is itself one of those (positive) interventions into the conceptual repertoire of stylistic (and material culture) analysis that will, furthermore, take on greater efficacy in that it comes from an originating author.

Dobres's chapter (chapter 2) is an excellent example of "why we don't have to throw out the baby with the bath water," despite her lengthy critique of Upper Paleolithic systematics and the kind of understandings of this period in southwestern Europe that these have engendered, at the cost—as she well argues—of all sorts of other understandings and insights. Hers is not a position that advocates, as do some Paleolithic scholars (e.g., Rigaud and Simek 1987) that we must start over; Dobres does not send us back to the proverbial "square one" that either sets aside the so-called outmoded typologies or requires collection of more data with more scientific rigor. Instead, by advocating another way of shuffling the analytical cards (so to speak), that is, by undertaking another way to analyze the extant material culture, she suggests that we can push out the edges of the delimited views that we have inherited. We can introduce new concepts, such as gender and agency; we can mix previously separated categories of material culture (e.g., different "types" of bone and antler artifacts) using new conceptual orientations (e.g., *chaîne opératoire*), and we can adjust the scale of analysis (to the site level). In this case the critical leads to a constructive reframing, and there are comparable implications for almost every region (as the chapter by Chilton shows so effectively).

Stark (chapter 3) strikes out on a constructive path as well, without belaboring the analytical programs, much less the specific weaknesses, of most material culture studies, which she finds either lacking in theoretical cohesion or, contrarily, overdetermined by what she calls (mistakenly) "postmodern" approaches. Specifically, she wants to forge a synthesis of a North American ("technological style") and a European (*"techniques et culture"*) technologically oriented approach to material culture and its patterning. Drawing from each of these approaches, she revisits her ethnoarchaeological ceramic data from the Philippines and uses the overall study to assess one of the key issues that have motivated archaeological studies of material culture: the identification of social bound-

aries and that which such boundaries have been assumed to imply, namely, "ethnicity." Although Stark suggests that the two technological approaches she wants to synthesize are "opposed," it is neither necessary nor warranted to counterpose them. As is clear from her own beginning "synthesis," the two approaches are ripe for mutual elaboration and the substantive conceptual frameworks that lie behind each provide much of the reason for why (see Dobres and Hoffman 1994) they are particularly suitable to archaeological theories of and for material culture, something that Stark calls for in her conclusions.[2]

Arnold's chapter (chapter 7) is most notably a critical engagement with two very specific and widespread theoretical approaches—the production stages approach and the selectionist approach—to the study of pottery production, an area of archaeological inquiry that has, perhaps, dominated the archaeological study of material culture. This is a model for an effective and parsimonious critical approach: the two different approaches are presented in the context of the author's own approach, and the critiques are drawn in reference to what Arnold takes to be the goals of archaeological and ethnoarchaeological inquiry and to what he understands to be the nature of human culture. The reader is always clear on the position of the author, and the critiques are shown to "hold" if one agrees with Arnold's assumptions. He then "ices the cake" by wedding an ethnoarchaeological study to an archaeological example.

As with Arnold, Chilton (chapter 4) is concerned about the masking of variation, that is, about the double-edged sword of archaeological analysis: how our methods (in this case, ceramic typologies in Late Woodland New England) that purportedly make sense of variation simultaneously mask variation. Is there any way out of this seemingly inevitable dilemma? To critique the foundational typologies for a regional culture history is a bold move, but the insights that Chilton draws here, based on taking a different approach (akin to the "technological style" of Lechtman [1977]), are suggestive enough to warrant taking on the ancestors.

In chapter 6 Costin takes up a fundamental arena of archaeological study—mortuary analysis—and expands the scope of what mortuary analysis might entail, focusing on intraburial variation rather than the usual interburial analysis. By considering everything that goes into the burial "assemblage" to be as much social labor as some sort of (passive) reflection of social structure or of symbolic significance, Costin's study becomes an important critique of how limited and limiting our own frames of reference can be and simultaneously brings out something new, something scrutinized, and something heretofore unconsidered.

In chapter 5 Arnold et al. also provide an example of positive critique in the sense that they hold firm to the position that despite the increasing sophistication of physical science methods in the archaeological study of material culture, there must always be anthropological problems and issues well in hand. On the one hand, the rigorous science methods—such as neutron activation analysis, which they employ here—must themselves be understood as open to change, problems, and ambiguities. On the other hand, they insist that—and show specific instances of when and how—we cannot assume that these methods are always the big and effective analytical "hammers" we might want. Thus, they too are interested in stressing the limits and limitations of our specific analytical approaches and in using the benefits of a longitudinal study to assess "results," reassess, and assess yet again. This is especially the case because these observational results are explicitly situated by the analysts within a past cultural matrix of cognizant human actors within changing sociohistorical circumstances.

Although one might suggest that this volume should offer some sorts of new, end-of-the-millennium methods or borrowable case studies for the central archaeological concern with material culture and its "meanings," this volume is less a "toolbox" than it is about the more difficult aspects of archaeology, namely, the thinking part of it. By thinking things through again, by reconsidering typology, ethnicity, style, ethnoarchaeology, scale, variation, and agency—among other issues and specific analytical methods—the contributors have met the challenge of what critical approaches can do to not only reinvigorate but redefine and reorient research. In each case we have learned something new.

KEEPING "VARIATION" IN FOCUS

Each paper reminds us that one of our key platforms for the archaeological study of material culture has been a concern for understanding "variation." All the authors here have been trained since the 1960s, a time in which the early Binfordian claims for the new archaeology marked quite clearly a programmatic focus on "variation" (e.g., the nature and significance of variation; see Binford [1962]). Long before those rousing cries of "we should partition our observational fields" (Binford 1965) and the like, archaeologists were certainly concerned with variation, if seen only in their emphases on classification and on their development of foundational principles of archaeological analysis, such as seriation. Of course, most contemporary archaeologists, no matter what theoretical persuasion, still must confront and use the differences and similarities in archaeological materials. So what's different here?

First, although the volume includes several notable attempts to recast our thinking about variation in archaeological analysis and interpretation, we are far from the needed purging of archaeological discourse to focus more on the makers, doers, thinkers, and people of the past and less on "formal variation," "assemblage variability," and "material culture patterning" as our objects of knowledge. This reorientation—as exemplified so powerfully in Spector's consideration of the dehumanized nomenclature of bone awls (Spector 1993:30)—does not mean less rigor or mere speculation.

Many archaeologists still hold all too tightly to the idea that our focus is (necessarily) on the *patterning* more than it is on the material, to say nothing of the human makers and users. Any review of material culture studies in archaeology tends to be a review of how we have understood—and methodologically tried to access—patterning. Although Wobst does not quite say as much, one can read here (in his reassessment of "Wobst 1977") his frustration that adopters of that approach were interested in it because it seemed to give them some specific methodological guidelines to elucidate patterning more so than because, as he rather eloquently states it here, it brought to our attention not just the primacy of "style" in human life but simultaneously the contextual nuances and possibilities for cultural practice that "style" provokes and how these might be played out in specific sociohistorical instances. In the "Wobst 1977" case the ethnographic data set at hand was Yugoslavian dress, which, if taken up again today in light of what has become of and been done with ethnicity and difference in contemporary post-Yugoslavia, takes on an especially poignant and pointed historical and anthropological significance. Such issues get masked, ignored, or avoided all too readily in the face of studies that zoom in on "formal variation," "assemblage variability," and "material culture patterning" in and of themselves.

There are distinct signs here that it is material culture as embedded in human life that is under consideration, more so than the "analysis of variation" in its method-idolatry guise. Yes, almost all of the authors in this volume have a consideration of "variation" close at hand. Arnold revisits the long important approach of ethnoarchaeology, not so much, as he states, to validate source-side models with the archaeological record but to use causal relationships to investigate variation in ancient production organization. In fact, his critique of the two prevalent models in pottery production studies is presented precisely because he is concerned that both mask significant variation in production activities, variation that derives from and is enacted by potters who made "intentional conscious choices based on short-term and

long-term perceptions of their circumstances" (Arnold, this volume).

Chilton is also specifically motivated to revisit (or perhaps visit for the first time in this culture area) the issue of ceramic typologies precisely because she seeks to better understand variation and co-variation across objects—not between (predetermined) groups of objects. On the one hand, it is amazing that we are still having to work away critically at such notions as "types" (see also Dobres, this volume), but given their ingrained and historic primacy in archaeological research, perhaps they will never go away. This state of affairs is a pointed reminder of the astute observations of Wobst and Keene (1983) about the research cone: those who define the point of the cone—in this case, those who defined the basic analytical categories or "types"—control or at least structure all subsequent work. Nonetheless, to move "beyond" types one must review all that the types are and do, citing and appeasing ancestors along the way. By taking up a combination of alternative categories and groupings with a more contextual, microscalar, and social characterization of differing Late Woodland peoples, Chilton—as does Dobres with Magdalenian-period peoples—points the way toward a new understanding of variation, one that invites the query: "what is it about these variations that made them meaningful to the makers and users?"

THERE ARE NO "CONCLUSIONS" HERE
The volume is a success in that there is, with each chapter, immediately more to be read, another step to take in the research and thinking. Wobst's chapter motivates one to go back and get that Bogatyrev (1971) data about dress and hats in Yugoslavia and reconsider them from the point of view of style as interference, style as intervention. Dobres's chapter cries out for one to see just how her reconceptualizations played out in the analysis of the bone and antler assemblages (see Dobres 1995b); what is it about a relatively open and flexible "making system"

that was meaningful to these bone and antler workers, especially in comparison with some of the very constrained or standardized bone/antler making that also went on during Magdalenian times in the French Midi-Pyrénées, as evidenced by the tiny animal head "cutouts" (*découpés;* Buisson et al. 1996), for example?

Chilton's chapter is also a prelude to a closer look at the very cultural contexts that she (rightly) claims to be crucial: this calls for a "zoom in" (so to speak) on some of the more specific and microscalar contexts that are included within the higher-order characterizations of Algonquians as mobile, the Iroquois as settled. Can we glean any closer looks at why the varying attributes were at work in the "referential contexts of social action" (after Hodder 1982a:14)? For example, what is it about the ceramic cooking-jar lip decorations on the big pots hanging in the midst of the house that made them meaningful in the specific contexts of daily life, as she suggests?

Costin herself begins some of the next questions at hand for the study of the North Peru burial assemblages: "What does it mean?" she asks about several of her findings. For example, she asks, "What does it mean to have members of a large labor pool each produce a few objects, when the technology and organizational structure are available for specialized, 'mass' production?" These are the kinds of questions we all should ask as we move along in the interpretive process. All analyses should stop at several points in the process and ask, "What does it or what might it mean?" For Costin's future study she might explore what the abundant ethnographic literature on mortuary practices suggests about the kind of material practices that the making of hundreds and thousands of little *crisoles* seems to be about. It is hard to imagine that the flurry of *crisole* making is not a good deal more than a "reflection of certain aspects of social structure," as Costin suggests.

As with most of the studies here that focus on specific sets of material culture, Arnold's interesting observations about the Comoapan pottery production activities invite him to seek other lines of (hopefully converging) evidence to support the first-round interpretations he presents here. This is when our notions of what constitutes material culture should be stretched, as Arnold suggests, to include such things as the very spatial settings within which production takes place. This is when the dedicated ceramicist must become (or collaborate with, in order to approximate) a multitalented archaeologist. The same is a next step in the study by D. Arnold et al.: What might be the contemporary potters' observations about clay composition? What about an archaeological analysis, even though the probable results as to what one would find and what one would probably miss are plausibly anticipated here? With this solid compositional study now at hand, especially one of such unusual and important time-depth, Arnold et al. could be emboldened to take the next step and ask how they might infer the ways in which the technological activities they now know so well create(d) worlds of value and meaning.

As with any ambitious attempt to bring together diverse and new theoretical approaches with a rich body of empirical observations, Stark's chapter challenges us to take up some of her concepts and inspirations. Although it served her purposes well to combine "technological style," "*habitus,*" and "cultural diacritics" in order to get some general reorientations about "making" onto the table, these theoretical goldmines are, I believe, not so readily conflated. A deeper reading, a sustained inquiry into the nuances and referents of each approach, might elevate the insights about Kalinga ceramics to an even more complex but provocative level. What other aspects, for example, of Kalinga daily practice are—or are not—resonant with the technological styles of ceramic making? Are the particular technological styles elucidated here actively deployed as "cultural diacritics" into some—and not other—referential contexts of social action? And if so, what might this mean?

And so it goes: Go back to our original conceptual inspirations and see how they stand up to our first-round "results"; push ahead and try to find additional lines of evidence that we hope will point toward and reinforce our first-round interpretation; stop and ask ourselves, along the way and at the end, "What is it about these forms, shapes, attributes, uses, techniques, and technologies that might have made them meaningful for the sociohistorical contexts and past peoples we are investigating?"

A CODA

In the Society for American Archaeology symposium that spawned this edited volume two other papers that are not included here presented some ideas that are useful as "bookends" to the volume at hand. On the one hand, Skibo and Schiffer (1996) made a strong argument (not surprisingly) for their behavioral archaeology approach to material culture as *the* primary one that we should adopt. On the other hand, Pfaffenberger (1996) discussed the anthropology of technology in the context of contemporary sociocultural anthropology and ethnography. Both approaches are well published (e.g., Pfaffenberger 1988, 1992; Schiffer 1976, 1992; Schiffer and Skibo 1987) and widely available. But from each I have drawn a few caveats as a platform for some ending remarks.

First, from Pfaffenberger (1996) came the provocative claim that perhaps the greatest achievement of the social and cultural anthropology of the latter half of the twentieth century is the demonstration that people actively construct the social and cultural worlds in which they live. Unfortunately, it still takes an impassioned and informed voice like his to make sure that this approach includes technological activities and the material world, although there is an increasing literature along these lines (e.g., Ingold 1990; MacKenzie 1991; the new *Journal of Material Culture;* and a new publication series, Materializing Culture [Berg Publishers]). In making palpable that an archaeological study of material culture must be connected

to a wider theoretical matrix from the human sciences, contemporary studies, including those in this volume, have contributed not only to the idea that people actively construct their social and cultural worlds but to showing precisely how this happens.

The resonating perspective that has stimulated the kinds of studies included in this volume holds that technological activities create worlds of meaning and value, even if all studies have yet to provide the specificity of meanings at issue in any instance. This perspective holds for archaeology the very real possibility of collapsing the old linear ladder of inference (as identified with Hawkes [1954]) into not only a more multidimensional but a very operational set of premises, whereby the materials of the archaeological record are understood as embedded in multiple referential contexts of social action and produced out of cultural significance.

Second, from Skibo and Schiffer (1996), who advocated behavioral archaeology as a "remedy" to the extremes of theoretical positioning in contemporary archaeology, I take their position as a springboard. Behavioral archaeology is an important and relevant perspective that has much to offer to the archaeological study of material culture, especially for certain scales of analysis. So far it has not been particularly at home once we edge toward engaging with the fields of meaning—cultural meaning(s)—that are surely integral to the making and using of the material world by humans. In the proposition that behavioral archaeology be taken as a "remedy" to the extremes of theoretical positioning in contemporary archaeology, Skibo and Schiffer (1996) evoke the ongoing theoretical angst (or at least a healthy theoretical introspection) that characterizes the discipline of archaeology today. In this regard what is striking about the chapters in this edited volume is that they are not very bothered or dissuaded by such angst and, indeed, "get on with it" in most productive ways.

Despite any programmatic offer of *a* remedy, there is probably not nor should there be any *one* way to do archaeology. There are no remedies, only multiple pathways "in" to the understandings of the pasts of humans. Although it might be reassuring indeed to think that we could isolate either "behavior" or "ideas" as the source for what we take as the archaeological record, surely archaeology is more complex than that. Surely it is a complex interplay of ideas, ideology, and long-standing cultural premises with individual human actors who are just as likely to be engaged in cultural production—whether it be of things or of social relations, if not both simultaneously—that is as situational and opportunistic as it is "rule-bound behavior." This is precisely why the *archaeological* study of and inquiry into material culture—in the broadest sense of the term—is so much more crucial than paradigmatic posturing.

Because humans worked from within their own mundane worlds, they invented and created materials, forms, images, and objects. They, thus, simultaneously invented their worlds. What they made and the processes by which this happened galvanized the production of meanings; making (as so many of the papers in this volume show) *is* social practice. As such, our inquiry can be simultaneously about the making *and* the circumstances of the objects and material world. To do this we may bring in the technical details of ceramic production or bone/antler working, the closely honed study of variation in differing contexts, and/or inspiration from ethnoarchaeological observations.

This volume underlines why, at least at this point in the development of the field, there need not be one programmatic stance for the study of material culture from an archaeological perspective. Of necessity, each so-called approach has its foci, its scale(s) of analysis, its interpretive goals, its ways of working, its so-called methods. Although some will yield "results" that are more satisfactory to some, this too will depend on what we want from our archaeologies. Most of us would probably agree that we seek an empirically grounded set of understandings that

can inform on the human condition and experiences in the past, which can be the basis for inferring both large-scale cultural processes and more microscalar practices of people in the world—whether these understandings are then used to explore such things as our relationship with the past or to tell an informed narrative of human lives in the past, or both. To these ends, this volume makes a significant contribution.

Notes

1. With a new or newly recognized (if not celebrated) instability of "group" in the cultural whirls of social anthropology at the end of the millennium—and therefore a subject matter that defies being "fixed" for study—it is not surprising that attention has been turned by some to the study of material culture, the objects of culture, and the "social life of things" (after Appadurai 1986) that have, for many past decades, been marginalized or flat out ignored (see Stocking 1985). In archaeology excavation has long held high preferential status as the primary means of research (e.g., Gero 1985, 1994). With the challenge to the primacy of excavation, especially in those archaeologies contested by indigenous peoples (e.g., in Australia, North America), museums and collections have increased in value and research interest. Thus in both subdisciplines—social anthropology and archaeology—there has been a turn to new engagements with materiality.

2. For the *techniques et culture* approach the conceptual motivations go back to at least Mauss (1979) and certainly center on the work of the archaeologist, prehistorian, and ethnologist André Leroi-Gourhan (e.g., 1943, 1945, 1964, and, in English translation, 1993). Many "disciples" of this approach have been helpful to the North American audience by often publishing in English for at least a decade (e.g., Lemonnier 1986, 1993; see other references as listed in Dobres and Hoffman 1994). For the "technological style" approach the conceptual bases can be found in Lechtman and Merrill (1977) and center on ethnographic and anthropological studies of art, technology (Merrill 1968), and material culture, along with the work of Cyril Stanley Smith (1978), most of which seem to have been at least somewhat influenced by structuralist perspectives, as was Leroi-Gourhan.

References

Adams, W. Y., and E. W. Adams
1991 *Archaeological Typology and Practical Reality.* Cambridge University Press, Cambridge.

Agger, B.
1991 Critical Theory, Poststructuralism, Postmodernism: Their Sociological Relevance. *Annual Review of Sociology* 17:105–131.

Alix, P., A. Averbouh, L. Binter, P. Bodu, A. Boguszewski, C. Cochin, V. Deloze, P. Gouge, V. Krier, C. Leroyer, D. Mordant, M. Philippe, J.-L. Rieu, P. Rodriquez, and B. Valentin
1993 Nouvelles Recherches sue le Peuplement Magdalénien de l'Interfluve Seine-Yonne: Le Grand Canton et Le Tureau des Gardes à Marolles-sur-Seine (Seine-et-Marne). *Bulletin de la Société Préhistorique Française* 90(3):196–218.

Alonso, A. M.
1994 The Politics of Space, Time, and Substance: State Formation, Nationalism, and Ethnicity. *Annual Review of Anthropology* 23:379–405.

Ames, K. M.
1995 Chiefly Power and Household Production on the Northwest Coast. In *Foundations of Social Inequality,* edited by T. D. Price and G. M. Feinman, pp. 155–187. Plenum Press, New York.

Anderson, B.
1991 *Imagined Communities.* Revised ed. Verso, London.

Annis, M. B.
1985 Resistance and Change: Pottery Making in Sardinia. *World Archaeology* 17(2):240–255.

Appadurai, A.
1986 *The Social Life of Things: Commodities in Cultural Perspective.* Cambridge University Press, Cambridge.

Arnold, D. E.
1971 Ethnomineralogy of Ticul, Yucatán Potters: Etics and Emics. *American Antiquity* 36:20–40.

1975 Principles of Paste Analysis: A Preliminary Formulation. *Journal of the Steward Anthropological Society* 6(1):33–47.

1980 Localized Exchange: An Ethnoarchaeological Perspective. In *Models and Methods in Regional Exchange,* SAA Papers No. 1, edited by R. E. Fry, pp. 147–150. Society for American Archaeology, Washington, D.C.

1981 A Model for the Identification of Non-local Ceramic Distribution: A View from the Present. In *Production and Distribution: A Ceramic Viewpoint,* edited by H. Howard and E. L. Morris, pp. 31–44. BAR International Series 120, Oxford.

1985 *Ceramic Theory and Cultural Process.* Cambridge University Press, Cambridge.

1993 *Ecology and Ceramic Production in an Andean Community.* Cambridge University Press, Cambridge.

Arnold, D. E., and B. F. Bohor
1977 An Ancient Clay Mine at Yo' K'at, Yucatán. *American Antiquity* 42:575–582.

Arnold, D. E., H. Neff, and R. L. Bishop
  1991 Compositional Analysis and "Sources" of Pottery: An Ethnoarchaeological Approach. *American Anthropologist* 93:70–90.

Arnold, D. E., and A. L. Nieves
  1992 Factors Affecting Ceramic Standardization. In *Ceramic Production and Distribution: An Integrated Approach,* edited by G. J. Bey III and C. A. Pool, pp. 93–113. Westview Press, Boulder.

Arnold, D. E., P. M. Rice, W. A Jester, W. N. Deutsch, B. K. Lee, and R. I. Kirsh
  1978 Neutron Activation Analysis of Contemporary Pottery and Pottery Materials from the Valley of Guatemala. In *The Ceramics of Kaminaljuyu,* edited by R. K. Wetherington, pp. 543–586. Pennsylvania State University Press, University Park.

Arnold, P. J., III
  1988 Household Ceramic Assemblage Attributes in the Sierra de los Tuxtlas, Veracruz, Mexico. *Journal of Anthropological Research* 44:357–383.
  1989 Prehispanic Household Ceramic Production Variability at Matacapan, Veracruz, Mexico. In *Households and Communities,* edited by S. MacEachern, D. Archer, and R. Gavin, pp. 388–397. Archaeological Association of the University of Calgary, Calgary.
  1990 The Organization of Refuse Disposal and Ceramic Production Within Contemporary Mexican Houselots. *American Anthropologist* 92:915–932.
  1991a *Domestic Ceramic Production and Spatial Organization: A Mexican Case Study in Ethnoarchaeology.* Cambridge University Press, Cambridge.
  1991b Dimensional Standardization and Production Scale in Mesoamerican Ceramics. *Latin American Antiquity* 2:363–370.
  1994 Ceramic Ecology: Discussion. Presented at the 91st Annual Meeting of the American Anthropological Association, Washington, D.C.
  1998 Ceramic Ethnoarchaeology: Caught between "Coming of Age" and "Showing Its Age." *Reviews in Anthropology* 27(1):17–32.

Arnold, P. J., III, C. A. Pool, R. R. Kneebone, and R. S. Santley
  1993 Intensive Ceramic Production and Classic-Period Political Economy in the Sierra de los Tuxtlas, Veracruz, Mexico. *Ancient Mesoamerica* 4:175–191.

Arnold, P. J., III, and R. S. Santley
  1993 Household Ceramics Production at Middle Classic Period Matacapan. In *Prehispanic Domestic Units in Western Mesoamerica,* edited by R. S. Santley and K. G. Hirth, pp. 227–248. CRC Press, Boca Raton, Fla.

Aronson, M., J. M. Skibo, and M. T. Stark
  1994 Production and Use Technologies in Kalinga Pottery. In *Kalinga Ethnoarchaeology,* edited by W. A. Longacre and J. M. Skibo, pp. 83–112. Smithsonian Institution Press, Washington, D.C.

Audouze, F.
  1987 The Paris Basin in Magdalenian Times. In *The Pleistocene Old World: Regional Perspectives,* edited by O. Soffer, pp. 183–200. Plenum Press, New York.
  1988 Les Activités de Boucherie à Vérberie. *Technologie Préhistorique* 25:97–111.
  1992 L'Occupation Magdalénienne du Bassin Parisien. In *Le Peuplement Magdalénien: Paléogeographie Physique et Humaine,* edited by J.-P. Rigaud, H. Laville, and B. Vandermeersch, pp. 345–356. Editions du Comité des Travaux Historiques et Scientifiques, Paris.

Bacdayan, A.
  1967 *The Peace Pact System of the Kalingas in the Modern World.* Ph.D. dissertation, Cornell University. University Microfilms, Ann Arbor.

Bahn, P.
  1977 Seasonal Migration in Southwest France during the Late Glacial Period. *Journal of Archaeological Science* 4(3):245–257.
  1982 Inter-Site and Inter-Regional Links during the Upper Palaeolithic: The Pyrenean Evidence. *Oxford Journal of Archaeology* 1(3):247–268.

1984 *Pyrenean Prehistory: A Palaeoeconomic Survey of the French Sites.* Aris and Phillips, Wiltshire.

Baker, V. G.
1980 Archaeological Visibility of Afro-American Culture: An Example from Black Lucy's Garden, Andover. In *Archaeological Perspectives on Ethnicity in America: Afro-American and Asian-American Culture History,* edited by R. L. Schuyler, pp. 29–37. Baywood, New York.

Baldwin, S. J.
1987 Roomsize Patterns: A Quantitative Method for Approaching Ethnic Identification in Architecture. In *Ethnicity and Culture,* edited by R. Auger, M. Glass, S. MacEachern, and P. McCartney, pp. 163–174. Archaeological Association of the University of Calgary, Calgary.

Baram, U.
1989 "Boys, Be Ambitious": Landscape Manipulation in Nineteenth Century Western Massachusetts. Unpublished Master's thesis, Department of Anthropology, University of Massachusetts.

Barrett, J. C.
1990 The Monumentality of Death: The Character of Early Bronze Age Mortuary Mounds in Southern Britain. *World Archaeology* 22:179–189.

Barth, F.
1969 Introduction. In *Ethnic Groups and Boundaries,* edited by F. Barth, pp. 9–38. Little, Brown, Boston.

Barton, R. F.
1949 *The Kalingas, Their Institutions and Custom Law.* University of Chicago Press, Chicago.

Beck, L. A. (editor)
1995 *Regional Approaches to Mortuary Analysis.* Plenum Press, New York.

Bégouën, R., and J. Clottes
1981 Nouvelles Fouilles dans la Salle des Morts de la Caverne d'Enlène à Montesquieu-Avantès (Ariège). *Congrès Préhistorique de France,* XXIeme Session (Quercy):33–69.

Beier, T., and H. Mommsen
1994 Modified Mahalanobis Filters for Grouping Pottery by Chemical Composition. *Archaeometry* 36:287–306.

Benco, N.
1988 Morphological Standardization: An Approach to the Study of Craft Production. In *A Pot for All Reasons: Ceramic Ecology Revisited,* edited by C. C. Kolb and L. M. Lackey, pp. 57–71. Laboratory of Anthropology, Temple University, Philadelphia, Pa.

Bendremer, J. C. M.
1993 Late Woodland Settlement and Subsistence in Eastern Connecticut. Unpublished Ph.D. dissertation, University of Connecticut, Storrs.

Bendremer, J. C. M., and R. E. Dewar
1994 The Advent of Prehistoric Maize in New England. In *Corn and Culture in the Prehistoric New World,* edited by S. Johannessen and C. A. Hastorf, pp. 369–393. Westview, Boulder, Colo.

Berger, J.
1973 *Ways of Seeing.* Viking, New York.

Bernbeck, R.
1995 Lasting Alliances and Emerging Competition: Economic Developments in Early Mesopotamia. *Journal of Anthropological Archaeology* 14:1–25.

Bernstein, D. J.
1992 Prehistoric Use of Plant Foods in the Narragansett Bay Region. *Man in the Northeast* 44:1–13.

Bey, G. J., III, and C. A. Pool (editors)
1992 *Ceramic Production and Distribution: An Integrated Approach.* Westview Press, Boulder, Colo.

Bieber, A. M., Jr., D. W. Brooks, G. Harbottle, and E. V. Sayre
1976 Application of Multivariate Techniques to Analytical Data on Aegean Ceramics. *Archaeometry* 18:59–74.

Bijker, W., T. Hughes, and T. Pinch (editors)
1987 *The Social Construction of Technological Systems: New Directions in the Sociology and History of Technology.* MIT Press, Cambridge, Mass.

Binford, L. R.
1962 Archaeology as Anthropology. *American Antiquity* 28:217–225.

1965 Archaeological Systematics and the Study of Culture Process. *American Antiquity* 31:203–210.

1966 A Preliminary Analysis of Functional Variability in the Mousterian of Levallois Facies. *American Anthropologist* 68:238–259.

1968 Some Comments on Historical versus Processual Archaeology. *Southwestern Journal of Anthropology* 24(3):267–275.

1971 Mortuary Practices: Their Study and Their Potential. In *Approaches to the Social Dimensions of Mortuary Practices,* edited by J. A. Brown, pp. 6–29. Memoirs No. 25. Society for American Archaeology. Washington, D.C.

1972 Model Building-Paradigms, and the Current State of Palaeolithic Research. In *An Archaeological Perspective,* edited by L. Binford, pp. 252–294. Academic Press, New York.

1973 Interassemblage Variability–The Mousterian and the 'Functional' Argument. In *Explanation of Culture Change: Models in Prehistory,* edited by C. Renfrew, pp. 227–254. Duckworth, London.

1977a Forty-Seven Trips: A Case Study in the Character of Archaeological Formation Processes. In *Contributions to Anthropology: The Interior Peoples of Northern Alaska,* edited by E. Hall, pp. 299–351. Ottawa National Museum of Man, Mercury Series, No. 49.

1977b General Introduction. In *For Theory Building in Archaeology,* edited by L. R. Binford, pp. 1–10. Academic Press, New York.

1978 *Nunamiut Ethnoarchaeology.* Academic Press, New York.

1980 Willow Smoke and Dog's Tails: Hunter-Gatherer Settlement Systems and Archaeological Site Formation. *American Antiquity* 45:4–20.

1981 Middle-Range Research and the Role of Actualist Studies. In *Bones: Ancient Men and Modern Myths,* edited by L. R. Binford, pp. 21–30. Academic Press, New York.

1982 Objectivity, Explanation, and Archaeology 1980. In *Theory and Explanation in Archaeology,* edited by A. C. Renfrew, M. J. Rowlands, and B. Segraves-Whallon, pp. 125–138. Academic Press, New York.

1983 *In Pursuit of the Past: Decoding the Archaeological Record.* Thames and Hudson, New York.

1989 *Debating Archaeology.* Academic Press, San Diego.

Binford, L. R. (editor)
1981 *Bones: Ancient Men and Modern Myths.* Academic Press, New York.

1983 *Working at Archaeology.* Academic Press, New York.

Binford, S. R. and L. R. Binford (editors)
1968 *New Perspectives in Archaeology.* Aldine, Chicago.

Bishop, R. L.
1975 *Western Lowland May Ceramic Trade: An Archaeological Application of Nuclear Chemistry and Geological Data Analysis.* Unpublished Ph. D. dissertation, Department of Anthropology, Southern Illinois University, Carbondale.

1980 Aspects of Ceramic Compositional Modeling. In *Models and Methods in Regional Exchange,* SAA Papers No. 1, edited by R. E. Fry, pp. 47–66. Society for American Archaeology, Washington, D.C.

Bishop, R. L., and H. Neff
1989 Compositional Data Analysis in Archaeology. In *Archaeological Chemistry IV,* edited by R. O. Allen, pp. 576–586. Advances in Chemistry Series 220, American Chemical Society, Washington, D.C.

Bishop, R. L., R. L. Rands, and G. R. Holley
1982 Ceramic Compositional Analysis in Archaeological Perspective. In *Advances in Archaeological Method and Theory,* vol. 5, edited by M. B. Schiffer, pp. 275–330. Academic Press, New York.

Blackman, M. J., G. J. Stein, and P. B. Vandiver
1993 The Standardization Hypothesis and Ceramic Mass Production: Technological, Compositional, and Metric Indexes of Craft Specialization at Tell Leilan, Syria. *American Antiquity* 58:60–80.

Blanton, R., G. M. Feinman, S. A. Kowalewski, and P. N. Peregrine

1996 A Dual-Processual Theory for the Evolution of Mesoamerican Civilization. *Current Anthropology* 37:1–15.

Boast, R.

1997 A Small Company of Actors. A Critique of Style. *Journal of Material Culture* 2(2):173–198.

Bodenhorn, B.

1990 "I'm Not the Great Hunter, My Wife Is": Iñupiat and Anthropological Models of Gender. *Inuit Studies* 14(1–2):55–74.

Bogatyrev, P.

1971 *The Functions of Folk Costume in Moravian Slovakia.* Mouton, The Hague.

Bonfante, L.

1989 Nudity as a Costume in Classical Art. *American Journal of Archaeology* 93(4):543–570.

Bordes, F.

1961 Mousterian Cultures in France. *Science* 134:803–810.

1972 *A Tale of Two Caves.* Harper and Row, New York.

Bourdieu, P.

1977 *Outline of a Theory of Practice.* Cambridge University Press, Cambridge.

Bragdon, K. J.

1996 *Native People of Southern New England, 1500–1650.* University of Oklahoma Press, Norman.

Braun, D. P.

1977 Middle Woodland–(Early) Woodland Social Change in the Prehistoric Central Midwestern U.S. Unpublished Ph.D. dissertation, Department of Anthropology, University of Michigan, Ann Arbor.

1980 Experimental Interpretation of Ceramic Vessel Use on the Basis of Rim and Neck Formal Attributes. In *The Navajo Project: Archaeological Investigations, Page to Phoenix 500 KV Southern Transmission Line,* edited by D. Fiero et al., pp. 171–231. Museum of Northern Arizona Research Paper No. 11. Flagstaff, Ariz.

1983 Pots as Tools. In *Archaeological Hammers and Theories,* edited by J. A. Moore and A. S. Keene, pp. 107–134. Academic Press, New York.

1987 Coevolution of Sedentism, Pottery Technology, and Horticulture in the Central Midwest, 200 B.C.–A.D. 600. In *Emergent Horticultural Economies of the Eastern Woodlands,* edited by W. F. Keegan, pp. 153–216. Center for Archaeological Investigations Occasional Paper No. 7. Southern Illinois University, Carbondale.

1995 Style, Selection, and Historicity. In *Style, Society, and Person: Archaeological and Ethnological Perspectives,* edited by C. Carr and J. E. Neitzel, pp. 123–141. Plenum Press, New York.

Braun, D. P., and S. Plog

1982 Evolution of "Tribal" Social Networks: Theory and Prehistoric North American Evidence. *American Antiquity* 47:504–523.

Breuil, H.

1912 Les Subdivisions du Paléolithique Supérieur et Leur Signification. *Congrès d'Anthropologie et d'Archéologie* 1:165–238.

Brown, J. A.

1995 On Mortuary Analysis—with Special Reference to the Saxe-Binford Research Program. In *Regional Approaches to Mortuary Analysis,* edited by L. Beck, pp. 3–28. Plenum Press, New York.

Brown, J. A. (editor)

1971 *Approaches to the Social Dimensions of Mortuary Practices.* Memoirs No. 25. Society for American Archaeology. Washington, D.C.

Brumbach, H.-J.

1975 "Iroquoian" Ceramics in "Algonkian" Territory. *Man in the Northeast* 10:17–28.

Brumfiel, E.

1991 Distinguished Lecture in Archaeology: Breaking and Entering the Ecosystem: Gender, Class, and Faction Steal the Show. *American Anthropologist* 94:551–567.

Brumfiel, E., and T. Earle

1987 Specialization, Exchange, and Complex Societies: An Introduction. In *Specialization, Exchange, and Complex Societies,* edited by E. Brumfiel and T. Earle, pp. 1–9. Cambridge University Press, Cambridge.

Buisson, D., C. Fritz, D. Kandel, G. Pinçon, G. Sauvet, and G. Tosello

1996 Analyse Formelle des Contours Découpés de Têtes de Chevaux: Implications Archéologiques. In *Pyrénées Préhistoriques: Arts et Sociétés,* edited by H. Delporte and J. Clottes, pp. 327–340. Editions du C. T. H. S., Paris.

Byers, D. S., and I. Rouse

1960 A Re-Examination of the Guida Farm. *Bulletin of the Archaeological Society of Connecticut* 30:5–39.

Cameron, C.

1998 Coursed Adobe Architecture, Style, and Social Boundaries in the American Southwest. In *The Archaeology of Social Boundaries,* edited by M. T. Stark. Smithsonian Institution Press, Washington, D.C.

Carr, C.

1986 Toward a Synthetic Theory of Artifact Design. Paper presented at the 51st Annual Meeting of the Society for American Archaeology, Denver.

Carr, C., and J. E. Neitzel

1995a Integrating Approaches to Material Style in Theory and Philosophy. In *Style, Society, and Person: Archaeological and Ethnological Perspectives,* edited by C. Carr and J. E. Neitzel, pp. 3–20. Plenum Press, New York.

1995b Future Directions for Material Style Studies. In *Style, Society, and Person: Archaeological and Ethnological Perspectives,* edited by C. Carr and J. E. Neitzel, pp. 437–59. Plenum Press, New York.

Carr, C., and J. E. Neitzel (editors)

1995 *Style, Society, and Person: Archaeological and Ethnological Perspectives.* Plenum Press, New York.

Cassedy, D., P. Webb, T. Mills, H. Mills, and Garrow and Associates

1993 New Data on Maize Horticulture and Subsistence in Southwestern Connecticut. Paper presented at the 33d Meeting of the Northeastern Anthropological Association, Danbury, Conn.

Castillo, L. J., and C. B. Donnan

1994 La Ocupación Moche de San José de Moro, Jequetepeque. In *Moche: Propuestas y Perspectivas,* edited by S. Uceda and E. Mujica, pp. 93–146. Travaux de l'Institut Francais d'Etudes Andines Vol. 79. Universidad Nacional de La Libertad, Trujillo, Lima.

Ceci, L.

1979 Maize Cultivation in Coastal New York: The Archaeological, Agronomical and Documentary Evidence. *North American Archaeologist* 1(1):45–74.

1990 Radiocarbon Dating "Village" Sites in Coastal New York: Settlement Pattern Change in the Middle to Late Woodland. *Man in the Northeast* 39:1–28.

Celerier, G.

1992 A Propos de Trois Habitats Magdaleniens de la Valée de la Dronne et la Notion de Site de Rassemblement. *Paleo* 4:155–159.

Chapman, R., I. Kinnes, and K. Randsborg (editors)

1981 *The Archaeology of Death.* Cambridge University Press, New York.

Childs, S. T.

1991 Style, Technology, and Iron Smelting in Bantu-Speaking Africa. *Journal of Anthropological Archaeology* 10:332–359.

1998 After All, a Hoe Bought a Wife: The Social Dimensions of Iron Working among the Toro of East Africa. In *Making Culture: Essays on Technological Practice, Politics, and World Views,* edited by M.-A. Dobres and C. Hoffman. Smithsonian Institution Press, Washington, D.C., in press.

Chilton, E. S.

1996 *Embodiments of Choice: Native American Ceramic Diversity in the New England Interior.* Unpublished Ph.D. dissertation, Department of Anthropology, University of Massachusetts, Amherst.

1998a The Cultural Origins of Technical Choice: Unraveling Algonquian and

Iroquoian Ceramic Traditions in the Northeast. In *The Archaeology of Social Boundaries,* edited by M. T. Stark. Smithsonian Institution Press, Washington.

1998b Mobile Farmers of Pre-Contact Southern New England: The Archaeological and Ethnohistoric Evidence. In *Current Northeast Paleoethnobotany,* edited by J. P. Hart, New York State Museum Bulletin, in press.

Chodoff, D.

1979 Investigaciones Arqueológicas en San José de Moro. In *Arqueología Peruana,* edited by R. Matos M., pp. 37–47. Universidad Nacional Mayor de San Marcos, Lima.

Christensen, M.

1995 In the Beginning Was the Potter: Material Culture as Mode of Expression and Anthropological Object. *Folk* 37:5–24.

Claassen, C. (editor)

1992 *Exploring Gender through Archaeology.* Prehistory Press, Madison, Wis.

1994 *Women in Archaeology.* University of Pennsylvania Press, Philadelphia.

Clark, G.

1991 A Paradigm Is Like an Onion: Reflections on My Biases. In *Perspectives on the Past: Theoretical Biases in Mediterranean Hunter-Gatherer Research,* edited by G. Clark, pp. 79–108. University of Pennsylvania Press, Philadelphia.

Clark, J. E.

1991 Statecraft and State Crafts: A Reconsideration of Mesoamerican Obsidian Industry. Paper presented at the 56th Annual Meeting of the Society for American Archaeology, Chicago.

1995 Craft Specialization as an Archaeological Category. In *Research in Economic Anthropology,* vol. 16, edited by B. L. Isaac, pp. 267–294. JAI Press, Greenwich.

Clark, J. E., and W. Parry

1990 Craft Specialization and Cultural Complexity. *Research in Economic Anthropology* 12:289–346.

Clark, J. G. D.

1953 The Economic Approach to Prehistory. Reprinted in *Contemporary Archaeology: A Guide to Theory and Contributions,* edited by M. Leone, pp. 62–77. Southern Illinois University Press, Carbondale.

Clarke, D. L.

1968 *Analytical Archaeology.* Methuen, London.

1972 *Models in Archaeology.* Methuen, London.

Clottes, J.

1989 Le Magdalénien des Pyrénées. In *Le Magdalénien en Europe: La Structuration du Magdalénien,* edited by J.-P. Rigaud, pp. 281–360. ERAUL No. 38, Université de Liège, Liège.

1990 The Parietal Art of the Late Magdalenian. Translated by P. Bahn. *Antiquity* 64:527–648.

Clottes, J., and F. Rouzaud

1983 La Caverne des Eglises à Ussat (Ariège): Fouilles 1964–1977. *Bulletin de la Société Préhistorique Ariège-Pyrénées* 38:23–81.

1984 Grotte des Eglises. In *L'Art des Cavernes: Atlas des Grottes Ornées Paléolithiques Françaises,* pp. 428–432. Imprimerie Nationale, Paris.

Cockburn, C.

1985 The Material of Male Power. In *The Social Shaping of Technology: How the Refrigerator Got Its Hum,* edited by D. MacKenzie and J. Wajcman, pp. 125–146. Open University Press, Milton Keynes.

Cockburn, C., and S. Ormrod

1993 *Gender and Technology in the Making.* Sage, London.

Cogswell, J. W., H. Neff, and M. D. Glascock

1996 The Effect of Firing Temperature on the Elemental Characterization of Pottery. *Journal of Archaeological Science* 23:283–287.

Cohen, A.

1974 *Two-dimensional Man: An Essay on the Anthropology of Power and Symbolism in Complex Society.* University of California Press, Berkeley.

Cohen, R.

1981 Evolutionary Epistemology and Values. *Current Anthropology* 22:201–218.

Coleman, S., and J. Elsner
1994 The Pilgrim's Progress: Art, Architecture and Ritual Movement at Sinai. *World Archaeology* 26(1): 73–89.

Collins, D., and J. Onians
1978 The Origins of Art. *Art History* 1(1):1–25.

Conkey, M. W.
1978 *An Analysis of Design Structure: Variability among Magdalenian Engraved Bones from North Coastal Spain.* Unpublished Ph.D. dissertation, Department of Anthropology, University of Chicago.
1980 The Identification of Prehistoric Hunter-Gatherer Aggregation Sites: The Case of Altamira. *Current Anthropology* 21:609–630.
1982 Boundedness in Art and Society. In *Symbolic and Structural Archaeology,* edited by I. Hodder, pp. 115–128. Cambridge University Press, Cambridge.
1989 The Place of Material Culture Studies in Contemporary Anthropology. In *Perspectives on Anthropological Collections from the American Southwest: Proceedings of a Symposium,* edited by A. L. Hedlund, pp. 13–32. Anthropological Research Papers No. 40. Arizona State University, Tempe.
1991 Does It Make a Difference? Feminist Thinking and Archaeologies of Gender. In *The Archaeology of Gender,* edited by D. Walde and N. Willows, pp. 24–33. Proceedings of the 1989 Chacmool Conference. Archaeological Association of the University of Calgary, Calgary.
1992a Preface. *Kroeber Anthropological Society Papers* 73–74:iii–iv.
1992b Les Sites d'Agrégation et la Réparation de l'Art Mobilier, Ou: Y-a-t-il des Sites d'Agrégation Magdalénien? In *Le Peuplement Magdalénien: Paléogeographie Physique et Humaine,* edited by J.-P. Rigaud, H. Laville, and B. Vandermeersch, pp. 19–25. Editions du Comité des

Travaux Historiques et Scientifiques, Paris.

Conkey, M. W., and J. M. Gero
1991 Tensions, Pluralities, and Engendering Archaeology: An Introduction to Women and Prehistory. In *Engendering Archaeology: Women and Prehistory,* edited by J. M. Gero and M. W. Conkey, pp. 3–30. Basil Blackwell, Oxford.

Conkey, M. W., and C. A. Hastorf
1990 Introduction. In *The Uses of Style in Archaeology,* edited by M. W. Conkey and C. A. Hastorf, pp. 1–4. Cambridge University Press, Cambridge.

Conkey, M. W., and C. A. Hastorf (editors)
1990 *The Uses of Style in Archaeology.* Cambridge University Press, Cambridge.

Conkey, M. W., and J. Spector
1984 Archaeology and the Study of Gender. In *Advances in Archaeological Method and Theory,* vol. 7, edited by M. B. Schiffer, pp. 1–38. Academic Press, New York.

Conrad, G.
1982 The Burial Platforms of Chan Chan: Some Social and Political Implications. In *Chan Chan: Andean Desert City,* edited by M. E. Moseley and K. C. Day, pp. 87–118. University of New Mexico Press, Albuquerque.

Cordell, L. S., and V. J. Yannie
1991 Ethnicity, Ethnogenesis, and the Individual: A Processual Approach Toward Dialogue. In *Processual and Postprocessual Archaeologies: Multiple Ways of Knowing the Past,* edited by R. W. Preucel, pp. 96–107. Center for Archaeological Investigations Occasional Paper No. 10. Southern Illinois University, Carbondale.

Costin, C.
1986 *From Chiefdom to Empire State: Ceramic Economy among the Pre-Hispanic Wanka of Highland Peru.* Ph.D. dissertation, University of California, Los Angeles. University Microfilms, Ann Arbor.
1991 Craft Specialization: Issues in Defining, Documenting, and Explaining

the Organization of Production. In *Archaeological Method and Theory,* vol. 3, edited by M. B. Schiffer, pp. 1–56. University of Arizona Press, Tucson.

1996 Exploring the Relationship between Gender and Craft in Complex Societies: Methodological and Theoretical Issues of Gender Attribution. In *Gender and Archaeology,* edited by R. Wright, pp. 111–137. University of Pennsylvania Press, Philadelphia.

1998a Housewives, Chosen Women, and Skilled Men: Cloth Production and Social Identity in the Late Pre-Hispanic Andes. In *Craft and Social Identity,* edited by C. Costin and R. Wright. Archaeological Papers of the American Anthropological Association No. 8. Washington, D.C.

1998b Introduction. In *Craft and Social Identity,* edited by C. Costin and R. Wright. Archaeological Papers of the American Anthropological Association No. 8. Washington, D.C.

Costin, C., and M. Hagstrum

1995 Standardization, Labor Investment, Skill, and the Organization of Ceramic Production in Late Prehispanic Peru. *American Antiquity* 60:619–639.

Cowgill, G. L.

1982 Clusters of Objects and Associations between Variables: Two Approaches to Archaeological Classification. In *Essays on Archaeological Typology,* edited by R. Whallon and J. A. Brown, pp. 30–55. Center for American Archaeology Press, Evanston, Ill.

1993 Distinguished Lecture in Archaeology: Beyond Criticizing New Archaeology. *American Anthropologist* 95:551–573.

Cresswell, R.

1990 "A New Technology" Revisited. *Archaeological Review from Cambridge* (1):39–54.

Cronon, W.

1983 *Changes in the Land: Indians, Colonists, and the Ecology of New England.* Hill and Wang, New York.

Cross, J.

1990 *Specialized Production in Non-*

Stratified Society: An Example from the Late Archaic in the Northeast. Unpublished Ph.D. dissertation, Department of Anthropology, University of Massachusetts, Amherst.

Csikszentmihalyi, M., and E. Rochberg-Halton

1981 *The Meaning of Things: Domestic Symbols and the Self.* Cambridge University Press, Cambridge.

Culler, J.

1994 Introduction: What's the Point? In *The Point of Theory: Practices of Cultural Analysis,* edited by M. Bal and I. E. Boer, pp. 13–17. Amsterdam University Press, Amsterdam.

D'Altroy, T., and T. Earle

1985 Staple Finance, Wealth Finance, and Storage in the Inka Political Economy. *Current Anthropology* 26:187–206.

David, F., and J. Enloe

1992 Chasse Saisonnière des Magdaléniens du Bassin Parisien. *Bulletin et Mémoire de la Société d'Anthropologie de Paris* 4(3–4): 167–174.

1993 L'Exploitation des Animaux Sauvages de la Fin du Paléolithique Moyen au Magdalénien. In *Exploitation des Animaux Sauvages à Travers le Temps,* pp. 29–47. Editions APDCA, Juan-les-Pins.

David, N., and H. David-Hennig

1972 The Ethnography of Pottery: A Fulani Case Study Seen in Archaeological Perspective. *McCaleb Module in Anthropology* 21, pp. 1–29. Addison-Wesley Modular Publications, Reading, Mass.

David, N., and A. S. MacEachern

1988 The Mandara Archaeological Project: Preliminary Results of the 1984 Season. In *Le Milieu et les Hommes: Recherches Comparatives et Historiques dans le Bassin du Lac Tchad,* edited by D. Barreteau and H. Tourneux, pp. 51–80. Editions de l'ORSTOM, Paris.

David, N., and I. Robertson

1996 Competition and Change in Two Traditional African Iron Industries. In *The Culture and Technology of African Iron Working,* edited by P.

Schmidt, pp. 128–144. University Press of Florida, Gainesville.

David, N., J. Sterner, and K. Gavua
1988   Why Pots Are Decorated. *Current Anthropology* 29:365–389.

David, S., F. Séara, and A. Thevenin
1994   Territoires Magdaléniens: Occupation et Exploitation de l'Espace à la Fin du Paléolithique Supérieur dans l'Est de la France. *L'Anthropologie* 98:666–673.

Dean, J. S.
1988   The View from the North: An Anasazi Perspective on the Mogollon. *The Kiva* 53:197–199.

DeBoer, W. R.
1974   Ceramic Longevity and Archaeological Interpretation: An Example from the Upper Acayali, Peru. *American Antiquity* 39:335–343.
1986   Pillage and Production in the Amazon: A View through the Conibo of the Ucayali Basin, Eastern Peru. *World Archaeology* 18:231–246.
1990   Interaction, Imitation, and Communication as Expressed in Style: The Ucayali Experience. In *The Uses of Style in Archaeology,* edited by M. W. Conkey and C. A. Hastorf, pp. 82–104. Cambridge University Press, Cambridge.

DeBoer, W. R., and D. Lathrap
1979   The Making and Breaking of Shipibo-Conibo Ceramics. In *Ethnoarchaeology: Implications of Ethnography for Archaeology,* edited by C. Kramer, pp. 102–138. Columbia University Press, New York.

DeBoer, W. R., and J. A. Moore
1982   The Measurement and Meaning of Stylistic Diversity. *Nawpa Pacha* 20:147–162.

Deetz, J. F., and E. S. Dethlefsen
1967   Death's Head, Cherub, Urn and Willow. *Natural History* 76(3):29–37.

de Lauretis, T.
1987   *Technologies of Gender: Essays on Theory, Film, and Fiction.* Indiana University Press, Bloomington.

Demeritt, D.
1991   Agriculture, Climate, and Cultural Adaptation in the Prehistoric Northeast. *Archaeology of Eastern North America* 19:183–202.

de Mortillet, G.
1869   Essai d'une Classification des Cavernes et des Stations Sous Abris, Fondée sur les Produits de l'Industrie Humaine. *Matériaux pour l'Histoire Primitive* 5(2eme série): 172–179.

De Raedt, J.
1991   Similarities and Differences in Lifestyles in the Central Cordillera of Northern Luzon, Philippines. In *Profiles in Cultural Evolution,* edited by A. T. Rambo and K. Gillogly, pp. 353–372. University of Michigan Museum of Anthropology Anthropological Papers No. 85. Ann Arbor.

Dietler, M., and I. Herbich
1989   *Tich Matek:* The Technology of Luo Pottery Production and the Definition of Ceramic Style. *World Archaeology* 21(1):148–164.
1994   Ceramics and Ethnic Identity: Ethnoarchaeological Observations on the Distribution of Pottery Styles and the Relationship between the Social Contexts of Production and Consumption. In *Terre Cuite et Societé: La Ceramique, Document Technique, Economique, Cultural,* pp. 459–472. XIVth Rencontres Internationales d'Archéologie et d'Histoire d'Antibes. Editions APDCA, Juan-les-Pins.
1998   *Habitus,* Techniques, Style: An Integrated Approach to the Social Understanding of Material Culture and Boundaries. In *The Archaeology of Social Boundaries,* edited by M. T. Stark. Smithsonian Institution Press, Washington, D.C.

Dillehay, T. D. (editor)
1995   *Tombs for the Living: Andean Mortuary Practices.* Dumbarton Oaks, Washington, D.C.

Dincauze, D. F.
1975   Ceramic Sherds from the Charles River Basin. *Bulletin of the Archaeological Society of Connecticut* 39:5–17.
1990   A Capsule Prehistory of Southern New England. In *The Pequot: The Fall and Rise of an American Indian Nation,* edited by L. Hauptman and

J. Wherry, pp. 19–32. University of Oklahoma Press, Norman.

Disselhoff, H. D.

1958a Cajamarca-Keramik von der Pama von San José de Moro (Prov. Pacasmayo). *Baessler-Archiv* 6:181–193. Museum fur Volkerkunde, Berlin.

1958b Tumbas de San José de Moro (Provincia de Pacasmayo, Perú). *Proceedings of the 32d International Congress of Americanists, 1956*, pp. 364–367. Copenhagen.

Dobres, M.-A.

1995a Gender and Prehistoric Technology: On the Social Agency of Technical Strategies. *World Archaeology* 27(1):25–49.

1995b *Gender in the Making: Late Magdalenian Social Relations of Production in the French Midi-Pyrénées.* Unpublished Ph.D. dissertation, Department of Anthropology, University of California, Berkeley.

1995c Beyond Gender Attribution: Some Methodological Issues for Engendering the Past. In *Gendered Archaeology,* edited by J. Balme and W. Beck, pp. 51–66. ANH Publications, RSPAS, Australian National University, Canberra. Research Papers in Archaeology and Natural History, No. 26.

1996 Variabilité des Activités Magdaléniennes en Ariège et en Haute-Garonne, d'après les Chaînes Opératoires dans l'Outillage Osseux. *Bulletin de la Société Préhistorique Ariège-Pyrénées* 51:149–194.

1998 Technology's Links and *Chaînes:* The Processual Unfolding of Technique and Technician. In *Making Culture: Essays on Technological Practice, Politics, and World Views,* edited by M.-A. Dobres and C. R. Hoffman. Smithsonian Institution Press, Washington, D.C., in press.

Dobres, M.-A., and C. R. Hoffman

1994 Social Agency and the Dynamics of Prehistoric Technology. *Journal of Archaeological Method and Theory* 1:211–258.

1998 Editors' Introduction: A Context for the Present and Future of Technol-ogy Studies. In *Making Culture: Essays on Technological Practice, Politics, and World Views,* edited by M.-A. Dobres and C. R. Hoffman. Smithsonian Institution Press, Washington, in press.

Donnan, C. B.

1971 Ancient Peruvian Potter's Marks and Their Interpretation through Ethnographic Analogy. *American Antiquity* 36:460–466.

1995 Moche Funerary Practice. In *Tombs for the Living: Andean Mortuary Practices,* edited by T. Dillehay, pp. 111–160. Dumbarton Oaks, Washington, D.C.

Donnan, C. B., and L. J. Castillo

1992 Finding the Tomb of a Moche Priestess. *Archaeology* 45(6):38–42.

1994 Excavaciones de Tumbas de Sacerdotisas Moche en San José de Moro, Jequetepeque. In *Moche: Propuestas y Perspectivas,* edited by S. Uceda and E. Mujica, pp. 415–424. Travaux de l'Institut Francais d'Etudes Andines Vol. 79. Universidad Nacional de La Libertad, Trujillo, Lima.

Donnan, C. B., and G. A. Cock

1985 Proyecto Pacatnamu: Segundo Informe Parcial—2da Temporada de Excavaciones (Junio–Setiembre 1984). Unpublished field report submitted to the Instituto Nacional de Cultura, Lima.

Donnan, C. B., and D. McClelland

1979 *The Burial Theme in Moche Iconography.* Studies in Pre-Columbian Art and Archaeology 21. Dumbarton Oaks, Washington, D.C.

Donnan, C. B., and C. J. Mackey

1978 *Ancient Burial Patterns of the Moche Valley, Peru.* University of Texas Press, Austin.

Doran, J. E., and F. R. Hodson

1975 *Mathematics and Computers in Archaeology.* Harvard University Press, Cambridge, Mass.

Dozier, E.

1966 *Mountain Arbiters: The Changing Life of a Hill People.* University of Arizona Press, Tucson.

Drucker, Charles

1977 To Inherit the Land: Descent and

Decision in Northern Luzon. *Ethnology* 16(1):1–20.

Drygulski Wright, B., M. Marx Ferree, G. Mellow, L. Lewis, M.-L. Daza Samper, R. Asher, and K. Claspell (editors)

1987 *Women, Work, and Technology: Transformations.* University of Michigan Press, Ann Arbor.

Dunnell, R. C.

1971 *Systematics in Prehistory.* Free Press, New York.

1978 Style and Function: A Fundamental Dichotomy. *American Antiquity* 43:192–202.

1981 Comments on Cohen's "Evolutionary Epistemology and Values." *Current Anthropology* 22:210.

1986 Methodological Issues in Americanist Artifact Classification. In *Advances in Archaeological Method and Theory,* vol. 9, edited by M. B. Schiffer, pp. 149–207. Academic Press, Orlando, Fla.

1989 Aspects of the Application of Evolutionary Theory in Archaeology. In *Archaeological Thought in America,* edited by C. C. Lamberg-Karlovsky, pp. 35–49. Cambridge University Press, New York.

Engelbrecht, W.

1972 The Reflection of Patterned Behavior in Iroquois Pottery. *Pennsylvania Archaeologist* 42(3):1–15.

1978 Ceramic Patterning between New York Iroquois Sites. In *The Spatial Organization of Culture,* edited by I. Hodder, pp. 141–152. University of Pittsburgh Press, Pittsburgh.

Enloe, J., F. David, and T. Hare

1994 Patterns of Faunal Processing at Section 27 of Pincevent: The Use of Spatial Analysis and Ethnoarchaeological Data in the Interpretation of Archaeological Site Structure. *Journal of Anthropological Archaeology* 13(2):105–124.

Faris, J. C.

1972 *Nuba Personal Art.* Duckworth, London.

Feinman, G.

1980 *The Relationship between Administrative Organization and Ceramic Production in the Valley of Oaxaca.* Unpublished Ph.D. dissertation, Department of Anthropology, City University of New York, Graduate Center.

1985 Changes in the Organization of Ceramic Production in Pre-Hispanic Oaxaca, Mexico. In *Decoding Prehistoric Ceramics,* edited by B. Nelson, pp. 195–224. Southern Illinois University Press, Carbondale, Ill.

Feinman, G., and J. Neitzel

1984 Too Many Types: An Overview of Sedentary Prestate Societies in the Americas. In *Advances in Archaeological Method and Theory,* vol. 7, edited by M. B. Schiffer, pp. 39–102. Academic Press, New York.

Feinman, G., S. Upham, and K. Lightfoot

1981 The Production Step Measure: An Ordinal Index of Labor Input in Ceramic Manufacture. *American Antiquity* 46:871–874.

Fenton, W. N.

1940 Problems Arising from the Northeastern Position of the Iroquois. *Smithsonian Miscellaneous Collections* 100:159–251.

1978 Northern Iroquoian Culture Patterns. In *Northeast,* edited by B. G. Trigger, pp. 296–321. Handbook of North American Indians, vol. 15, W. C. Sturtevant, general editor. Smithsonian Institution Press, Washington, D.C.

Ferguson, L.

1992 *Uncommon Ground: Archaeology and Early African America, 1650–1800.* Smithsonian Institution Press, Washington, D.C.

Flannery, K. V.

1972 The Cultural Evolution of Civilizations. *Annual Review of Ecology and Systematics* 3:399–426.

Fletcher, R.

1984 Identifying Spatial Disorder: A Case Study of a Mongol Fort. In *Intrasite Spatial Analysis in Archaeology,* edited by H. J. Hietala, pp. 196–223. Cambridge University Press, Cambridge.

Fontana, B. L., W. J. Robinson, C. W. Cormack, and E. E. Leavitt Jr.

1962 *Papago Indian Pottery.* University of Washington Press, Seattle.

Forge, A.
1970 Learning to See in New Guinea. In *Socialization: The Approach from Social Anthropology,* edited by P. Mayer, pp. 269–291. Tavistock, London.

Frank, B.
1998 *Mande Potters and Leatherworkers: Art and Heritage in West Africa.* Smithsonian Institution Press, Washington, D.C.

Fritz, J. M., and G. Mitchell
1987 Interpreting the Plan of a Medieval Hindu Capital, Vijanagara. *World Archaeology* 19(1):105–129.

Funk and Wagnalls
1973 *Funk and Wagnalls Standard College Dictionary.* Funk and Wagnalls Publishing, New York.

Fyfe, G., and J. Law
1988 On the Invisibility of the Visual: Editors' Introduction. In *Picturing Power: Visual Depictions and Social Relations,* edited by G. Fyfe and J.Law, pp. 1–14. Routledge, London.

Gallay, A.
1992 On the Study of Habitat Structures: Reflections Concerning the Archaeology-Anthropology-Science Transition. In *Representations in Archaeology,* edited by J.-C. Gardin and C. Peebles, pp. 107–121. Indiana University Press, Bloomington.

George, D. R., and J. C. M. Bendremer
1995 *Late Woodland Subsistence and the Origins of Maize Horticulture in New England.* Paper presented at the 60th Annual Meeting of the Society for American Archaeology, Minneapolis.

Gero, J.
1983 *Material Culture and the Reproduction of Social Complexity: A Lithic Example from the Peruvian Formative.* Ph.D. dissertation, University of Massachusetts, Amherst. University Microfilms, Ann Arbor.
1985 Socio-Politics and the Woman-At-Home Ideology. *American Antiquity* 50:342–350.
1994 Excavation Bias and the Woman-at-Home Ideology. In *Equity Issues for Women in Archaeology,* edited by

M. Nelson, S. Nelson, and A. Wylie, pp. 37–41. American Anthropological Association, Washington, D.C.

Gero, J. M., and M. W. Conkey (editors)
1991 *Engendering Archaeology: Women in Prehistory.* Basil Blackwell, Oxford.

Giddens, A.
1979 *Central Problems in Social Theory.* University of California Press, Berkeley.
1982 *Sociology: A Brief but Critical Introduction.* McMillan, London.

Gladwell, M.
1997 Annals of Style: The Coolhunt. *New Yorker.* 17 March:78–88.

Glascock, M. D.
1992 Characterization of Archaeological Ceramics at MURR by Neutron Activation Analysis and Multivariate Statistics. In *Chemical Characterization of Ceramic Pastes in Archaeology,* edited by H. Neff, pp. 11–26. Prehistory Press, Madison, Wis.

Glick, T. F.
1977 Noria Pots in Spain. *Technology and Culture* 18(4):644–650.

Goldstein, L. G.
1976 *Spatial Structure and Social Organization: Regional Manifestations of Mississippian Society.* Ph.D. dissertation, Northwestern University. University Microfilms, Ann Arbor.

Goodby, R. G.
1992 Diversity as a Typological Construct: Understanding Late Woodland Ceramics from Narragansett Bay. Paper presented at the 32d Meeting of the Northeastern Anthropological Association, Bridgewater, Mass.
1998 Technological Patterning and Social Boundaries: Ceramic Variability in Southern New England, A.D. 1000–1675. In *The Archaeology of Social Boundaries,* edited by M. T. Stark. Smithsonian Institution Press, Washington, D.C.

Gosselain, O. P.
1992a Technology and Style: Potters and Pottery among the Bafia of Cameroon. *Man* (N.S.) 27:559–586.
1992b Bonfire of the Enquiries. Pottery Fir-

ing Temperatures in Archaeology: What For? *Journal of Archaeological Science* 19:243–259.

1998 Social and Technical Identity in a Clay Crystal Ball. In *The Archaeology of Social Boundaries,* edited by M. T. Stark. Smithsonian Institution Press, Washington, D.C.

Goucher, C., and E. Herbert

1996 The Blooms of Banjeli: Technology and Gender in West African Iron Making. In *The Culture and Technology of African Iron Production,* edited by P. Schmidt, pp. 40–57. University Press of Florida, Gainesville.

Gould, R.

1978 *Explorations in Ethno-Archaeology.* University of New Mexico Press, Albuquerque.

Gould, S. J.

1997 A Tale of Two Worksites. *Natural History* October 106(9):18–68.

Gould, S. J., and R. Lewontin

1979 The Spandrels of San Morco and the Panglossian Paradigm: A Critique of the Adaptationist Programme. *Proceedings of the Royal Society of London* B205:581–598.

Graham, M.

1994 *Mobile Farmers: An Ethnoarchaeological Approach to Settlement Organization among the Rarámuri of Northwestern Mexico.* International Monographs in Prehistory, *Ethnoarchaeological Series* 3. Ann Arbor.

Graves, M. W.

1981 Ethnoarchaeology of Kalinga Ceramic Design. Unpublished Ph.D. dissertation, Department of Anthropology, University of Arizona, Tucson.

1985 Ceramic Design Variation within a Kalinga Village: Temporal and Spatial Processes. In *Decoding Prehistoric Ceramics,* edited by B. A. Nelson, pp. 9–34. Southern Illinois University Press, Carbondale.

1991 Pottery Production and Distribution among the Kalinga: A Study of Household and Regional Organization and Differentiation. In *Ceramic Ethnoarchaeology,* edited by W. A.

Longacre, pp. 112–143. University of Arizona Press, Tucson.

1994 Kalinga Social and Material Culture Boundaries: A Case of Spatial Convergence. In *Kalinga Ethnoarchaeology,* edited by W. A. Longacre and J. M. Skibo, pp. 13–50. Smithsonian Institution Press, Washington, D.C.

Guss, D.

1989 *To Weave and Sing: Art, Symbol, and Narrative in the South American Rain Forest.* University of California Press, Berkeley.

Haefeli, E., and K. Sweeney

1993 Revisiting *The Redeemed Captive:* New Perspectives on the 1704 Attack on Deerfield. *The William and Mary Quarterly* (3d Series) 52(1): 3–46.

Hägerstrand, T.

1967 *Innovation Diffusion as a Spatial Process.* University of Chicago Press, Chicago.

Hagstrum, M.

1988 Ceramic Production in the Central Andes, Peru: An Archaeological and Ethnographic Comparison. In *A Pot for All Reasons: Ceramic Ecology Revisited,* edited by C. C. Kolb and L. M. Lackey, pp. 127–145. Laboratory of Anthropology, Temple University, Philadelphia, Pa.

Hallifax, C. J.

1894 Pottery and Glass Industries of the Punjab. *Journal of Indian Art and Industry* 5(41):163–196.

Hamilton, W. L.

1998 The School Uniform as Fashion Statements. How Students Crack the Dress Code. *New York Times,* 2 February:A19.

Handsman, R.

1991 What Happened to the Heritage of the Weantinock People. *Artifacts* 19(1):3–9.

Handsman, R. G., and M. P. Leone

1989 Living History and Critical Archaeology in the Reconstruction of the Past. In *Critical Traditions in Contemporary Archaeology: Essays in the Philosophy, History and Socio-Politics of Archaeology,* edited by V. Pinsky and A. Wylie, pp. 117–135.

Cambridge University Press, Cambridge.

Hanson, N. R.

1958   *Patterns of Discovery: An Inquiry into the Conceptual Foundations of Science.* Cambridge University, Cambridge.

Harbottle, G.

1976   Activation Analysis in Archaeology. *Radiochemistry* 3:33–72. The Chemical Society, London.

Hardin, M.

1970   Design Structure and Social Interaction: Archaeological Implications of an Ethnographic Analysis. *American Antiquity* 35:332–343.

1977   Individual Style in San Jose Pottery Painting: The Role of Deliberate Choice. In *The Individual in Prehistory,* edited by J. N. Hill and J. Gunn, pp. 109–136. Academic Press, New York.

1979   The Cognitive Basis of Productivity in a Decorative Art Style: Implications of an Ethnographic Study for Archaeologists' Taxonomies. In *Ethnoarchaeology: Implications of Ethnography for Archaeology,* edited by C. Kramer, pp. 75–101. Columbia University Press, New York.

1983   The Structure of Tarascan Pottery Painting. In *Structure and Cognition in Art,* edited by D. K. Washburn, pp. 8–24. Cambridge University Press, Cambridge.

Harding, S.

1987   Introduction: Is There a Feminist Method? In *Feminism and Methodology,* edited by S. Harding, pp. 1–14. Indiana University Press and Open University Press, Bloomington and Milton Keynes.

Hargrave, M. L., C. R. Cobb, and P. A. Webb

1991   Late Prehistoric Ceramic Style Zones in Southern Illinois. In *Stability, Transformation, and Variation: The Late Woodland Southeast,* edited by M. S. Nassaney and C. R. Cobb, pp. 149–176. Plenum Press, New York.

Hasenstab, R. J.

1990   *Agriculture, Warfare, and Tribaliza-*
tion in the Iroquois Homeland of New York: A G.I.S. Analysis of Late Woodland Settlement. Unpublished Ph.D. dissertation, Department of Anthropology, University of Massachusetts, Amherst.

Hastings, C. M., and M. E. Moseley

1975   The Adobes of Huaca del Sol and Huaca de la Luna. *American Antiquity* 40:196–203.

Hastorf, C.

1991   Gender, Space, and Food in Prehistory. In *Engendering Archaeology: Women and Prehistory,* edited by J. M. Gero and M. W. Conkey, pp. 132–159. Blackwell, Oxford.

Hawkes, C.

1954   Archaeological Theory and Method: Some Suggestions from the Old World. *American Anthropologist* 56:155–168.

Hayashida, F. M.

1995   *State Pottery Production in the Inka Provinces.* Unpublished Ph.D. dissertation, Department of Anthropology, University of Michigan, Ann Arbor.

Hayden, B.

1987   *Lithic Studies among the Contemporary Highland Maya.* University of Arizona Press, Tucson.

Heckenberger, M. J., J. B. Petersen, and N. A. Sidell

1992   Early Evidence of Maize Agriculture in the Connecticut River Valley of Vermont. *Archaeology of Eastern North America* 20:125–149.

Hegmon, M.

1992   Archaeological Research on Style. *Annual Review of Anthropology* 21:517–536.

1998   Technology, Style, and Social Practices: Archaeological Approaches. In *The Archaeology of Social Boundaries,* edited by M. T. Stark. Smithsonian Institution Press, Washington, D.C.

Hegmon, M., W. Hurst, and J. R. Allison

1995   Production for Local Consumption and Exchange: Comparison of Early Red and White Ware Ceramics in the San Juan Region. In *Ceramic Production in the American South-*

west, edited by B. Mills and C. Crown, pp. 30–62. University of Arizaon Press, Tucson.

Herbert, E.
1993   *Iron, Gender, and Power: Rituals of Transformation in African Societies.* Indiana University Press, Bloomington.

Heyerdahl, T., D. H. Sandweiss, and A. Narváez
1995   *Pyramids of Tucumé: The Quest for Peru's Forgotten City.* Thames and Hudson, London.

Higgs, E. (editor)
1972   *Papers in Economic Prehistory.* Cambridge University Press, Cambridge.

Hill, C. W.
1989   Who Is What? A Preliminary Enquiry into Cultural and Physical Identity. In *Archaeological Approaches to Cultural Identity,* edited by S. Shennan, pp. 233–241. Unwin Hyman, London.

Hill, J. N.
1979   Individual Variability in Ceramics and the Study of Prehistoric Social Organization. In *The Individual in Prehistory,* edited by J. N. Hill and J. Gunn, p. 55–108. Academic Press, New York.

1985   Style: A Conceptual Evolutionary Framework. In *Decoding Prehistoric Ceramics,* edited by B. A. Nelson, pp. 362–385. Southern Illinois University Press, Carbondale.

Hill, J. N., and R. K. Evans
1972   A Model for Classification and Typology. In *Models in Archaeology,* edited by D. L. Clarke, pp. 231–273. Methuen, London.

Hodder, I.
1977   The Distribution of Material Culture Items in the Baringo District, Western Kenya. *Man* 12:239–269.

1979   Economic and Social Stress and Material Culture Patterning. *American Antiquity* 44:446–454.

1980   Social Structure and Cemeteries: A Critical Appraisal. In *Anglo-Saxon Cemeteries,* edited by P. Rahtz, T. Dickinson, and L. Watts, pp. 161–169. BAR British Series 82, Oxford.

1981   Society, Economy and Culture: An Ethnographic Case amongst the Lozi. In *Pattern of the Past: Studies in Honour of David Clarke,* edited by I. Hodder, G. Isaac, and N. Hammond, pp. 67–96. Cambridge University Press, Cambridge.

1982a Theoretical Archaeology: A Reactionary Review. In *Symbolic and Structural Archaeology,* edited by I. Hodder, pp. 1–16. Cambridge University Press, Cambridge.

1982b *Symbols in Action.* Cambridge University Press, Cambridge.

1984   Burials, Houses, Women and Men in the European Neolithic. In *Ideology, Power and Prehistory,* edited by D. Miller and C. Tilley, pp. 51–68. Cambridge University Press, Cambridge.

1986   *Reading the Past: Current Approaches to Interpretation in Archaeology.* Cambridge University Press, Cambridge.

1991a The Decoration of Containers: An Ethnographic and Historical Study. In *Ceramic Ethnoarchaeology,* edited by W. A. Longacre, pp. 71–94. University of Arizona Press, Tucson.

1991b *Reading the Past: Current Approaches to Interpretation in Archaeology.* 2d ed. Cambridge University Press, Cambridge.

Hodder, I. (editor)
1989   *The Meanings of Things: Material Culture and Symbolic Expression.* Unwin Hyman, London.

Hodder, I., and C. Orton
1976   *Spatial Analysis in Archaeology.* Cambridge University Press, Cambridge.

Hodson, F. R.
1982   Some Aspects of Archaeological Classification. In *Essays in Archaeological Typology,* edited by R. Whallon and J. A. Brown, pp. 21–29. Center for American Archaeology Press, Evanston, Ill.

Holmes, W. H.
1903   *Aboriginal Pottery of the Eastern United States.* 20th Annual Report of the Bureau of American Ethnol-

ogy to the Secretary of the Smithsonian Institution, pp. 1–237. U.S. Government Printing Office, Washington, D.C.

Hosler, D.
  1995 Sound, Color and Meaning in the Metallurgy of Ancient West Mexico. *World Archaeology* 27(1):100–115.
  1996 Technical Choices and Style: Two Examples from New World Production Technologies. Paper presented at the 61st Meeting of the Society for American Archaeology, New Orleans.

Hutterer, K. L.
  1991 Losing Track of the Tribes: Evolutionary Sequences in Southeast Asia. In *Profiles in Cultural Evolution,* edited by A. T. Rambo and K. Gillogly, pp. 219–246. University of Michigan Museum of Anthropology Anthropological Papers No. 85. Ann Arbor.

Ingold, T.
  1990 Society, Nature, and the Concept of Technology. *Archaeological Review from Cambridge* 9(1):5–17.

Jameson, J. F.
  1909 *Narratives of New Netherland, 1609–1664.* Barnes and Noble, New York.

Jenks, A. E.
  1905 *The Bontoc Igorot.* Ethnological Survey Publications Volume 1. Bureau of Public Printing, Department of Interior, Manila.

Johnson, E. S.
  1993 *Some by Flatteries and Others by Threatening: Political Strategies in Seventeenth Century Native New England.* Unpublished Ph.D. dissertation, Department of Anthropology, University of Massachusetts, Amherst.

Jones, G. T., R. D. Leonard, and A. L. Abbott
  1995 The Structure of Selectionist Explanations in Archaeology. In *Evolutionary Archaeology: Methodological Issues,* edited by P. A. Teltser, pp. 13–32. University of Arizona Press, Tucson.

Jones, S.
  1997 *The Archaeology of Ethnicity: Constructing Identities in the Past and Present.* Routledge, London.

Jordan, D.
  1975 Factors Affecting New England Archaeology. *Man in the Northeast* 10:71–74.

Jordanova, L.
  1980 Natural Facts: A Historical Perspective on Science and Sexuality. In *Nature, Culture, and Gender,* edited by R. MacCormack and M. Strathern, pp. 42–69. Cambridge University Press, Cambridge.
  1993 Gender and the Historiography of Science. *British Journal for the History of Science* 26:469–483.

Josselyn, J.
  1988 [1674] Two Voyages to New-England. In *John Josselyn, Colonial Traveler: A Critical Edition of Two Voyages to New-England,* edited by P. J. Lindholdt, pp. 1–200. University Press of New England, Hanover, New Hampshire.

Joyce, R., and C. Claassen
  1997 Women in the Ancient Americas: Archaeologists, Gender, and the Making of Prehistory. In *Women in Prehistory: North America and Mesoamerica,* edited by C. Claassen and R. A. Joyce, pp. 1–14. University of Pennsylvania Press, Philadelphia.

Keesing, F. M.
  1962 *The Ethnohistory of Northern Luzon.* Stanford University Press, Stanford.

Keesing, F. M., and M. Keesing
  1934 *Taming Philippine Headhunters: A Study of Government and Cultural Change in Northern Luzon.* Stanford University Press, Palo Alto.

Kenyon, V. B.
  1979 A New Approach to the Analysis of New England Prehistoric Pottery. *Man in the Northeast* 18:81–84.

Kertzer, D. I.
  1988 *Ritual, Politics, and Power.* Yale University Press, New Haven.

Kneebone, R. R.
  1990 *Energy Flow, Spatial Organization, and Community Structure at Matacapan, Veracruz, Mexico.* Unpub-

lished Ph.D. dissertation, Department of Anthropology, University of New Mexico, Albuquerque.

Kramer, C.
1982 *Village Ethnoarchaeology: Rural Iran in Archaeological Perspective.* Academic Press, New York.
1985 Ceramic Ethnoarchaeology. *Annual Review of Anthropology* 14:77–102.

Kramer, C. (editor)
1979 *Ethnoarchaeology: Implications of Ethnography for Archaeology.* Columbia University Press, New York.

Krieger, A. D.
1944 The Typological Concept. *American Antiquity* 9:271–288.

Kroeber, A. L.
1943 *Peoples of the Philippines.* Handbook Series No. 8. American Museum of Natural History, New York.

Kuhn, R. D., and R. E. Funk
1994 The Mohawk Klock and Smith Sites. Ms. on file, New York State Historic Preservation Office, Waterford, New York.

Kuhn, S.
1991 New Problems, Old Glasses: Methodological Implications of an Evolutionary Paradigm for the Study of Palaeolithic Technologies. In *Perspectives on the Past: Theoretical Biases in Mediterranean Hunter-Gatherer Research,* edited by G. Clark, pp. 242–257. University of Pennsylvania Press, Philadelphia.

Kuhn, T. S.
1962 *The Structure of Scientific Revolutions.* University of Chicago Press, Chicago.

Lamarck, J. B.
1984 [1809] *Zoological Philosophy.* University of Chicago Press, Chicago.

Laqueur, T.
1990 *Making Sex: Body and Gender from the Greeks to Freud.* Harvard University Press, Cambridge.

Larick, R.
1987 Men of Iron and Social Boundaries in Northern Kenya. In *Ethnicity and Culture,* edited by R. Auger, M. Glass, S. MacEachern, and P. McCartney, pp. 67–76. Archaeological Association of the University of Calgary, Calgary.

Lathrap, D. W.
1983 Recent Shipibo-Conibo Ceramics and Their Implications for Archaeological Interpretation. In *Structure and Cognition in Art,* edited by D. K. Washburn, pp. 25–39. Cambridge University Press, Cambridge.

Latta, M. A.
1991 The Captive Bride Syndrome: Iroquoian Behavior or Archaeological Myth? In *The Archaeology of Gender,* edited by D. Walde and N. Willows, pp. 375–383. Archaeological Association of the University of Calgary, Calgary.

Lavin, L.
1986 Pottery Classification and Cultural Models in Southern New England Prehistory. *North American Archaeologist* 7(1):1–14.
1988a Coastal Adaptation in Southern New England and Southern New York. *Archaeology of Eastern North America* 16:101–120.
1988b The Morgan Site, Rocky Hill, Connecticut: A Late Woodland Farming Community in the Connecticut River Valley. *Bulletin of the Archaeological Society of Connecticut* 51:7–22.

Lavin, L., and L. Miroff
1992 Aboriginal Pottery from the Indian Ridge Site, New Milford, Connecticut. *Bulletin of the Archaeological Society of Connecticut* 55:39–61.

Lawless, R.
1978 Impinging Extra-Kalinga Forces and Change in Pasil Municipality. In *Social Change in the Modern Philippines,* edited by M. D. Zamora, D. J. Baxter, and R. Lawless, pp. 145–159. Filipiniana Book Guild, Manila.

Lechtman, H.
1977 Style in Technology—Some Early Thoughts. In *Material Culture: Styles, Organization, and Dynamics of Technology,* edited by H. Lechtman and R. Merrill. 1975 Proceedings of the American Ethnological Society, pp. 3–20. West Publishing, St. Paul, Minn.

Lechtman, H., and R. Merrill (editors)
    1977 *Material Culture: Styles, Organization, and Dynamics of Technology.* 1975 Proceedings of the American Ethnological Society. West Publishing, St. Paul, Minn.

Leese, M. N. and P. L. Main
    1994 The Efficient Computation of Unbiased Mahalanobis Distances and Their Interpretation in Archaeometry. *Archaeometry* 36:307–316.

Lemonnier, P.
    1986 The Study of Material Culture Today: Towards an Anthropology of Technical Systems. *Journal of Anthropological Archaeology* 5:147–186.

    1989 Bark Capes, Arrowheads and Concord: On Social Representations of Technology. In *The Meanings of Things,* edited by I. Hodder, pp. 156–171. One World Archaeology, vol. 6, Unwin Hyman, London.

    1992 *Elements for an Anthropology of Technology.* Museum of Anthropology, University of Michigan, Ann Arbor.

    1993 Introduction. In *Technological Choices: Transformation in Material Cultures since the Neolithic,* edited by P. Lemonnier, pp. 1–35. Routledge, London.

Lemonnier, P. (editor)
    1993 *Technological Choices: Transformation in Material Cultures since the Neolithic.* Routledge, London.

Lenig, D.
    1965 The Oak Hill Horizon and Its Relation to the Development of Five Nations Iroquois Culture. *Research and Transactions of the New York State Archaeological Association* 15(1):1–114.

Leonard, R. D., and H. E. Reed
    1996 Theory, Models, Explanation, and the Record: Response to Kohler and Sebastian. *American Antiquity* 61:603–608.

Leone, M. P.
    1972 Issues in Contemporary Archaeology. In *Contemporary Archaeology,* edited by M. Leone, pp. 14–27. Southern Illinois University Press, Carbondale.

    1984 Interpreting Ideology in Historical Archaeology: Using the Rules of Perspective in the William Paca Garden in Annapolis, Maryland. In *Ideology, Power, and Prehistory,* edited by D. Miller and C. Tilley, pp. 25–35. Cambridge University Press, Cambridge.

    1992 Epilogue: The Productive Nature of Material Culture and Archaeology. *Historical Archaeology* 26(3):130–133.

Leone, M. P., P. B. Potter Jr., and P. A. Shackel
    1987 Toward a Critical Archaeology. *Current Anthropology* 28:283–302.

Leone, M. P., E. K. Reid, J. H. Ernstein, and P. A. Shackel
    1989 Power Gardens of Annapolis. *Archaeology* 42:34–39, 74–75.

Leroi-Gourhan, A.
    1943 *Evolution et Techniques: L'Homme et la Matière.* A. Michel, Paris.

    1945 *Evolution et Techniques: Milieu et Techniques.* A. Michel, Paris.

    1964 *Le Geste et la Parole I: Technique et Langage.* A. Michel, Paris

    1982 *The Dawn of European Art.* Cambridge University Press, Cambridge.

    1993 *Gesture and Speech (Geste et la Parole).* Translated by Anna Bostock Berger. MIT Press, Cambridge, Mass.

Leroi-Gourhan, A., and M. Brézillion
    1972 *Fouilles de Pincevent, Essai d'Analyse Ethnographique d'un Habitat Magdalénien.* VII Supplément à *Gallia Préhistoire.* CNRS, Paris.

Lewis, M. W.
    1991 Elusive Societies: A Regional-Cartographical Approach to the Study of Human Relatedness. *Annals of the Association of American Geographers* 81(4):605–626.

Linnekin, J., and L. Poyer
    1990 Introduction. In *Cultural Identity and Ethnicity in the Pacific,* edited by J. Linnekin and L. Poyer, pp. 1–16. University of Hawaii Press, Honolulu.

Little, B.
    1992 Explicit and Implicit Meanings in Material Culture. *Historical Archaeology* 26(3):85–94.

Little, E. A., and M. J. Schoeninger
  1995 The Late Woodland Diet on Nantucket Island and the Problem of Maize in Coastal New England. *American Antiquity* 60:351–368.

Longacre, W. A.
  1981 Kalinga Pottery: An Ethnoarchaeological Study. In *Pattern of the Past: Studies in Honor of David Clarke,* edited by I. Hodder, G. Isaac, and N. Hammond, pp. 49–66. Cambridge University Press, Cambridge.
  1991 Sources of Ceramic Variability among the Kalinga of Northern Luzon. In *Ceramic Ethnoarchaeology,* edited by W. A. Longacre, pp. 95–111. University of Arizona Press, Tucson.

Longacre, W. A. (editor)
  1991 *Ceramic Ethnoarchaeology.* University of Arizona Press, Tucson, Arizona.

Longacre, W. A., and J. E. Ayres
  1968 Archeological Lessons from an Apache Wickiup. In *New Perspectives in Archaeology,* edited by L. R. Binford and S. R. Binford, pp. 151–159. Aldine, Chicago.

Longacre, W. A., and J. M. Skibo
  1994 An Introduction to Kalinga Ethnoarchaeology. In *Kalinga Ethnoarchaeology,* edited by W. A. Longacre and J. M. Skibo, pp. 1–11. Smithsonian Institution Press, Washington, D.C.

Longacre, W. A., and J. M. Skibo (editors)
  1994 *Kalinga Ethnoarchaeology: Expanding Archaeological Method and Theory.* Smithsonian Institution Press, Washington, D.C.

Lubar, S., and W. D. Kingery
  1993 Introduction. In *History from Things,* edited by S. Lubar and W. D. Kingery, pp. viii–xvii. Smithsonian Institution Press, Washington, D.C.

Lyons, P. J.
  1987 Language and Style in the Peruvian Montaña. In *Ethnicity and Culture,* edited by R. Auger, M. Glass, S. MacEachern, and P. McCartney, pp. 101–114. Archaeological Association of the University of Calgary, Calgary.

McBride, K. A.
  1984 *Prehistory of the Lower Connecticut River Valley.* Unpublished Ph.D. dissertation, Department of Anthropology, University of Connecticut, Storrs.

MacEachern, A. S.
  1992 Ethnicity and Ceramic Variation around Mayo Plata, Northern Cameroon. In *An African Commitment: Papers in Honour of Peter Lewis Shinnie,* edited by J. Sterner and N. David, pp. 211–230. University of Calgary Press, Calgary.
  1998 Scale, Style, and Cultural Variation: Technological Traditions in the Northern Mandara Mountains. In *The Archaeology of Social Boundaries,* edited by M. T. Stark. Smithsonian Institution Press, Washington, D.C.

McGaw, J.
  1989 No Passive Victims, No Separate Spheres: A Feminist Perspective on Technology's History. In *In Context,* edited by R. Cutliffe and S. Post, pp. 172–191. Research in Technology Studies Volume 1. Lehigh University Press, Bethlehem.
  1996 Reconceiving Technology: Why Feminine Technologies Matter. In *Gender and Archaeology,* edited by R. Wright, pp. 52–75. University of Pennsylvania Press, Philadelphia.

McGrew, W. C.
  1992 *Chimpanzee Material Culture: Implications for Human Evolution.* Cambridge University Press, Cambridge.

McGuire, R. H.
  1988 Dialogues with the Dead: Ideology and the Cemetery. In *The Recovery of Meaning: Historical Archaeology in the Eastern United States,* edited by M. P. Leone and P. B. Potter, pp. 435–480. Smithsonian Institution Press, Washington, D.C.
  1992 *A Marxist Archaeology.* Academic Press, New York.

MacKenzie, M.
  1991 *Androgynous Objects: String Bags and Gender in Central New Guinea.* Harwood Academic Publishers, Chur, Switzerland.

MacNeish, R. S.

1952   *Iroquois Pottery Types: A Technique for the Study of Iroquois Pottery.* National Museum of Canada Bulletin 124. Minister of Resources and Development, Ottawa.

McPherron, A.

1967   On the Sociology of Ceramics. In *Iroquois Culture, History, and Prehistory: Proceedings of the 1965 Conference on Iroquois Research,* edited by Elisabeth Tooker, pp. 101–108. New York State Museum and Science Service, Albany.

Magannon, E.

1984   Cognition of Time, Change, and Social Identity: Kalinga History and Historical Consciousness. In *History and Peasant Consciousness in South East Asia.* Senri Ethnological Studies 13. National Museum of Ethnology, Senri, Osaka.

Mahias, M.-C.

1993   Pottery Techniques in India: Technical Variants and Social Choice. In *Technological Choices: Transformation in Material Cultures since the Neolithic,* edited by P. Lemonnier, pp. 157–180. Routledge, London.

Margolis, H.

1993   *Paradigms and Barriers: How Habits of Mind Govern Scientific Beliefs.* University of Chicago Press, Chicago.

Marquardt, W.

1992   Dialectical Archaeology. *Archaeological Method and Theory,* vol. 4, edited by M. B. Schiffer, pp. 101–140. University of Arizona Press, Tucson.

Mauss, M.

1979   Les Technique du Corps. In *Sociology and Psychology: Essays of Marcel Mauss.* Translated by B. Brewster. Routledge and Kegan Paul, London. Originally published 1936.

Mayr, E.

1982   *The Growth of Biological Thought: Diversity, Evolution, and Inheritance.* Harvard University Press, Cambridge.

1988   *Towards a New Philosophy of Biology: Observations of an Evolution-ist.* Harvard University Press, Cambridge.

Méroc, L.

1953   La Conquête de Pyrénées par l'Homme. *Premier Congrès International de Spéléologie* Paris IV(4):35–53.

Merrill, R.

1968   The Study of Technology. In *International Encyclopedia of the Social Sciences,* vol. 15, edited by David Sills, pp. 576–589. MacMillan, New York.

Miller, D.

1982   Explanation and Social Theory in Archaeological Practice. In *Theory and Explanation in Archaeology,* edited by C. Renfrew, M. J. Rowlands, B. A. Segraves, pp. 83–95. Cambridge University Press, Cambridge.

1983   Things Ain't What They Used to Be. *Royal Anthropological Institute Newsletter,* no. 59, pp. 5–7.

1985   *Artefacts as Categories: A Study of Ceramic Variability in Central India.* Cambridge University Press, Cambridge.

1986   Exchange and Alienation in the Jajmani System. *Journal of Anthropological Research* 42(4):535–556.

1987   *Material Culture and Mass Consumption.* Basil Blackwell, Oxford.

Mills, B. J.

1989   Integrating Functional Analyses of Vessels and Sherds through Models of Ceramic Assemblage Formation. *World Archaeology* 21:133–147.

Mizoguchi, K.

1993   Time in the Reproduction of Mortuary Practices. *World Archaeology* 25(2):223–235.

Moore, H.

1982   The Interpretation of Spatial Patterning in Settlement Residues. In *Symbolic and Structural Archaeology,* edited by I. Hodder, pp. 74–79. Cambridge University Press, Cambridge.

1986   *Space, Text, and Gender: An Anthropological Study of the Marakwet of Kenya.* Cambridge University Press, Cambridge.

Moore, J. A., and A. S. Keene
1983 Archaeology and the Law of the Hammer. In *Archaeological Hammers and Theories,* edited by J. A. Moore and A. S. Keene, pp. 3–13. Academic Press, New York.

Morgan, L. H.
1901 *League of the HO-DE-NO-SAU-NEE or Iroquois,* edited by H. M. Lloyd. Burt Franklin, New York.

1965 *House and House-life of the American Aborigines.* University of Chicago Press, Chicago.

Morris, I.
1992 *Death Ritual and Social Structure in Classical Antiquity.* Cambridge University Press, Cambridge.

Mossman, B. M., and M. Selsor
1988 A Utilitarian Pottery Tradition and the Modern Spanish Kitchen. In *A Pot for All Reasons: Ceramic Ecology Revisited,* edited by C. C. Kolb and L. M. Lackey, pp. 213–237. Laboratory of Anthropology, Temple University, Philadelphia, Pa.

Murray, T. A.
1987 Remembrance of Things Present: Appeals to Authority in the History and Philosophy of Archaeology. Unpublished Ph.D. dissertation, University of Sidney, New South Wales, Australia.

Neff, H.
1992a Introduction. In *Chemical Characterization of Ceramic Pastes in Archaeology,* edited by H. Neff, pp. 1–10. Prehistory Press, Madison, Wis.

1992b Ceramics and Evolution. In *Archaeological Method and Theory,* vol. 4, edited by M. B. Schiffer, pp. 141–193. University of Arizona Press, Tucson.

1993 Theory, Sampling, and Analytical Techniques in the Archaeological Study of Prehistoric Ceramics. *American Antiquity* 58:23–44.

Neff, H., R. L. Bishop, and E. V. Sayre
1988 Simulation Approach to the Problem of Tempering in Compositional Studies of Archaeological Ceramics. *The Journal of Archaeological Science* 15:159–172.

1989 More Observations on the Problem of Tempering in Compositional Studies of Archaeological Ceramics. *Journal of Archaeological Science* 16:57–69.

Neiman, F.
1995 Stylistic Variation in Evolutionary Perspective: Inferences from Decorative Diversity and Interassemblage Distance in Illinois Woodland Ceramic Assemblages. *American Antiquity* 60:7–36.

Nelson, M. C.
1991 The Study of Technological Organization. In *Archaeological Method and Theory,* vol. 3, edited by M. B. Schiffer, pp. 57–100. University of Arizona Press, Tucson.

Nelson, S.
1997 *Gender in Archaeology: Analyzing Power and Prestige.* AltaMira Press, Walnut Creek, Calif.

Newell, R. R., D. Kielman, T. S. Constandse-Westermann, W. A. B. van der Sanden., and A. van Gijn
1990 *An Inquiry into the Ethnic Resolution of Mesolithic Regional Groups: The Study of Their Decorative Ornaments in Time and Space.* Brill, Leiden, the Netherlands.

Niemczycki, M. P.
1984 *The Origin and Development of the Seneca and Cayuga Tribes of New York State.* Research Records 17, Rochester Museum and Science Center, Rochester, New York.

Nougier, L.-R.
1968 Une Grotte-Type des Pyrénées: La Grotte de 'La Vache' à Alliat (Ariège). *L'Information de l'Histoire de l'Art* 13th année (5):199–207.

Nougier, L.-R., and R. Robert
1956 Un 'Foyer Tribal' du Magdalénien Pyrénéen. *La Nature* 3253:190–194.

O'Brien, M. J., and T. D. Holland
1992 The Role of Adaptation in Archaeological Explanation. *American Antiquity* 57:36–59.

O'Brien, M. J., T. D. Holland, R. J. Hoard, and G. L. Fox
1994 Evolutionary Implications of Design and Performance Characteristics of Prehistoric Pottery. *Journal of*

Archaeological Method and Theory
1:259–304.

Olive, M.
1992   En Marge des Unités d'Habitations
       d'Etiolles: Les Foyers d'Activité
       Satellites. *Gallia Préhistoire* 34:85–
       140.

Olive, M., and N. Pigeot
1992   Les Tailleurs de Silex Magdaléniens
       d'Etiolles: Vers l'Identification d'une
       Organisation Sociale Complexe? In
       La Pierre Préhistorique, edited by
       M. Menu and P. Walter, pp. 173–
       185. Laboratoire de Recherche des
       Musées de France, Paris.

O'Shea, J. M.
1984   *Mortuary Variability: An Archaeo-
       logical Investigation.* Academic
       Press, New York.

1996   *Villagers of the Maros: A Portrait
       of an Early Bronze Age Society.*
       Plenum Press, New York.

Pacey, A.
1983   *The Culture of Technology.* Black-
       well, Oxford.

Parker, A. C.
1968   *Parker on the Iroquois.* Syracuse
       University Press, Syracuse.

Paynter, R.
1988   Steps to an Archaeology of Capital-
       ism: Historical Change and Class
       Analysis. In *The Recovery of Mean-
       ing: Historical Archaeology in the
       Eastern United States,* edited by
       M. P. Leone and P. B. Potter Jr., pp.
       407–433. Smithsonian Institution
       Press, Washington, D.C.

Peacock, D. P. S.
1982   *Pottery in the Roman World: An
       Ethnoarchaeological Approach.*
       Longman, London.

Pearson, M. P.
1982   Mortuary Practices, Society, and
       Ideology: An Ethnoarchaeological
       Study. In *Symbolic and Structural
       Archaeology,* edited by I. Hodder,
       pp. 99–113. Cambridge University
       Press, Cambridge.

Pelegrin, J.
1985   Reflexion sur le Comportement
       Technique. In *La Signification Cul-
       turelle des Industries Lithiques,*
       edited by M. Otte, pp. 72–82. BAR
       International Series 239, Oxford.

Perlman, I., and F. Asaro
1969   Pottery Analysis by Neutron Activa-
       tion. In *Science and Archaeology,*
       edited by R. H. Brill, pp. 182–195.
       MIT Press, Cambridge, Mass.

Petersen, J. B., and D. Sanger
1991   An Aboriginal Ceramic Sequence for
       Maine and the Maritime Provinces.
       In *Prehistoric Archaeology in the
       Maritime Provinces: Past and Pres-
       ent Research,* edited by M. Deal and
       S. Blair, pp. 121–178. The Council
       of Maritime Premiers, Maritime
       Committee on Archaeological Co-
       operation, Fredericton, New
       Brunswick.

Peyrony, D.
1950   Passage du Paléolithique au Mé-
       solithique dans la Sud-Ouest Eu-
       ropéen: Magdalénien Final et
       Azilien Ancien. *Congrès Préhis-
       torique de France* XIIIeme ses-
       sion:536–541.

Pfaffenberger, B.
1988   Fetishised Objects and Humanised
       Nature: Towards an Anthropology
       of Technology. *Man* 23(2):236–252.

1992   Social Anthropology of Technology.
       Annual Review of Anthropology
       21:491–516.

1996   Material Culture and the Techno-
       Social Construction of Intersubjec-
       tive Meaning: A Perspective from
       Social Anthropology. Paper pre-
       sented at the 61st Meeting of the So-
       ciety for American Archaeology,
       New Orleans.

Phillips, P., and G. Willey
1953   Method and Theory in American
       Archaeology: An Operational Basis
       for Culture-Historical Integration.
       American Anthropologist
       55:615–633.

Pigeot, N.
1987   *Magdaléniens d'Etiolles: Débitage et
       Organisation Sociale.* XXV Supplé-
       ment à *Gallia Préhistoire.* CNRS,
       Paris.

Pinch, T. J., and W. E. Bijker
1987   The Social Construction of Facts
       and Artifacts: Or How the Sociology
       of Science and the Sociology of
       Technology might Benefit Each
       Other. In *The Social Construction of*

Technological Systems, edited by W. E. Bijker, T. P. Hughes, and T. J. Pinch, pp. 17–50. MIT Press, Cambridge, Mass.

Plog, S.
1980 *Stylistic Variation in Prehistoric Ceramics: Design Analysis in the American Southwest.* Cambridge University Press. Cambridge.

Pollock, S.
1983 *The Symbolism of Prestige.* Ph.D. dissertation, University of Michigan. University Microfilms, Ann Arbor.

Pool, C. A.
1990 *Ceramic Production, Resource Procurement, and Exchange at Matacapan, Veracruz, Mexico.* Unpublished Ph.D. dissertation, Department of Anthropology, Tulane University, New Orleans.
1997 Prehispanic Kilns at Matacapan, Veracruz, Mexico. In *The Prehistory and History of Ceramic Kilns,* edited by P. Rice, pp. 149–171. Ceramics and Civilization, vol. 7. The American Ceramic Society, Westerville, Ohio.

Pool, C. A., and R. S. Santley
1992 Middle Classic Pottery Economics in the Tuxtla Mountains, Southern Veracruz, Mexico. In *Ceramic Production and Distribution: An Integrated Approach,* edited by G. J. Bey III and C. A. Pool, pp. 205–234. Westview Press, Boulder, Colo.

Quiñones, H., and R. Allende
1974 Formation of the Lithified Carapace of Calcareous Nature Which Covers Most of the Yucatán Peninsula and Its Relation to the Soils and Geomorphology of the Region. *Tropical Agriculture* 51(2):94–101.

Raab, L., and A. Goodyear
1984 Middle-Range Theory in Archaeology: A Critical Review of Origins and Applications. *American Antiquity* 49:255–268.

Rands, R. L., and R. L. Bishop
1980 Resource Procurement Zones and Patterns of Ceramic Exchange in the Palenque Region, Mexico. In *Models and Methods in Regional Exchange,* SAA Papers No. 1, edited by R. E. Fry, pp. 19–46. Society for American Archaeology, Washington, D.C.

Redman, C. L., E. Curtin, N. Versaggi, and J. Wanser
1978 Social Archaeology: The Future of the Past. In *Social Archaeology: Beyond Subsistence and Dating,* edited by C. L. Redman, M. J. Berman, E. V. Curtin, W. T. Langhorne Jr., N. M. Versaggi, J. C. Wanser, pp. 1–18. Academic Press, New York.

Reedy, C. L., and T. J. Reedy
1994 Relating Visual and Technological Styles in Tibetan Sculpture Analysis. *World Archaeology* 25(3):304–320.

Reents-Budet, D.
1994 *Painting the Maya Universe: Royal Ceramics of the Classic Period.* Duke University Press, Durham.
1998 Elite Maya Pottery and Artisans as Social Indicators. In *Craft and Social Identity,* edited by C. Costin and R. Wright. Archaeological Papers of the American Anthropological Association No. 8. Washington, D.C.

Reid, L. A.
1972 Wards and Working Groups in Guinaang, Bontoc, Luzon. *Anthropos* 67:530–563.
1994 Terms for Rice Agriculture and Terrace Building in Some Cordilleran Languages of the Philippines. In *Austronesian Terminologies: Continuity and Change,* edited by A. K. Pawley and M. D. Ross, pp. 363–388. Pacific Linguistics C-127.

Reina, R. E., and R. M. Hill II
1978 *The Traditional Pottery of Guatemala.* University of Texas Press, Austin.

Reinach, S.
1903 L'Art et la Magie: A Propos des Peintures et des Gravures de l'Age du Renne. *L'Anthropologie* 14:257–266.

Rice, P. M.
1978 Clear Answers to Vague Questions: Some Assumptions of Provenance Studies of Pottery. In *The Ceramics of Kaminaljuyu,* edited by R. K. Wetherington, pp. 511–542. Pennsylvania State University Press, University Park.
1981 Evolution of Specialized Pottery

Production: A Trial Model. *Current Anthropology* 22:219–240.

1984 Change and Conservatism in Pottery Producing Systems. In *The Many Dimensions of Pottery: Ceramics in Archaeology and Anthropology*, edited by S. E. van der Leeuw and A. C. Pritchard, pp. 231–288. University of Amsterdam, Amsterdam.

1987 *Pottery Analysis: A Sourcebook*. University of Chicago Press, Chicago.

1991 Specialization, Standardization, and Diversity: A Retrospective. In *The Ceramic Legacy of Anna O. Shepard*, edited by R. L. Bishop and F. W. Lange, pp. 257–279. University Press of Colorado, Niwot, Colo.

1996a Recent Ceramic Analysis: 2. Composition, Production, and Theory. *Journal of Archaeological Research* 4:165–202.

1996b Recent Ceramic Analysis: 1. Function, Style, and Origins. *Journal of Archaeological Research* 4:133–163.

Rigaud, J.-P., and J. Simek
1987 'Arms Too Short to Box With God': Problems and Prospects for Palaeolithic Prehistory in the Dordogne, France. In *The Pleistocene Old World: Regional Perspectives*, edited by O. Soffer, pp. 47–62. Plenum Press, New York.

Ritchie, W. A.
1958 *An Introduction to Hudson Valley Prehistory*. New York State Museum and Science Service Bulletin 367. Albany, New York.

Ritchie, W. A., and R. S. MacNeish
1949 Pre-Iroquoian Pottery of New York State. *American Antiquity* 15:97–124.

Roaf, M., and J. Galbraith
1994 Pottery and *p*-values: "Seafaring Merchants of Ur?" Re-examined. *Antiquity* 68:770–783.

Robert, R., M. Malvesin-Fabre, and L.-R. Nougier
1953 Sur l'Existence Possible d'une Ecole d'Art dans le Magdalénien Pyrénéen. *Bulletin Archéologique du Comité des Travaux Historiques et Scientifiques*, pp. 187–193.

Roe, P. G.
1980 Art and Residence among the Shipibo Indians of Peru: A Study in Microacculturation. *American Anthropologist* 82:42–71.

Rood, S.
1991 Issues on Creating An Autonomous Region for the Cordillera, Northern Philippines. *Ethnic and Racial Studies* 14(4):516–544.

Root, D.
1984 Material Dimensions of Social Inequality in Non-stratified Societies: An Archaeological Perspective. Unpublished Ph.D. dissertation, Department of Anthropology, University of Massachusetts, Amherst.

Rosaldo, R.
1988 Ethnic Concentrations: The Ilongots in Upland Luzon. In *Ethnic Diversity and the Control of Natural Resources in Southeast Asia*, edited by A. T. Rambo, K. Gillogly, and K. L. Hutterer, pp. 161–171. Michigan Papers on South and Southeast Asia, Center for South and Southeast Asian Studies No. 32. University of Michigan, Ann Arbor.

Rouse, I.
1947 Ceramic Traditions and Sequences in Connecticut. *Bulletin of the Archaeological Society of Connecticut* 21:10–25.

1960 The Classification of Artifacts in Archaeology. *American Antiquity* 25:313–323.

1964 *Prehistory in Haiti: A Study in Method*. Reprinted. Yale University Publication in Anthropology 21, New Haven. Originally published 1939, Yale University Press, New Haven, Conn.

Roveland, B.
1989 Ritual as Action. The Production and Use of Art at the Magdalenian Site, Goennersdorf. Unpublished Master's thesis, Department of Anthropology, University of Massachusetts, Amherst.

Rozoy, J.
1992 The Magdalenian in Europe: Demography, Regional Groups. *Préhistoire Europeenne* 1:67–82.

Rye, O. S.

1976 Keeping Your Temper under Control. *Archaeology and Physical Anthropology in Oceania* 11(2):106–137.

1981 *Pottery Technology: Principles and Reconstruction.* Manuals on Archaeology 4. Taraxacum, Washington, D.C.

Sackett, J. R.

1973 Style, Function and Artifact Variability in Paleolithic Assemblages. In *The Explanation of Culture Change,* edited by C. Renfrew, pp. 316–325. Duckworth, London.

1977 The Meaning of Style in Archaeology. *American Antiquity* 42:369–380.

1982 Approaches to Style in Lithic Archaeology. *Journal of Anthropological Archaeology* 1:59–112.

1985 Style and Ethnicity in the Kalahari: A Reply to Wiessner. *American Antiquity* 50:154–159.

1986 Isochrestism and Style: A Clarification. *Journal of Anthropological Archaeology* 5:266–277.

1990 Style and Ethnicity in Archaeology: The Case for Isochrestism. In *The Uses of Style in Archaeology,* edited by M. W. Conkey and C. A. Hastorf, pp. 32–43. Cambridge University Press, Cambridge.

Sahlins, M.

1976 *Culture and Practical Reason.* University of Chicago Press, Chicago.

Salisbury, N.

1993 Facing the Eastern Door: New England Algonquians and the Iroquois. Paper presented at the 2d Mashantucket Pequot History Conference, Mystic, Conn.

Santley, R. S., P. J. Arnold III, and C. A. Pool

1989 The Ceramic Production System at Matacapan, Veracruz, Mexico. *Journal of Field Archaeology* 16:107–132.

Santley, R. S., P. Ortiz C., and C. A. Pool

1987 Recent Archaeological Research at Matacapan, Veracruz: A Summary of the 1982–1986 Field Seasons. *Mexicon* 9:41–48.

Saxe, A.

1970 *Social Dimensions of Mortuary Practices.* Ph.D. dissertation, University of Michigan. University Microfilms, Ann Arbor.

Sayre, E. V., and R. W. Dodson

1957 Neutron Activation Study of Mediterranean Potsherds. *American Journal of Archaeology* 61:35–41.

Schiebinger, L.

1993 *Nature's Body: Gender in the Making of Modern Science.* Beacon, Boston.

Schiffer, M. B.

1972 Archaeological Context and Systemic Context. *American Antiquity* 37:156–165.

1976 *Behavioral Archaeology.* Academic Press, New York.

1983 Toward the Identification of Site Formation Processes. *American Antiquity* 48:675–706.

1987 *Formation Processes of the Archaeological Record.* University of New Mexico Press, Albuquerque.

1991 *The Portable Radio in American Life.* University of Arizona Press, Tucson.

1992 *Technological Perspectives on Behavioral Change.* University of Arizona Press, Tucson.

1995 *Behavioral Archaeology: First Principles.* University of Utah Press, Salt Lake City.

Schiffer, M. B., and J. M. Skibo

1987 Theory and Experiment in the Study of Technological Change. *Current Anthropology* 28:595–622.

1997 The Explanation of Artifact Variability. *American Antiquity* 62:27–50.

Schultz, L. G., A. O. Shepard, P. D. Blackmon, and H. C. Starkey

1971 Mixed-layer Kaolinite-montmorillonite from the Yucatán Peninsula, Mexico. *Clays and Clay Minerals* 19:137–150.

Schwartz Cowan, R.

1983 *More Work for Mothers: The Ironies of Household Technology from the Hearth to the Microwave.* Basic Books, New York.

Scott, W. H.

1969 *On the Cordillera.* MCS Enterprises, Manila.

1977 *The Discovery of the Igorots:*

Spanish Contact with the Pagans of Northern Luzon. Revised ed. New Day, Quezon City.

Sellet, F.
1993 Chaîne Opératoire: The Concept and Its Applications. *Lithic Technology* 18(1–2):106–112.

Shackel, P. A.
1993 *Personal Discipline and Material Culture: An Archaeology of Annapolis, Maryland, 1695–1870.* University of Tennessee Press, Knoxville.

Shanks, M., and C. Tilley
1987a *Social Theory and Archaeology.* Polity Press, Cambridge.
1987b *Re-Constructing Archaeology: Theory and Practice.* Cambridge University Press, Cambridge.

Sharp, H.
1991 Dry Meat and Gender: The Absence of Chipewyan Ritual for the Regulation of Hunting and Animal Numbers. In *Hunters and Gatherers 2: Property, Power, and Ideology,* edited by T. Ingold, D. Riches, and J. Woodburn, pp. 183–191. Berg, New York.

Sheehy, J.
1988 Ceramic Ecology and the Clay/Fuel Ratio: Modeling Fuel Consumption in Tlajinga 33, Teotihuacan, Mexico. In *Ceramic Ecology Revisited, 1987: The Technology and Socioeconomics of Pottery,* edited by C. Kolb, pp. 199–226. BAR International Series 436(ii), Oxford.

Shennan, S.
1988 *Quantifying Archaeology.* Academic Press, San Diego.
1989a Introduction: Archaeological Approaches to Cultural Identity. In *Archaeological Approaches to Cultural Identity,* edited by S. Shennan, pp. 1–32. Unwin Hyman, London.
1989b Cultural Transmission and Cultural Change. In *What's New? A Closer Look at the Process of Innovation,* edited by S. E. van der Leeuw and R. Torrence, pp. 330–346. Unwin Hyman, London.

Shepard, A. O.
1956 *Ceramics for the Archaeologist.* Publication 609. Carnegie Institu-

tion of Washington, Washington, D.C.

Shepard, A. O., and H. E. D. Pollock
1971 *Maya Blue: An Updated Record.* Notes from a Ceramic Laboratory 4. Carnegie Institution of Washington, Washington, D.C.

Siefert, D. J.
1991 Gender in Historical Archaeology. *Historical Archaeology* 25(4):1–155.

Sieveking, A.
1976 Settlement Patterns in the Later Magdalenian in the Central Pyrenees. In *Problems in Economic and Social Archaeology,* edited by G. de G. Sieveking, I. Longworth, and K. Wilson, pp. 583–603. Duckworth, London.

Silver, A.
1980 Comment on Maize Cultivation in Coastal New York. *North American Archaeologist* 2(2):117–130.

Silverblatt, I.
1988 Women in States. *Annual Review of Anthropology* 17:427–460.

Simek, J.
1984 *A K-Means Approach to the Analysis of Spatial Structure in Upper Palaeolithic Habitation Sites.* BAR International Series 205, Oxford.

Sinclair, A.
1995 The Technique as a Symbol in Late Glacial Europe. *World Archaeology* 27:50–62.

Sinopoli, C. M.
1988 The Organization of Craft Production at Vijayanagara, South India. *American Anthropologist* 90:580–597.
1991 *Approaches to Archaeological Ceramics.* Plenum Press, New York.

Skibo, J. M.
1992 *Pottery Function: A Use-Alteration Perspective.* Plenum Press, New York.

Skibo, J. M., and M. B. Schiffer
1996 People and Things: A Behavioral Approach. Paper presented at the 61st Meeting of the Society for American Archaeology, New Orleans.

Smith, C. E.
1994 Situating Style. An Ethnoarchaeo-

logical Study of Social and Material Context in an Australian Aboriginal Artistic System. Unpublished Ph.D. dissertation, University of New England, Armidale, New South Wales, Australia.

Smith, C. S.

1947 An Outline of the Archaeology of Coastal New York. *Bulletin of the Archaeological Society of Connecticut* 21:3–9.

1978 Structural Hierarchy in Science, Art and History. In *On Aesthetics in Science,* edited by Judith Wechsler, pp. 9–53. MIT Press, Cambridge, Mass.

Snow, D. R.

1980 *The Archaeology of New England.* Academic Press, New York.

1994 *The Iroquois.* Blackwell, Cambridge, Mass.

Sollas, E.

1911 *Ancient Hunters and Their Modern Representatives.* McMillan, London.

Spaulding, A. C.

1953 Statistical Techniques for the Discovery of Artifact Types. *American Antiquity* 18:305–313.

1954 Reply to Ford. *American Antiquity* 19:391–393.

Spector, J.

1993 *What This Awl Means: Feminist Archaeology in a Dakota Wahpeton Village.* Minnesota Historical Society, Minneapolis, Minn.

Spiess, A.

1979 *Reindeer and Caribou Hunters: An Archaeological Study.* Academic Press, New York.

Stark, B.

1995 Problems in Analysis of Standardization and Specialization in Pottery. In *Ceramic Production in the American Southwest,* edited by B. Mills and P. Crown, pp. 231–267. University of Arizona Press, Tucson.

Stark, M. T.

1991 Ceramic Production and Community Specialization: A Ceramic Ethnoarchaeological Study. *World Archaeology* 23(1):64–78.

1993a *Pottery Economics: A Kalinga Ethnoarchaeological Study.* Unpublished Ph.D. dissertation, Depart-

ment of Anthropology, University of Arizona, Tucson.

1993b Review of *Ceramic Production and Distribution: An Integrated Approach,* edited by G. J. Bey III and C. A. Pool. *Antiquity* 67:184–188.

1994 Pottery Exchange and the Regional System: A Dalupa Case Study. In *Kalinga Ethnoarchaeology,* edited by W. A. Longacre and J. M. Skibo, pp. 169–197. Smithsonian Institution Press, Washington, D.C.

1995 Cultural Identity in the Archaeological Record: The Utility of Utilitarian Ceramics. In *The Roosevelt Community Development Study, Volume 2: Ceramic Chronology, Technology, and Economics,* edited by J. M. Heidke and M. T. Stark, pp. 331–362. Anthropological Papers No. 14. Center for Desert Archaeology, Tucson.

1998 Technical Choices and Social Boundaries in Material Culture Patterning: An Introduction. In *The Archaeology of Social Boundaries,* edited by M. T. Stark, pp. 1–11. Smithsonian Institution Press, Washington, D.C.

Stark, M. T. (editor)

1998 *The Archaeology of Social Boundaries.* Smithsonian Institution Press, Washington, D.C.

Stark, M. T., J. J. Clark, and M. D. Elson

1995 Causes and Consequences of Migration in the 13th Century Tonto Basin. *Journal of Anthropological Archaeology* 14:212–246.

Stark, M. T., and W. A. Longacre

1993 Kalinga Ceramics and New Technologies: An Ethnoarchaeological Perspective. In *The Social and Cultural Contexts of New Ceramic Technologies,* edited by W. D. Kingery, pp. 1–32. Ceramics and Civilization 6. American Ceramics Society, Waterville, Ohio.

Steele, J., and S. Shennan (editors)

1996 *The Archaeology of Human Ancestry: Power, Sex and Tradition.* Routledge, London.

Steinberg, A.

1977 Technology and Culture: Technological Styles in the Bronzes of Shang

China, Phrygia and Urnfield Central Europe. In *Material Culture: Style, Organization, and Dynamics of Technology,* edited by H. Lechtman and R. S. Merrill, pp. 53–86. West Publishing, St. Paul, Minn.

Sterner, J.
1989 Who Is Signaling Whom? Ceramic Style, Ethnicity and Taphonomy among the Sirak Bulahay. *Antiquity* 63:451–459.

Stocking, G.
1985 *Objects and Others: Essays on Museums and Material Culture.* University of Wisconsin Press, Madison.

Straus, L.
1986 Late Würm Adaptive Systems in Cantabrian Spain: The Case of Eastern Asturias. *Journal of Anthropological Archaeology* 5:330–368.

1990– An Essay at Synthesis: Tardiglacian
1991 Adaptive Systems in the Vasco-Cantabrian and Pyrenean Regions of S. W. Europe. *Kobie (Serie Paleoantropologia) Bilbao* 19:9–22.

1991 Paradigm Found? A Research Agenda for Study of the Upper and Post-Palaeolithic in Southwest Europe. In *Perspectives on the Past: Theoretical Biases in Mediterranean Hunter-Gatherer Research,* edited by G. Clark, pp. 56–78. University of Pennsylvania Press, Philadelphia.

Sturdy, D., and D. Webley
1988 Palaeolithic Geography: Or, Where Are the Deer? *World Archaeology* 19(3):262–280.

Tainter, J. A.
1978 Mortuary Practices and the Study of Prehistoric Social Systems. *Advances in Archaeological Method and Theory,* vol. 1, edited by M. B. Schiffer, pp. 105–141. Academic Press, new York.

Takaki, M.
1977 *Aspects of Exchange in a Kalinga Society, Northern Luzon.* Ph.D. dissertation, Yale University. University Microfilms, Ann Arbor.

Teltser, P. A.
1995a Culture History, Evolutionary Theory, and Frequency Seriation. In *Evolutionary Archaeology: Method-*

ological Issues, edited by P. A. Teltser, pp. 51–68. University of Arizona Press, Tucson.

1995b The Methodological Challenge of Evolutionary Theory in Archaeology. In *Evolutionary Archaeology: Methodological Issues,* edited by P. A. Teltser, pp. 1–11. University of Arizona Press, Tucson.

Teltser, P. A. (editor)
1995 *Evolutionary Archaeology: Methodological Issues.* University of Arizona Press, Tucson.

Terrell, J. E., T. L. Hunt, and C. Gosden
1997 The Dimensions of Social Life in the Pacific. *Current Anthropology* 38:155–195.

Thomas, J.
1990 Monuments from the Inside: The Case of the Irish Megalithic Tombs. *World Archaeology* 22(2):168–178.

Thomas, N.
1991 *Entangled Objects: Exchange, Material Culture, and Colonialism in the Pacific.* Harvard University Press, Cambridge, Mass.

Thomas, P. A.
1979 *In the Maelstrom of Change: The Indian Trade and Cultural Process in the Middle Connecticut River Valley: 1635–1665.* Ph.D. dissertation, University of Massachusetts, Amherst. University Microfilms, Ann Arbor.

Thompson, R. H.
1958 *Modern Yucatecan Maya Pottery Making.* Memoirs No. 15. Society for American Archaeology. Washington, D.C.

Thorbahn, P. F.
1988 Where Are the Late Woodland Villages in Southern New England? *Bulletin of the Massachusetts Archaeological Society* 49(2):46–57.

Thwaites, R. G. (editor)
1896– *The Jesuit Relations and Allied*
1901 *Documents.* 73 Vols. Burrows Brothers, Cleveland.

Tilley, C.
1984 Ideology and the Legitimation of Power in the Middle Neolithic of Southern Sweden. In *Ideology, Power, and Prehistory,* edited by

D. Miller and C. Tilley, pp. 114–146. Cambridge University Press, Cambridge.

1993 Interpretation and a Poetics of the Past. In *Interpretative Archaeology*, edited by C. Tilley, pp. 1–27. Berg, Providence, R.I.

Trescott, M.
1979 *Dynamos and Virgins Revisited: Women and Technological Change in History.* Scarecrow Press, Metuchen, N.J.

Trigger, B. G.
1989 *A History of Archaeological Thought.* Cambridge University Press, Cambridge.

Tringham, R.
1991 Households with Faces: The Challenge of Gender in Prehistoric Architectural Remains. In *Engendering Archaeology: Women and Prehistory,* edited by J. M. Gero and M. W. Conkey, pp. 93–131. Blackwell, Oxford.

1994 Engendered Places in Prehistory. *Gender, Place, and Culture* 1(2):169–203.

Tuck, J. A.
1971 *Onondaga Iroquois Prehistory: A Study in Settlement Archaeology.* Syracuse University Press, Syracuse.

1978 Northern Iroquoian Prehistory. In *Northeast,* edited by B. G. Trigger, pp. 322–333. Handbook of North American Indians, vol. 15, W. C. Sturtevant, general editor. Smithsonian Institution Press, Washington, D.C.

van der Leeuw, S. E.
1976 *Studies in the Technology of Ancient Pottery.* Organization for the Advancement of Pure Research, Amsterdam.

1977 Towards a Study of the Economics of Pottery Making. In *Ex Horreo,* edited by B. L. Beek, R. W. Brant, and W. Gruenman van Watteringe, pp. 68–76. Cingvla 4. Instituut voor Prae- en Protohistorie, Universiteit van Amsterdam, Amsterdam.

1984 Dust to Dust: A Transformational View of the Ceramic Cycle. In *The Many Dimensions of Pottery: Ceramics in Archaeology and Anthropology,* edited by S. E. van der Leeuw and A. C. Pritchard, pp. 707–773. Instituut voor Prae- en Protohistorie, Universiteit van Amsterdam, Amsterdam.

1991 Variation, Variability, and Explanation in Pottery Studies. In *Ceramic Ethnoarchaeology,* edited by W. A. Longacre, pp. 11–39. University of Arizona Press, Tucson.

1993 Giving the Potter a Choice: Conceptual Aspects of Pottery Techniques. In *Technological Choices: Transformation in Material Cultures since the Neolithic,* edited by P. Lemonnier, pp. 238–288. Routledge, London.

Vidale, M., J. M. Kenoyer, and K. K. Bhan
1992 A Discussion of the Concept of "Chaîne Opératoire" in the Study of Stratified Societies: Evidence from Ethnoarchaeology and Archaeology. In *Ethnoarchéologie: justification, problèmes, limits.* XIIeme Rencontres Internationales d'Archéologie et d'Histoire d'Antibes. Éditions APDCA, Juan-les-Pins.

Vinsrygg, S.
1988 Archaeology—As If People Mattered: A Discussion of Humanistic Archaeology. *Norwegian Archaeological Review* 21(1):1–12.

Vitelli, K. D., K. B. Tankersley, and N. R. Shaffer
1987 More Problems with Archaeometric Sourcing of Archaeological Ceramics: Are the Fingerprints Smudged? Paper presented at the 52d Annual Meeting of the Society for American Archaeology, Toronto.

Voss, J. A.
1980 Tribal Emergence during the Neolithic of Northwestern Europe. Unpublished Ph.D. dissertation, Department of Anthropology. University of Michigan, Ann Arbor.

Voss, J. A., and R. L. Young
1995 Style and the Self. In *Style, Society, and Person: Archaeological and Ethnological Perspectives,* edited by C. Carr and J. E. Neitzel, pp. 77–99. Plenum Press, New York.

Wailes, B. (editor)
   1996   *Craft Specialization and Social Evo-
          lution: In Memory of V. Gordon
          Childe.* University of Pennsylvania
          Museum, Philadelphia.
Walde, D., and N. D. Willows (editors)
   1991   *The Archaeology of Gender: Pro-
          ceedings of the 22d Annual Confer-
          ence of the Archaeological Associa-
          tion of the University of Calgary.*
          Archaeological Association of the
          University of Calgary, Calgary.
Washburn, D. K., and D. Crowe
   1989   *Symmetries of Culture: Theory and
          Practice of Plane Pattern Analysis.*
          University of Washington Press,
          Seattle.
Watson, J. B.
   1990   Other People Do Other Things:
          Lamarckian Identities in the
          Kainantu Subdistrict, Papua New
          Guinea. In *Cultural Identity and
          Ethnicity in the Pacific,* edited by
          J. Linnekin and L. Poyer, pp. 17–42.
          University of Hawaii Press, Hon-
          olulu.
Watson, P. J., and M. Kennedy
   1991   The Development of Horticulture in
          the Eastern Woodlands of North
          America: Women's Role. In *Engen-
          dering Archaeology: Women and
          Prehistory,* edited by J. M. Gero and
          M. W. Conkey, pp. 255–275. Black-
          well, Oxford.
Watson, P. J., S. Le Blanc, and C. Redman
   1971   *Explanation in Archaeology: An Ex-
          plicitly Scientific Approach.* Colum-
          bia University Press, New York.
Weigand, P. C., G. Harbottle, and E. V. Sayre
   1977   Turquoise Sources and Source
          Analysis: Mesoamerica and the
          Southwestern U.S.A. In *Exchange
          Systems in Prehistory,* edited by
          T. K. Earle and J. E. Ericson, pp.
          15–34. Academic Press, New York.
Weiner, A., and J. Schneider
   1989   *Cloth and Human Experience.*
          Smithsonian Institution Press, Wash-
          ington, D.C.
Welsch, R. L., and J. Terrell
   1991   Continuity and Change in Economic
          Relations along the Aitape Coast of
          Papua New Guinea, 1909–1990.
          Pacific Studies 14(4):113–128.

   1998   Material Culture, Social Fields, and
          Social Boundaries on the Sepik
          Coast of New Guinea. In *The Ar-
          chaeology of Social Boundaries,*
          edited by M. T. Stark. Smithsonian
          Institution Press, Washington, D.C.
Whallon, R., Jr.
   1965   *The Owasco Period: A Reanalysis.*
          Unpublished Ph.D. dissertation, De-
          partment of Anthropology, Univer-
          sity of Chicago, Chicago.
   1968   Investigations of Late Prehistoric
          Social Organization in New York
          State. In *New Perspectives in Ar-
          chaeology,* edited by S. R. Binford
          and L. R. Binford, pp. 223–244.
          Aldine, Chicago.
   1972   A New Approach to Pottery Typol-
          ogy. *American Antiquity* 37:13–33.
   1982   Variables and Dimensions: The Crit-
          ical Step in Quantitative Typology.
          In *Essays on Archaeological Typol-
          ogy,* edited by R. Whallon and J. A.
          Brown, pp. 127–161. Center for
          American Archaeology Press,
          Evanston, Ill.
Whallon, R., and J. A. Brown
   1982   Preface. In *Essays in Archaeological
          Typology,* edited by R. Whallon and
          J. A. Brown, pp. xv–xix. Center for
          American Archaeology Press,
          Evanston, Ill.
White, R.
   1985   *Upper Palaeolithic Land Use in the
          Périgord: A Topographic Approach
          to Subsistence and Settlement.* BAR
          International Series 253, Oxford.
Wiessner, P.
   1983   Style and Social Information in
          Kalahari San Projectile Points.
          American Antiquity 48:253–276.
   1984   Reconsidering the Behavioral Basis
          for Style: A Case Study among the
          Kalahari San. *Journal of Anthropo-
          logical Archaeology* 3:190–234.
   1985   Style or Isochrestic Variation? A Re-
          ply to Sackett. *American Antiquity*
          50:160–166.
Willey, G. R., and P. Phillips
   1958   *Method and Theory in American
          Archaeology.* University of Chicago
          Press, Chicago.
Williams, R.
   1963   [1643] *The Complete Writings of*

Roger Williams, vol. 1. Russell and Russell, New York.

Wilson, L. L.
1956   Sapao: Walter Franklin Hale. In Memoriam. *Journal of East Asiatic Studies* 5(2):1–38.

Wobst, H. M.
1969   Stylistic Behavior and Information Exchange. Ms. on file, Department of Anthropology, University of Massachusetts, Amherst.

1977   Stylistic Behavior and Information Exchange. In *For the Director: Research Essays in Honor of James B. Griffin*, edited by C. E. Cleland, pp. 317–342. University of Michigan Museum of Anthropology Anthropological Papers No. 61. Ann Arbor.

1978   The Archaeo-Ethnology of Hunter-Gatherers or the Tyranny of the Ethnographic Record in Archaeology. *American Antiquity* 43:303–309.

1994   Anti-paradigmatic Typology, or the Repression of Variation in Archaeology. Paper presented at the 59th Annual Meeting of the Society for American Archaeology, Disneyland, Calif.

1997a Agency in (Spite of) Material Culture. Paper presented at the Symposium: Agency: Paradigm or Platitude. 62d Annual Meeting of the Society for American Archaeology, Nashville, Tennessee.

1997b Towards an "Appropriate Metrology" of Human Action in Archaeology. In *Time, Process, and Structured Transformation in Archaeology*, edited by S. E. van der Leeuw and J. McGlade, pp. 426–448. Routledge, London.

Wobst, H. M., and A. S. Keene
1983   Archaeological Explanation as Political Economy. In *The Socio-Politics of Archaeology*, edited by J. Gero, D. Lacy, and M. Blakey, pp. 59–65. Research Reports No. 23, University of Massachusetts, Amherst.

Wood, W.
1977   [1634] *New England's Prospect*, edited by A. T. Vaughan. The Commonwealth Series, Winfred E. A.

Bernhard, general editor. University of Massachusetts Press, Amherst, Mass.

Worcester, D. C.
1906   The Non-Christian Tribes of Northern Luzon. *The Philippine Journal of Science* 1:791–876.

Wrangham, R. W. (editor)
1994   *Chimpanzee Cultures*. Harvard University Press, Cambridge, Mass.

Wright, J. V.
1967   Type and Attribute Analysis: Their Application to Iroquois Culture History. In *Iroquois Culture, History, and Prehistory: Proceedings of the 1965 Conference on Iroquois Research*, edited by E. Tooker, pp. 99–100. New York State Museum and Science Service, Albany.

Wright, R. P.
1983   Standardization as Evidence for Craft Specialization: A Case Study. Paper presented at the 82d Annual Meeting of the American Anthropological Association, Chicago.

1993   Technological Styles: Transforming a Natural Material into a Cultural Object. In *History from Things: Essays on Material Culture*, edited by S. Lubar and W. D. Kingery, pp. 242–269. Smithsonian Institution Press, Washington, D.C.

1996   Technology, Gender, and Class: Worlds of Difference in Ur III Mesopotamia. In *Gender and Archaeology*, edited by R. P. Wright, pp. 79–110. University of Pennsylvania Press, Philadelphia.

Wright, R. P. (editor)
1996   *Gender and Archaeology*. University of Pennsylvania Press, Philadelphia.

Wylie, A.
1985   The Reaction against Analogy. In *Advances in Archaeological Method and Theory*, vol. 8, edited by M. B. Schiffer, pp. 63–111. Academic Press, New York.

1991   Gender Theory and the Archaeological Record: Why Is There No Archaeology of Gender. In *Engendering Archaeology: Women and Prehistory*, edited by J. M. Gero and M. W. Conkey, pp. 31–54. Basil Blackwell, Oxford.

1992   The Interplay of Evidential Constraints and Political Interests: Recent Archaeological Research on Gender. *American Antiquity* 55: 15–35.

Zubrow, E.
     1992   Formal Models of Ceramic Production. In *Ceramic Production and Distribution: An Integrated Approach,* edited by G. J. Bey III and C. A. Pool, pp. 115–129. Westview Press, Boulder, Colo.

Index

Adams, E. W., 44–45

Adams, W. Y., 44–45

Algonquians: ceramics, 54, 56, 58, 59–60; mutability of society, 59–60; in New England, 51–53, 58

Archaeology: defined, 1; new, 7. *See also* Ethnoarchaeology; Postprocessual archaeology; Processual archaeology

Archaeometry, 108, 109. *See also* Neutron activation analysis

Arnold, D. E. et al., 137, 139

Arnold, P. J., III, 136, 139

Artifacts: disuse and style of, 123–24; as material interferences, 120; production of, 123

Attributes, ceramic, 32, 46–49, 53–58

Boundaries: social, 26–27, 33, 35–38, 41–42; technological, 27, 29

Braun, D. P., 55

Burials: archaeological study of, 86–87; ideology and, 85; from North Coast of Peru, 87–90, 98–102

Ceramic production: ethnoarchaeology and, 109, 116; firing, 84n7, 111–13; household vs. household industry, 58–59; kiln wasters, 65; operational sequence of, 30–32; scales of, 58; selectionist approach to, 104, 106–9, 116; temper in, 69–70, 76, 78, 80; temper/clay ratio in, 76; typological approach to, 104–6

Ceramics: attribute analysis of, 32, 46–47; clay chemistry of, 62–63; "fitness" of, 107, 108; intended function of, 55, 58; mobility and diversity in, 58; typological approach to,

45–46, 60; vessel size, 58. *See also* Algonquians; *Crisoles;* Iroquois; Kalinga; Yucatán

Childs, S. T., 27

Chilton, E. S., 136–37, 139

Christensen, M., 1, 2

Clark, J. E., 105–6

Clarke, D. L., 46–47

Conkey, M. W., 6

Costin, C., 105–6, 137, 139

Crisoles, 88, 89; decorated, 94–98; plain, 90–94; size of, 92–93, 94, 95, 96; social meaning of, 100–102

Cultural diacritics, 28

Death, 85–86. *See also* Burials

Dincauze, D. F., 52

Dobres, M. -A., 5, 136, 138–39

Donnan, C. B., 100

Dunnell, R. C., 116

Enstructuration, 125

Eskimo, 13, 15

Ethnicity, 26–27. *See also* Boundaries

Ethnoarchaeology, 2, 109; of Kalinga, 35–42; Magdalenian studies and, 13–14; material culture studies and, 103; of technological style, 29; in Tuxtla Mountains, Mexico, 110, 111–13, 115–16; in Yucatán, 62–67, 68–83

Evans, R. K., 44

Fontana, B. L. et al., 29

Function: material culture and, 124–25; style and, 118; style in, 126

Contributors

DEAN E. ARNOLD, Department of Sociology and Anthropology, Wheaton College, Illinois

PHILIP J. ARNOLD III, Department of Sociology and Anthropology, Loyola University, Chicago

RONALD L. BISHOP, Conservation Analytical Laboratory, Smithsonian Institution, Washington, D.C.

ELIZABETH S. CHILTON, Department of Anthropology, Harvard University, Massachusetts

MARGARET W. CONKEY, Department of Anthropology, University of California, Berkeley

CATHY LYNNE COSTIN, Department of Anthropology, California State University, Northridge

MARCIA-ANNE DOBRES, Archaeological Research Facility, Department of Anthropology, University of California, Berkeley

MICHAEL D. GLASCOCK, Missouri University Research Reactor, University of Missouri, Columbia

HECTOR A. NEFF, Missouri University Research Reactor, University of Missouri, Columbia

MIRIAM T. STARK, Department of Anthropology, University of Hawaii

H. MARTIN WOBST, Department of Anthropology, University of Massachusetts, Amherst